CARAVANS OF SPLENDOR
NAVIGATING IDENTITY ON MY JOURNEY WITH JESUS AND MUSLIM FRIENDS

PRAISE FOR CARAVANS OF SPLENDOR

What a joy it was for me to read *Caravans of Splendor*.

I have known the author, Joseph Williams, and his family for years, visiting them once in their small central Asian town. I have heard some of these stories before and been aware of many of the issues Williams brings out in this fine study. It was therefore very special for me to see Joseph's journey presented in a single writing, enriched at every point by deep theological, biblical and intellectual insights and reflections.

The central question of this book is how people born Muslim can become committed disciples of Jesus and still remain part of the Muslim community and family of their birth. How can we as those called to share the good news of Jesus with others, bring that message without undermining or harming the social fabric of a Muslim's life? A final related question would be, what do we imagine Jesus would do if he walked the streets of Central Asian towns and villages today?

That actually is where this book begins. It opens with a very moving modern-day parable where Jesus visits a Central Asian man in the man's home. Seeing what Jesus says to this Muslim gentleman as they sit on the floor together, sets the tone for the entire book. The book ends with an excellent discussion on "religion, culture, ethnicity, Gentiles, Muslims, and Jews" where Joseph shows how complex the interaction of religion, culture and ethnic identity is, both in the Bible and our modern world. Between the opening parable and the closing discussion, the reader will see how Joseph interacted with Muslims like Hajji Akbar, Hajji Odan and Azizullah, and how Joseph's wife, Michelle, met countless women face-to-face in the safety of their homes where burqas are not required.

I urge you to read this book carefully and prayerfully. Carefully, in that many of these ideas go against what many of us have always assumed is simply "the way things are." And prayerfully—Joseph and Michelle and others like them need our prayers, as do the hundreds of Muslims they interact with regularly, who have never heard before that Jesus is truly *for* them – not just for others.

John Jay Travis, PhD, Affiliate Assistant Professor of Islamic Studies and Spiritual Dynamics, Fuller Seminary and author of *Understanding Insider Movements: Disciples of Jesus within Diverse Religious Communities*

Oh man, *Caravans of Splendor!* The hair on the back of my head stood straight up when I read what Joseph Williams envisions: Millions of Muslims arriving at the gates of the New Jerusalem, bringing caravans loaded with every imaginable kind of treasure fit for a king. They will bring it all to the throne of the Lord Jesus Christ. One treasure will be prized above all others: the splendor above all others is the knowledge of God that each Muslim nation has learned by listening to the missionary message, studying the truth of the Bible. In other words, each Muslim nation will "glorify God for His mercy" in ways known uniquely to each Muslim people group. There are aspects of mercy and dazzling facets of truth that will still be hidden after the English speakers have explained their understanding of God's love and mercy. After the nations of Europe explain it all there will still be more to explain. That is the big surprise of the caravans of splendor. Each Muslim community of Muslim believers will bring its own worship music, for one thing. For another, perhaps even more delightful, each nation will make known to all the others its own theology: each nation will present to the angels a unique, satisfying, wonderful study of God, of the cross of Christ, of Creation. We will listen to Muslim believers, and they will listen to us, in a wondrous realization that we all have made peace with one another through Jesus Christ We all have been saved by God, but having said that, we have not said all that it means until we hear from everyone. So we should be on tiptoes, looking to the horizon, for when the caravans of splendor begin to arrive, they will pile up jewels of glory that we have never dreamed of. Now we know in part; no doubt more will be made known on the day of the Lord. That day has already begun in Muslim communities where people like Joseph and Michelle are doing the work of making disciples.

Joseph is one of those happy few "who received grace and apostleship to bring the obedience of faith to the Gentiles." He is a man of much humility, a true brother, a beloved family man. He is also a man of sorrows and acquainted with grief. I don't know when two men cried so hard as Joseph and I cried when we saw each other after a long separation. There is a bond between brothers known only to those who have left home and taken up the cross in the regions beyond. Joseph and Michelle and others who have forsaken all will have their reward. God will answer their prayers. The Bible says, "Christ confirmed the promises made to the patriarchs, so **that the Gentiles might glorify God for his mercy**" (Romans 15:9-10). What I learned from my own years overseas and what Joseph Williams has written about in this magnificent book, has stirred my heart to pray that the day will come soon when caravans of splendor begin to arrive at the gates of glory.

Robert A. Blincoe, PhD President Emeritus, Frontiers US

"Williams is genuinely doing *fresh* thinking. He's pushing evangelicals into deep waters they haven't explored yet and it is exciting to read *Caravans of Splendor*. Williams *engages* his subject in a way that one can tell this is a matter of life and death for him. He is *passionate* about his subject in a way that galvanizes his intellect to search for the deepest truths about it and not settle for pat answers. Williams' effort to bridge his own context from Paul's is done carefully and with awareness of the hermeneutical challenge of applying an ancient text to a modern scene that Paul himself didn't envision. This is a very good book."

Rev. Wesley Hill, PhD, author of *Paul and the Trinity: Persons, Relations, and the Pauline Letters* and *Washed and Waiting: Reflections on Christian Faithfulness and Homosexuality*, associate professor of New Testament, Western Theological Seminary

I've known Joseph Williams (and Michelle) for almost twenty-five years now. Why should you care about that when considering reading this book that he's produced? Because I've seen Joseph's tenacious, fierce, self-sacrificing, and loving commitment up close for over a quarter-century to reach those far from Jesus. Which means that what you hold in your hands isn't mere words, it isn't just a philosophy or methodology for missions in complex times and situations (though it is that), **this has been lived**. And his sometimes surprising missiological conclusions have thus been arrived at through the refining filter of sometimes painful mistakes made, but learned from; and through the application of a lifetime of study worked out on the ground and in the lives of the lost. And as a pastor rooted in the local, Western church, Joseph's experience, passion, and instruction have been an invaluable treasure to me as I help our people understand Islam and Muslims, and what it means to reach them, both near and far.

Matthew Molesky, Lead Pastor, Grace Church, Salida, CO

Caravans of Splendor is long overdue. Joseph Williams expounds wise insights and principles that are essential to effective cross-cultural work. These insights and principles have been widely accepted and praised for more than a century when applied to secular and animistic people groups, but they unfortunately have been rejected when applied to Muslim people groups. Williams gently demonstrates how important it is to reverse that trend. His decades-long experience of living among Muslims, coupled with his extraordinary analytical skills, make him the perfect candidate to expand our vision for how God will make His glory known among the nations of Muslims.

Chuck Walker, Wycliffe Bible Translators, Central Asia

Every Christian assumes a confident answer to the question, What must I do to be saved? "Believe on the Lord Jesus Christ!" Still, in every culture, the question becomes inevitable prelude to a further pressing question, What must I do to live out my new allegiance? Many Christians are confident of the answer to that in the case of Muslims who turn to Jesus: leave behind your Muslim practice and culture, even your identity as a Muslim. The product of decades of living among Muslims, this book holds that second answer up to biblical scrutiny with missiological results that challenge assumptions for ministry among every people group.

No conversation about the call of the Gospel of Jesus on Muslim life and commitments can any longer be complete without wrestling with the issues Dr Williams lays on the table in this indispensable and thought-provoking book. If allegiance to Jesus did not require the Gentiles of the first century to abandon their Gentile identity and become Jews (as Paul argues in Galatians), and if allegiance to Jesus did not require the Jews to abandon their Jewish identity to become Christian (as Paul argues in Romans), then what becomes more important to a Muslim follower of Jesus? Trust in the promises and work of Jesus? Or identification with (culturally laden presumptions that tend to characterize our use of) the label "Christian"?

Each of these questions implicates hard and necessary work in exegesis of New Testament texts that grapple with the cross-cultural transmission of Jewish covenants to Gentiles of the Roman world. Each of these questions implicates hard and necessary work in day-to-day strategies of keeping open doors of witness without compromising essentials of fidelity to the Gospel. The book in your hands undertakes that hard and necessary thinking on both fronts with learned care and dedicated resolve to honor God in Christ at every step of the mature counsel it proposes.

I have assigned draft versions of Dr Williams' book to my college seminar on Islam for the past few years. Students find it accessible, eye-opening, and vital to a transformed vision of how the Good News of Jesus can be introduced and nurtured more effectively not only among Muslims but across cultural boundaries of every sort. The benefit they were not expecting to discover came in deeper reflection on their personal embrace of the Gospel amid their own cultural assumptions.

Don Westblade, Professor of Religion, Hillsdale College

Williams' writing is refreshingly accessible, not academic or theoretical or polemical. His approach—far from merely fitting recent categories or particular camps—is both innovative for his context and radically biblical and Jesus-centered. And his stories and examples from his years of experience among Muslims make it a compelling and fascinating read. I've been eagerly waiting for him to publish this book so I can share it with newcomers in this line of work.

Zechariah Davidson, cross-cultural linguist, Central Asia

Joseph William's book, *Caravans of Splendor*, is a fascinating pilgrimage to the leading edge of where the Kingdom of God is expanding today. With honesty, humility and wisdom, Joseph gives us a first-hand report of what he finds at this faith frontier: in his relationships and discussions with Muslims as he listens to them and shares the hope within himself. His insightful experience sheds light on our own faith and understanding of God at work in the world today.

Steve Holloway, Senior Leader, Frontiers

Caravans of Splendor presents a beautiful, generous, and challenging vision of what it means to follow Jesus. Williams' theological exploration intertwined with compelling stories ushers readers deep into scripture and allows for personal reflection and wrestling with the implications of this vision. This book removes cultural and even religious blinders, and asks readers to open our eyes and see the incredible work God is doing all over the world, especially in places we might not know to look for it.

Anonymous Author

CARAVANS OF SPLENDOR

NAVIGATING IDENTITY ON MY JOURNEY WITH JESUS AND MUSLIM FRIENDS

JOSEPH S. WILLIAMS

Foreword by
J. DUDLEY WOODBERRY

Copyright © 2023 by Joseph S. Williams

All rights reserved.

No part of this book may be reproduced in any form or by any electronic or mechanical means, including information storage and retrieval systems, without written permission from the author, except for the use of brief quotations in a book review.

Unless otherwise noted, Scripture quotations are taken from the Holy Bible, New Living Translation, copyright ©1996, 2004, 2015 by Tyndale House Foundation. Used by permission of Tyndale House Publishers, Carol Stream, Illinois 60188. All rights reserved.

Scripture quotations marked (ESV) are from The ESV® Bible (The Holy Bible, English Standard Version®), copyright © 2001 by Crossway, a publishing ministry of Good News Publishers. Used by permission. All rights reserved.

Scripture quotations marked (NIV) are taken from the Holy Bible, New International Version®, NIV®. Copyright © 1973, 1978, 1984, 2011 by Biblica, Inc.™ Used by permission of Zondervan. All rights reserved worldwide. www.zondervan.com The "NIV" and "New International Version" are trademarks registered in the United States Patent and Trademark Office by Biblica, Inc.™

ISBN 978-1-7387968-2-3 (print); 978-1-7387968-3-0 (e-book)

Published by MOF Publishing; mofpublishing@proinbox.com; mofpublishing.com

CONTENTS

Foreword	xv
Preface	xix
Introduction	xxv

PART I
THE JOURNEY BEGINS -- BLINDERS EXPOSED

1. Vision and Identity	3
2. Alphabets and Identity: The C-Spectrum Ruckus in the Muslim World	17
3. The Acts 15 Circumcision Controversy and Muslim Believers	29

PART II
THE VISION EXPANDS

4. An Expansive Vision of Christ in Mission	49
5. Loving People More Than Categories	61
6. Whose Story Do They Join?	73

PART III
APPLYING THE VISION

7. A Vision for Discipleship within Muslim Contexts	93
8. Demons, Meat, and the Discipleship of Cultural Discernment	115
Conclusion	136
Appendix A	145
Appendix B	153
References	175
About the Author	183

DEDICATION

For my teachers, who taught me to obey God's Word at all costs.

And for three friends who gave their lives in love of Central Asian Muslims.

FOREWORD

Muslims are confessing Christ as Lord and Savior in many contexts. The Kabyle Berber Muslims in Algeria and Morocco, who are a minority group in a dominant Arab majority, recently received the Bible in their own language and learned that in previous centuries they had been Christians. Subsequently there have been major conversions among them and the forming of Christian churches and reaching out to the Arab majority as well.

Other minority Muslims fled the fighting in Afghanistan led by the dominant Pashtuns and became followers of Jesus as they studied English in Pakistan or became refugees in places like Canada. Other Muslim refugees became followers of Jesus in Lebanon and Jordan as Christians cared for them when they fled fighting in Syria and Iraq. Many in Iran were attracted to Christianity after the Khomeini revolution which introduced a restrictive and militant form of Islam. In each case there was enough of a reaction to another expression of Islam to facilitate other groups breaking away and either attaching themselves to an existing Christian group or forming another expression of the Church.

What frequently happened, however, when there were not other factors to facilitate a larger group moving to faith in Christ, was illustrated by Habib, an Afghan friend of our family. He accepted Christ as his Savior and Lord when he was a student in the United States. When he returned to Afghanistan and shared his new faith, he was poisoned, apparently by his own family to blot out the shame. In his death, however, he still bore witness to Christ. A friend said, "I have never seen a Christian die. There must be something real." But he was not able to share more gradually how the Bible and his new faith enriched the references the Quran made to the biblical characters from Adam to Jesus so that his family and friends could see and perhaps experience growth into biblical faith as he had.

There could be support for this approach from the Quranic verse, "If you are in doubt about what We [God] have sent down to you, ask those who received the Book before you [Jews and Christians]" (10:94). There were Jews and Christians in Arabia at that time who could fill in the biblical details behind the references to the many biblical persons and events mentioned in the Quran.

The present book by Joseph Williams describes this more gradual approach where Muslims are following Christ. The author is not dogmatic about his approach which was unexpected when he first went to serve in two different Central Asian countries. This approach gradually developed, as it has with some other Muslim evangelists, as he worked with Muslims and studied various patterns of witness in Scripture.

The author is an evangelical who believes in the supremacy of the Bible, the need of faith in Christ for salvation, the divine Trinity, and justification by faith alone. Although he has not seen the development of groups yet, his focus is on helping inquirers and converts share what they are learning from the Bible with others. And the ultimate focus is on Jesus, not the Quran and Mohammad. Enquirers are encouraged to maintain a relationship with their families and friends in order to demonstrate the power of Jesus to change lives. The original results are encouraging.

He draws insight into how Muslims who are studying the Bible can look at their identity from passages like Acts 15 on the circumcision controversy between early Jewish and Gentile followers of Christ. He notes how followers of Jesus might act based on the flexible guidelines in different contexts for eating meat offered to idols.

On the practical level, he shows how his wife's wearing of the burqa opened many avenues for both of them to have fellowship in Muslim homes with entire families. And even as the early followers of Jesus were identified by various names in biblical times, they found that identifying themselves as "followers of Jesus" rather than "Christians" kept more doors open because it was not associated with any issues, such as foreignness, that local Muslims might connect with the latter term. The emphasis is on families and social networks. However, any aspect of Islamic theology that is incompatible with the Bible is rejected, or reinterpreted if legitimately possible.

What could also be added to the author's reasoning is that the most celebrated Sunni Muslim theologian, Abu Hamid al-Ghazali (d. 1111), is recorded in two places as saying that it is legitimate for people to alter the second half of the Muslim confession of faith, "There is no god but God (Allah), and Mohammad is the Apostle of God (Allah)" to "Jesus is the Apostle of God."[1]

The emphasis is to stay as much as possible, with integrity, in the Muslim community and study with Muslims what the Bible teaches about the biblical characters mentioned in the Quran, and God's interaction with them. This is facilitated by the Quran's giving them as examples but saying very little about then. Then the biblical injunctions are applied to Muslims' lives. By the time the study reaches Jesus in the New Testament, they are prepared in many ways to follow him. Meanwhile Muslims who are studying the Bible with the author or other believers are encouraged to share what they are learning with their family and friends.

As we have seen, this is not the only way God is working to draw Muslims to Christ, but it is proving more fruitful, particularly than some of the extractionist practices of the past. And I wonder if Habib, the Afghan friend of our family who was killed by his family, might have been able to lead them to faith if he had concentrated on sharing what the Bible taught about the people mentioned in the Quran, culminating in Jesus, as the present book suggests.

J. Dudley Woodberry
Dean Emeritus & Sr. Prof. of Islamic Studies
School of Intercultural Studies
Fuller Theological Seminary

---

1. *Al-Qustas al-Mustaqim*, ed. V. Chelhot, 68, in Chelhot, "La Balance Juste," *Bulletin d'Etudes Orientales*, XV (1958), 62; *al-Munqidh min dalal* (*The Deliverer from Error*), ed. J. Saliba and K. 'Ayyad (3rd ed.; Damascus, 1358/1939), 101; trans. In W.M. Watt, *The Faith and Practice of al-Ghazali* (London: George Allen and Unwin Ltd., 1953), 39.

PREFACE

This book has a ten-year history.

It began in 2013 when I took three months to write during a transition between jobs on-site in Central Asia. At the time, I wanted to respond to a fury of controversies over missionary engagement with Muslims. These controversies were from Christians concerned about missionary compromise. There were news articles, blog posts, and even a change.org petition. I had been living in Central Asia for nearly ten years by this point with very little time in the US. So, this was all disorienting to me.

At this time, churches and mission agencies started to publish policy statements that they required those working among Muslims to sign. These struck me as pulling strategy for very complex and nuanced issues away from the context in which the discussions needed to be held. I loved the evangelical community that had sent me overseas in the first place and longed for them to understand the deep waters into which we were wading to show Jesus' love among Muslims. I wanted them to understand better the daily dynamics of religious identity and how it was as an American to understand it within the Muslim context. I wanted to share what I had learned by living among Muslims with my Bible and heart open to expand my vision.

So, in the spring of 2013, I spent mornings writing about my experiences and trying to address the concerns that I thought my supporters might have as they read these articles and heard about these controversies. I tried at the time to also find a publisher, writing and sending out proposals. I got only rejection letters or silence. Then my new job started. I didn't have time to continue.

In 2016 I was able to draft the entirety of the book and send it off to a publisher for consideration. The publisher scrutinized the manuscript and agreed to publish it. I was elated. But around the time I received that positive news, I also encountered some challenges. I had been telling people openly about the book. A leader of a church with which we were associated asked to read a pre-publication copy of the book. This church asked for a time to read and discuss the book with us, a process that took three years' time. Based on feedback from the church, I revised the book to address points of confusion. I was glad for this point in the process as they helped me refine the book to say what I meant, rather than to just respond to the controversies. During that time, however, the publisher changed editors and the new editor decided against publishing it. So in 2019, after all the discussion and delays, I simply decided to informally distribute the book and see what happened.

Over the next four years, I shared the manuscript with various friends, colleagues, and supporters. I got good feedback. Some readers asked, "Can I share this with someone?" I was pleased to see the book helping others. Some even started using it in training new people in their work among Muslims. A professor friend used it in his college class on Islam.

Then came another disruption to our lives. Civil war in our host country intensified. A new power, unfriendly to our passport country, now had control. We had been out of the country at the time but were now unable to return. That story is for another time, but the long and short is that it provided a fresh opportunity to complete this project and make it more broadly available. MOF Publishing made this all the more possible by providing an avenue for releasing the book to those who had been asking for copies over the years.

I have found that the book has served those preparing for or currently engaged in ministry among Muslims and other non-Christian contexts. The questions asked by churches in the West, particularly the questions that emerged in the controversies of the early 2010s, are different than those faced by in-person conversations with Muslims. Indeed, some of those questions prevent a person from listening to, understanding, and ministering to Muslims or those from other religious backgrounds within their own context. This new version of the book has focused on addressing the questions those in face-to-face ministry encounter with non-Christians, even as I welcome the curious and open, as well as those of any background and vocation to listen in.

A note about language and names—throughout the book, there are terms and names which vary in spelling in English as the origin of these words and names is based in the Arabic language. I have chosen to remain faithful to the preferred English spellings in the geographical context where I was located in Central Asia. In cases where the books of the Bible are abbreviated, I have followed the preferred abbreviations of the Society of Biblical Literature. In referring to holy writings, depending on the context of the situation, these are referred to as "the Scriptures" or simply "Scripture." Additionally, the names and situations within the book have been changed to preserve the safety of those whose stories I share within this book.

I am deeply grateful to the many friends along the way who have made this project possible. Most of those to whom I am indebted cannot be named but I want to give them credit. I was deeply informed by the biblical rigor and love of my college mentor and my seminary mentor who gave me a framework for loving the Bible and loving people. Thank you.

Other dear friends worked side-by-side with us processing the questions, challenges, and sufferings in our efforts to share Jesus' love with Muslims in ways that they could understand. Most are still persevering in that work. You have shaped me and changed me. A few of you got your hands dirty looking sentence-by-sentence at this book. Thank you.

I am also grateful to worshipping communities that supported and nourished us during dark times. Without you, we could not have persevered. Thank you.

Wes and Elaine made possible a dream of mine that I didn't think was possible. Thank you for the extensive effort you made to bring this project to life and make it better than I imagined.

Finally, to my wife, Michelle. You continue to amaze me. You've supported me in so many immeasurable ways. And you have truly been a pioneer of love who pushes into the unknown to see people and Jesus in new and powerful ways. I am more indebted to you than I can ever express. Thanks for walking this journey with me.

J. S. Williams

Look and see, for everyone is coming home!
Your sons are coming from distant lands;
your little daughters will be carried home.
Your eyes will shine,
and your heart will thrill with joy,
for merchants from around the world will come to you.
They will bring you the wealth of many lands.
Vast caravans of camels will converge on you,
the camels of Midian and Ephah.
The people of Sheba will bring gold and frankincense
and will come worshiping the LORD.
The flocks of Kedar will be given to you,
and the rams of Nebaioth will be brought for my altars.
I will accept their offerings,
and I will make my Temple glorious.

Isaiah 60:4-7

INTRODUCTION

A Parable

Jesus comes to the gate of a Central Asian home. Central Asian houses are all walls from the outside. The walls are white, the big metal gate is a bright green. I'm tagging along a few feet behind Jesus, watching. Jesus knocks on the gate. It takes a few minutes, but eventually a child comes to the door. Jesus asks if the head of the house is at home. The child leaves. The father comes back and opens the gate once again.

He looks carefully at Jesus. Jesus simply says, "May I come in?" The man looks at me and hesitates. Then he invites us in.

The yard has a small garden with roses and fruit trees. It's spring, so flowers and trees are just beginning to bloom. The man leads us to a room near the gate. This is the hosting room. The man removes his shoes. We remove ours also. The man steps in first. He opens the door and asks us to enter as well. He encourages Jesus to go to the front of the room, far from the door we just entered. Jesus sits there. The man points to a place on the side for me to sit. I do so.

Then the man sits down near to the door. A child, the one who answered the gate, steps into the room carrying a tray. It has three small mugs, a dish of candy, a small empty dish, and a thermos of tea. No one speaks. The man pours a little tea into a cup. He swishes it and dumps it into the next cup. Again, he swishes the cup and dumps it into the third cup. He swishes the third cup and dumps the tea into the empty dish. Then he fills up a cup with tea and hands it to Jesus. He fills up another cup and hands it to me. He pours a cup for himself.

Jesus and the man begin to talk. At times I ask a question or make a comment, but mostly I listen. I understand some things, but others are a mystery to me. Sometimes I don't understand because of the limitations of language. Sometimes I just don't understand what they are talking about, though I understand each word of the sentence. They just don't make sense. They talk like old friends using short-hand and clipped sentences. They make references to the past, to the future, to the city, and to family that I just don't know enough about to piece together. The man started by sitting down next to the door, ten feet from Jesus' place as the guest of honor. He's now sitting right next to him, leaning forward as he listens. They begin to talk faster and faster, too fast for me to follow. Sometimes the man laughs. Sometimes he tears up. But increasingly, there's a look of wonder in his eyes. Consistently, there's a look of compassion in Jesus' eyes.

Then there's a pause. The man looks up and stares at me. He looks again at Jesus. And he says to Jesus, "I'll follow you." As he says this, he sighs. Again, a pause. Now he looks at me, the first follower of Jesus he had ever met, and asks, "Do I have to move to your house?"

"Do I have to move to your house?"

What would I answer? When I first moved to Central Asia my answer to this question would have been "Yes." I would have said at this point in the conversation, "Yes, it's time to move to my house to talk more."

This impulse, a natural impulse for reasons I'll discuss, was misconceived. In an effort to uphold Jesus and all that he stood for, I would have unintentionally interrupted what he was doing in this man's life. Now, when I get to watch Jesus meet with people, I gladly say, "You don't need to move to my house. Just keep talking with him and do what he tells you."

This book is about my journey to embrace this understanding of Christian evangelism. It's a process of following the lead of Jesus and the early church to see the Gospel—the announcement of Jesus' Global Authority inaugurated through his death, resurrection and ascension—and its transformative power *implanted* within a community rather than a tool for *extraction* from it. In other words, it's a process of watching and learning how Jesus woos people past barriers.

That journey involved a move across the globe to Muslim Central Asia. It involved learning language. It involved making mistakes and experiencing some successes. And it involved reading and discussing tough questions with others about how best to disciple people within Muslim contexts.

The questions we discussed, tough because they challenged presuppositions and expectations that I had, centered on the question of identity. Specifically, how do believers in Muslim contexts identify themselves. Can they still call themselves "Muslims" even if they are devoted to Jesus? For many readers, this very question will sound like an impossibility, an oxymoron. "Being Muslim," most of my American friends presume, *means* being devoted to the teachings of Mohammad and being in opposition to the teachings, sacrificial death, and deity of Jesus. A "Muslim" who is devoted to Jesus is simply impossible, they say.

I felt this way before I lived among Muslims, before I saw the complexities of the issue in the lives of actual Muslims, before I wrestled with how the Bible deals with issues of allegiance, identity, and association, and before I learned that the question itself is misleading. I came to realize the misunderstanding had to do with location, not allegiance. It was about *where* Jesus talked to people, not their submission to what he said.

Engaging Muslims in a Time of Conflict

This book comes in a time of conflict. Since 9/11/2001, many of our conversations about the world and personal security have involved Muslims. Very few Muslims are known by face-to-face experience. This conflict has only intensified through politics, wars, and experiences in the pandemic. During much of this time, I have lived in Muslim countries. My neighbors and friends have been Muslims. Apart from my family, I have spent more time with Muslims than I have with Americans. This colors my experience and expectations. It can also create gaps between me and the average American or European reader.

This book aims to serve as a bridge between worlds to create greater understanding. It seeks to bring you into my experiences among Muslims over the past twenty years. I arrived in the Muslim world with many expectations and assumptions—about Muslim identity and community, about myself and my personal sense of calling, and about what it means to be a true disciple of Jesus. Most of those expectations and assumptions have been challenged over the past twenty years. Remarkably, as I reflect on the challenges, I see my own love for Muslims and my devotion to the Gospel intensified. Most of all, I see the glory of God's abundant joy all the more clearly. I want to share that vision with you.

My own calling to the Muslim world came in 1995. After a season of grief from the death of my believing father, God swept me up into his arms of love. I still remember the feeling of walking on air as I realized that God was himself delight, ready to shower me with his pleasures in Jesus. I had seen God as a taskmaster that needed my service for his purposes. The bold claim in Isaiah 64:4 that God alone was the one who "works for those who wait for him" had flipped my world upside down. No longer did I need to serve God "as if he needed anything" (Acts 17:25). Rather I could serve God in pursuit of the delights he had for me as his child.

This prompted a strange calling on my life. I asked, "If this joy is real, could it be found while working among Muslims?" At the time Muslims were considered the most difficult to reach. That question thrust me down a path where I've spent most of my adult life in the Muslim world. I have found God faithful in good and often hard times.

My aim in this book, then, is to invite you into the understanding I've gained from my journey. I am an evangelical who believes in the supremacy of the Christian Scripture, the necessity of conscious faith in Jesus for salvation, the splendor of God as Trinity, and the world-shattering truth of justification by faith alone. As I've encountered Muslims and sought to tell them about these glorious truths, I've come to see how my own misconceptions about identity and community hindered me from living out and explaining the truths and practices I hold dear. This book is an attempt to reconcile those tensions.

But the book has limitations. In my own ministry, I have primarily been involved in sharing the Gospel with those that have never heard it and discipling first generation believers who say, "That's good *news*." I have yet to move onto the later stages of discipleship in which local believers begin to disciple other local believers—where expanding and multiplying groups of believers begin to face a variety of community issues related to their allegiance to Jesus. Thus, this book involves discussion about those front-end perceptions and problems I encountered in Muslim communities. As I've tried to reconcile those experiences with Scripture, I've also reflected on God's greater purposes in the world and how the Gospel breaks into a seemingly resistant community. This will be of value to readers because it offers a picture of the complex realities on the front-end of spiritual breakthrough that inform decisions made later in the process.

Defining the key issues

The Gospel is for every community in the world. God promised this to Abraham when he said that through his seed (Jesus) all the families of the earth would be blessed (Gen 12:1–3). Families, and by extension the communities they form together, are an avenue and even a goal for Gospel transformation rather than an enemy of it. I have first-hand experience of communities turning against me and my friends because of our association with Jesus. This is not a naïve assumption about how easy this process can be. Nor does it presume that persecution can be avoided. But the Gospel—the proclamation of Jesus as Lord because of his death and resurrection and the "Good News" of a restored relationship with God through Jesus—is meant to go to the core of Muslim communities. For this to happen, the first recipients of the Gospel within those communities must see the Gospel as being *for their community*. This has important implications for how I extend the invitation of the Gospel. From the first day, I must operate in such a way as to extend that invitation *to the whole community*. Even more, I have to disciple people in ways that cultivate and impact their existing relationships rather than automatically sever them. I also have to work to avoid turning the Gospel invitation into an invitation for people to join me and my community at the expense of their own. *They do not need to move into my house to encounter or follow Jesus.*

Key terms will pop up throughout the book—"identity," "community," "association," and "allegiance." "Identity" because helpful teaching about "finding our identity in Christ" can often be assumed to have an absolute meaning tied to one's sense of being and purpose. In this sense of the word, our identity needs to be in Christ. But that is not the way I will be using the word. Because of recent debates about "identity politics" and "sexual identity" in America, the term can also carry controversial connotations that imply every individual can choose his or her own identity, including sexual identity, regardless of bloodlines or community. I am not using the word in this way either.

For this book, when I talk about *identity*, I am referring to a person's relationship to his or her *community* of birth, to the basic social relationships that keep them going in life. "Identity" and "community" will overlap considerably throughout this book. I didn't always understand identity this way. As I lay out the original issues I encountered in the Muslim world, this point will not have immediate clarity. But the overlap between identity and community is what I argue for in the latter half of the book. Increasingly, the question about believers *identifying* as "Muslims" will become the question: "Do believers retain connections to the *community* of their birth?"

Everyone lives with multiple identities. They are known as certain things in certain places, e.g. American, New Yorker, white, black, Democrat, parent, spouse. Most of us are not bothered by the fact that we have multiple identities. What concerns us is our allegiances. To what, or whom, are we most loyal? At the end of the day, when we have competing voices telling us what to do, to whose voice do we listen? This book is going to argue that ultimate allegiance must be given to Jesus, not the Quran, not Mohammad, not the community, and certainly not to me. Indeed, God's call on the world is that this should be or is the case for all human beings, whether or not they self-identify as "Christian." All people, regardless of ethnic and religious origin and identity, are called to full, complete, and total allegiance to Jesus as Lord.

This point bears repeating particularly in the context of presumptions from the West about Muslims. Very often "identity" can be tied exclusively to "allegiance." Too quickly the term "Muslim" for an American audience connotes "full, complete, and total allegiance to Mohammad" or "allegiance to Allah as construed by Mohammad." Any association with Islam or Muslims is assumed to similarly retain that "full, complete, and total allegiance to Mohammad." This book is an attempt to challenge that fundamental assumption, just as my own assumption of it was challenged when I first went to the Muslim world.

This leads back into a discussion of *communities*. Communities can and do require allegiance. Sometimes their demands come into conflict with other allegiances. My assumption going overseas was that they *always* came into conflict. This fundamental assumption was challenged by my time befriending Muslims and reading Scripture with different lenses than my biased, individualistic eyes. I'm emphatically *not* saying that believers should retain and uphold all of the ideas, theologies, teachings and practices that their community propagates. It is possible, however, to maintain one's connection to a community without agreeing with everything for which that community stands. There will be tensions between staying connected to one's community and embracing the commonly held ideas of that community.

Finally, one of the greatest tension points in understanding how one's identity and community relates to one's allegiance is the issue of association. Does retaining connections to a community where false ideas and doctrines are propagated irredeemably contaminate faithful discipleship? I will argue no. This may be one of the toughest arguments to swallow once the words "Muslim" and "Islam" are introduced into the conversation. My experience among Muslims and engagement with Scripture will demonstrate the point.

Filling a Gap

The issues raised in this book are not new. Indeed, in many respects, they continue to ask the crucial question that Fuller Professor Donald McGavran asked in 1955: "How do peoples become Christian?" McGavran answered his own question by saying that the very social relationships of a community were the *bridge*, not an ultimate barrier, to seeing God's transformative work in a community.

Recent books continue this theme by showing how approaches to discipleship that focus on obedience to God's Word, on sharing Jesus within existing relationships, and on group processing of this new information are resulting in movements of people from seemingly resistant peoples to the transformation and joy promised in Jesus' Gospel. Jerry Trousdale's *Miraculous Movements*, David Garrison's *A Wind in the House of Islam*, and David Watson's *Contagious Disciple-Making* all provide descriptions of this process and some of the key principles involved in seeing large groups of people align themselves with Jesus' lordship.

These books do not tend to deal in depth with the ways such movements relate to their communal identities. Over the past decade a number of books have explored this dynamic. *Understanding Insider Movements: Disciples of Jesus within Diverse Religious Communities,* edited by Harley Talman and John Jay Travis, provides over 600 pages of articles on the issues of identity and community from a variety or perspectives. Secondly, Bryan Bishop's *Boundless: What Global Expressions of Faith Teach us about Following Jesus* explains in highly accessible terms Bishop's research about those grappling with issues of identity throughout the world, including believers from Muslim, Buddhist, Hindu, and Native American backgrounds. William Dyrness' *Insider Jesus* explores theological issues related to the issues of identity and religious association. More recently, Darren Duerkson's *Christ-followers in Other Religions* provides a broad explanation of the phenomenon of those following Jesus retaining their birth identity.

Caravans of Splendor approaches these same questions but incorporates a vital first-person encounter with Muslims in their own homes. I imagine us sitting down in my living room in Central Asia to talk about the issues we have faced in our ministry. The book provides a place to discuss the questions many have been forced to ask and explore the decisions of one practitioner on the journey to follow Jesus made in interaction with others. Although there are theories woven into these issues, I will bring the theories into the dynamic realities of human interaction. The theories will interplay with thousands of hours of conversation with Central Asian Muslims—at the local bazaar, in their workplace settings, in my living room, and in their homes. As these are questions asked in the context of dynamic, complex relationships, they have relevance for those outside of a Muslim context, as well. Many of the same principles for relating to others could be applied to any group with a collective identity, including indigenous peoples, other faith backgrounds, or other communities of deep loyalty and identity.

I hope my journey encountering these realities will bring greater understanding and effectiveness to your own ministry.

The book can also serve Christians supporting the work of missions or grappling with theological and missiological issues related to Muslims. God's Spirit is currently working across the world in ways that challenge historic stereotypes. This book prepares readers for conversations about God's work in the world. Some Muslim disciples of Jesus are maintaining their relationships with Muslim family and friends in order to demonstrate the power of Jesus' transformation in their lives. Disciples of Jesus in Muslim contexts can be hidden like wheat in a field of weeds; they do not show up on the nightly news and they rarely write books for Western audiences because they intend to maintain their relationships with their Muslim communities. But God's work in them is nonetheless dramatic and powerful. Though this book does not contain their stories, it aims to prepare readers to hear from these disciples as much as possible on their own terms. In raising the issue as I do, the treasures that they bring to the kingdom will be valued and even pursued.

Where we're going from here

You will find in the pages ahead my intellectual and experiential journey. I express that journey through biblical, theological, and sociological arguments for engaging Muslims and discipling believers with great sensitivity to maintain, rather than reject, on-going community relationships and identification. To get at this idea, you will have to walk with me through the process of removing lenses—presuppositions, ideals, assumptions, and cultural biases. I will help you do so by introducing flesh and blood Muslims—friends I've met over the years who have helped me see the world differently—and by walking with me into Central Asian homes. I pray you will understand and feel the challenges new believers in Muslim contexts face and the tough issues those working cross-culturally face in serving them. And if you are working with Muslims, I hope you will consider fresh ways of seeing how you relate to and describe religious identity.

The book is divided into three parts. The first three chapters look at the backdrop to self-identification as a central issue in discussions about sharing the Gospel with Muslims. Part of this background is personal. In chapter one I relate how my experiences with Muslims in Central Asia framed the issue for me. Initially I resisted the idea that believers could conceive of themselves as a new kind of "Muslim." I ended up asking a variety of questions.

Chapter two explains the main problem, identity, and a missiological rubric called the "C-Spectrum." For over 25 years , this descriptor has framed debates concerning the identity of Muslims who choose to follow Jesus. Chapter two explains the C-Spectrum descriptor and the debate surrounding it.

Chapter three focuses on community and identity by comparing the Acts 15 circumcision controversy to today's discussion about Muslim identity. This will address thoughtful concerns of missiological theologians.

The Acts 15 controversy allowed me to embrace flexibility on how believers identify themselves. Part two, chapters four through six, includes the foundational statements and the big picture argument for biblical and practical viability of this crucial topic. Chapter four presents an outline for a theology for diversity. Chapter five describes a series of relationships that challenged how I saw the issue of religious identity. Finally, chapter six deals with the conversion of believers.

In part three I look at the broader implications of this approach to identity, and particularly the issues of association that I raised above. Chapter seven describes the process of making disciples and counteracts the concern that my approach encourages passivity and shallow theological reflections. In chapter eight I look more closely at how the Apostle Paul dealt with his own missiological problem in the first century—whether or not Christians could eat meat sacrificed to idols. I reflect on the nuance and care with which Paul dealt with culture, drawing out implications for today's issues among disciples in Muslim contexts. I will particularly focus on the concern that association with false religion requires believers to dissociate from their community of birth. With this in view, I will demonstrate how providing space for disciples from Muslim contexts to sort out their theology and culture in light of Scripture allows them to remain consistent with the biblical vision. Lastly, I will present how all of this might look in practice and voice questions some will ask. This book is about following God's lead as disciples, both foreign and local, in the Muslim world. Following is always done in real time, not just in theory, which means I myself have lingering questions as I continue this journey. Those questions do not diminish the hopes I have for seeing more of God's splendor in the process and at the end of the age.

I hope to show you the challenges I have faced along the way and the reasons why I've come to certain conclusions in the face of those challenges. In this respect, this book is *my* contextualized approach to ministry for my own cross-cultural setting. Though I am in conversation with other practitioners and theoreticians working among Muslim peoples, I do not intend to represent others in my arguments. This approach is one that I've developed in conversation with my context, others ministering in similar contexts, and most important of all, the best missions text ever, the Bible. My aim for myself is the same as my aim for the people I disciples in Muslim contexts: I want Jesus to rule my past, present, and future and to give me a vision for him and his work in the world. This book is an invitation for you to do the same in whatever context you may be.

I invite you to join me on a journey to expand your vision. It requires removing blinders. It requires being uncomfortable. It may heighten fears and threaten stereotypes. My prayer is that this journey would open up new vistas of possibility for you, that it would undermine false images of Muslims, especially disciples in Muslim contexts, and that it would expand your vision for the height, depth, length, and width of Jesus' love and glory among all the peoples he created. Join me in seeing how the challenges of understanding and engaging Muslims expands our vision of God's love for us and them.

REFLECTION QUESTIONS

1. Have you ever felt like Jesus had a conversation with you? What did he say?
2. How do associations, identity, community, and allegiances intersect in your life? What is most important to you about each one?
3. What do you know, think, and feel about Muslims?
4. What does the idea of disciples of Jesus in Muslim contexts make you think about?

PART I
THE JOURNEY BEGINS -- BLINDERS EXPOSED

1

VISION AND IDENTITY

The man looked around. "Yes," he said, "I see people, but I can't see them very clearly."

The Gospel according to Mark 8:24

Obscured Vision

My wife wears a burqa.

The burqa, found primarily in conservative Muslim countries of Central and South Asia, is a large sheet that covers the whole of a woman's body—from head to toe. In front of the eyes, it has a fabric mesh through which a woman can see and breathe. It comes in multiple colors, but where I work in Central Asia, most of them are blue. A woman in a burqa often looks like a blue tent with feet.

For most Westerners, the burqa is interpreted as a sign of oppression—a symbol of demeaning women. Westerners tend to see it as hiding a woman's personality and beauty. Many see it as denying personhood and meaning to women in the Muslim world. I understand why it looks oppressive. It's hot, awkward, and overwhelming. And it hides the woman wearing it.

Although the burqa is oppressive in the eyes of the West and it does hide a woman's face and body, it also reveals. Indeed, for my wife and me, it has become a teacher and a key.

I will start with what the burqa teaches. Later in the chapter, I will talk about the door it unlocked.

As I step out of my gate where I have lived the past ten years in a small town of Central Asia, I see children playing and men talking. Sometimes one of the daughters of my seventy-five-year-old neighbor steps out at the same time. On few occasions we exchange words. Though I hear her voice, I cannot see her eyes.

Sometimes I walk the streets and go into back alleys. I pass the winding mud walls. I see an open field. But when I step into an unknown neighborhood, everyone stops. They look at me. They stop their conversations. If there are women around, they arrange their veils. If there are men, they look and pause. I have full range of vision. I can see in front of me and from both peripheries. And yet, some things are still hidden from my sight.

My wife, Michelle, has a different experience. She tells me how much she can see from behind that veil. She sees faces. And, when she walks through a neighborhood, no one hides. The men keep talking. The children keep playing. If another woman passes her and no men are around, they lift up the veil and look one another in the eyes, open-face to open-face. Her vision is limited. She can't see the peripheries. And yet, she often sees more than I do.

The burqa is only for outside of the home, not for inside. That's because strange men are limited in their access to the home. When I visit a neighbor he ushers me quickly into a hosting room. I stay in that room to drink tea with whoever comes to me. I cannot leave the room without permission. I cannot see the unveiled women that move freely outside the hosting room.

Michelle, however, has the burqa removed from her head as soon as she enters the home of another woman—friend or stranger. She is given access to nearly everything in the home. Kitchen. Bedrooms. The real living room. She sees women, children, and occasionally men come in and out freely. She sees the nuts and bolts of family life. I see only what the family brings into the hosting room.

The burqa is not much different than actual life. In Central Asia and America, we all veil ourselves from some and show ourselves to others. We see some things open-faced, clearly, without hindrance. But other things—other experiences, other people—are blocked from our view. From the outside, we think we see freely like I seemingly do on Central Asian streets. But this sense of freedom is an illusion. In a sense, we all wear burqas.

My journey to understand identity and discipleship is a journey of discovery. It is also a journey of exposure. I discovered a lot about myself and other people. I had my blinders and veils exposed. From the outside, the burqa seems to only limit the experience of women. From the inside, it opens up new sights. That was my experience moving into the Muslim world. Other things that I thought I saw were illusions. Some things that I knew nothing about came into sight as I learned to see.

This chapter is about learning to see.

Identity and Mission among Muslims

In 1997 I made my first trip to Muslim Central Asia. I was just out of college. Young. Excited. I spent two years teaching English and sensed the Lord's call to devote my life to seeing his Gospel spread among Muslim peoples. But I knew I needed more training. I returned to the U.S. and went to seminary.

Though most of the students were focused on becoming pastors, we still talked about missions. We were introduced to one of the hot button issues in missions for the day: how to respond to followers of Jesus that still called themselves "Muslims." This issue was fuzzy to all of us in the classroom. As I understood it, these believers didn't identify themselves with the name "Christian" because it led to persecution within their community.

I could understand some of this. During my two years in Central Asia, I was in a Muslim-majority country that had been part of the Soviet Union. Though many Russians were atheists, there were Christian churches as well. Those Christians were Russian.

For the most part, they were Russian Orthodox Christians. Their convictions and practices were so tied to formalities and liturgy that I, a Protestant evangelical, preferred to distance myself from them. So, when someone asked me about my religion, I didn't usually call myself a Christian. I described myself as a follower of Jesus or some similar phrase. I wanted to be distinguished from the Russian culture that Muslims associated with the term.

I learned in seminary about Muslims who took this approach a step further. They didn't just express concerns about calling themselves "Christians," they retained the term "Muslim." But Muslim meant a follower of the Quran, a disciple of Mohammad. How could they really be disciples of Jesus if they were telling everyone they were still following Mohammad?

In a class on 1 Peter, I remember reading Peter's words to the suffering church in chapter four:

> If you are insulted because you bear the name of Christ, you will be blessed, for the glorious Spirit of God[a] rests upon you. If you suffer, however, it must not be for murder, stealing, making trouble, or prying into other people's affairs. But it is no shame to suffer for being a Christian. Praise God for the privilege of being called by his name! (I 14-16)

This is one of the few places in the New Testament that uses the term "Christian."[1] In the New Testament, what we call "Christians" are usually called "believers," or "saints," or "followers of the Way." The same is the case today. Some "Christians" are called "Jesus people" or "Nazarenes" or "Catholic" or "Baptist" or any number of terms associated with Jesus or historical Christianity. Peter wasn't talking about the actual term "Christian" but about a kind of association. He was saying that association with Jesus was a good thing. And if association with Jesus means persecution, then "praise God."

But calling oneself a Muslim, rather than developing a Jesus-associated identity, seemed to contradict this point. It pointed in a different direction than Jesus. Muslims who identified as followers of Jesus, as I assessed them, were miscommunicating on the other end. They were expressing devotion to Mohammad and implicitly denying Jesus' authority in their lives. I concluded that this approach was unbiblical.

I wasn't alone in this assessment. Over the past twenty-five years, a number of critiques of believers that retain their Muslim identity have emerged. John Piper suggested in 2006 that missionaries adopting this philosophy, have concluded that the gap . . . between the glory of Christ and the religion of the nationals, is simply too great for the fullness of God's Word to overcome. The upshot seems to be the minimization of the Word of God in its robust and glorious fullness.[2]

Missiologist Tim Tennent summarized his assessment in the same year,

To encourage Muslim believers to retain their self-identity as Muslims and to not find practical ways to identify themselves with the larger community of those who worship Jesus Christ reveals a view of the church that is clearly sub-Christian.[3]

More recently, the book *Chrislam: How Missionaries are Promoting an Islamized Gospel*[4] received endorsements from Christian leaders and theologians like Josh McDowell, Dr. J. P. Moreland, and William Lane Craig.

All of these writers were concerned about "syncretism." Syncretism is the mixing of two religions so that the fundamental core of one or both religions is lost. One way people imagine syncretism is with Hinduism, which believes in a pluralism of deities. If Jesus is just added as another member of the pantheon of gods, then he's not being revered as the Bible intends. This, many would say, is syncretism.[5]

Those who said believers could somehow retain their identity as "Muslims" were being accused of a different kind of syncretism. In large measure, they were assumed to be leaving Mohammad on his pedestal and putting Jesus on equal or lower footing with him thus altering the core doctrines of biblical Christianity. Because Muslims don't usually recognize Jesus' deity but receive him as a mere prophet, critics suggested that these missionaries and missiologists were lowering Jesus' status. They were giving up too much of the truth of Scripture to fit in culturally.

This concerned me as well. When my family and I set out in 2004 for Central Asia to join a church-planting team, we were convinced that it was wrong for believers in Jesus to identify themselves as Muslims.

Paradigm Reinforced

My wife and I moved to Central Asia on a student visa. We were able to devote all of our time to language learning. Language learning is a fun and extremely challenging process. In our case, it allowed us to visit people, make new friends, and observe. I was itching to teach young believers, but on the whole, my role was just to learn.

I watched how local believers negotiated their own identity in a time of change. Our host country, as a part of the former Soviet Union, opened up to Westerners in the early 1990s. With this, those who had been seeking an opportunity to share the Gospel with the people of Central Asia flooded into the country. They were largely given free access and after 10 years started to see numerical fruit among the different ethnic groups of these countries, including Muslims. Muslims were coming to Jesus.

By the time I came to Central Asia in 2004, the government was increasingly scrutinizing these local believers. It was requiring them to register any gatherings as official churches but simultaneously refusing to register any churches made up of Muslim background believers (MBBs). This forced a number of small churches to take legal shelter for their meetings under the existing Russian Baptist or Russian Pentecostal churches that were registered with the government.

Registration challenged some of the religious identity issues to which I have alluded. On the one hand, many believers didn't want to be known as "Russian Baptist" or "Russian Pentecostal." They did not identify themselves as "Christian" but as "members of Jesus' community" or some other newly coined term. On the other hand, they didn't call themselves Muslim.

When the government started forcing them to meet in Russian Christian buildings, it was hard to maintain a distinctive identity. In most cases, they abandoned that distinctive and took on a religious identity associated with Russians. Overall, believers that I knew were comfortable with this shift. Some would have preferred to meet on their own and maintain a distinctive identity, but given the legal climate, they accepted it as a necessity.

Others, often from more conservative Muslim backgrounds, rejected it. They went underground or retained their Muslim identity. They called themselves "Muslims" and seemed to distance themselves from other believers. One of my close believing friends from a Muslim background scorned these "Muslim believers." He saw them as blending Islam and faithful Christianity.

Compounding this problem was that one American missionary had publicly professed Islam on TV and gone to Mecca to fulfill the pilgrimage obligation of a Muslim. I never met this man and only heard rumors about him—some of which may well have been false. This troubled my good friend, and I internalized his concerns.

Michelle's experience with a local believer also colored my perspective. Michelle was discipling a young woman who trusted Jesus with her life and heart, but this new believer was afraid to talk about her faith with her family. Some foreigners told her that she should start calling herself a Muslim again and even attend the mosque. We knew this young woman to have been a nominal Muslim at best before she came to faith. It seemed that these other missionaries were encouraging her to be "more Muslim" than she was before she came to faith. From Michelle's perspective, this sister just needed to overcome her fears and trust Jesus to take care of her.

These combined scenarios pushed me farther away from this approach to identity. After all, some believers were carving out for themselves a place in their community. The approach of making up a new term to describe their loyalty to Jesus seemed possible, however difficult it was in the current environment. Those suggesting that believers call themselves Muslim seemed to be encouraging people to be more Islamic rather than Jesus-like. My pre-field assumptions were reinforced.

Paradigm Challenged

After one year in Central Asia, my small family and I left the country for an agency conference. My wife and I signed up for a seminar on something called "Insider Movements." "Insider" was the term some people were using to describe this idea of believers retaining their Muslim identity. At this point, despite all of my preconceived ideas about Muslim identity issues before I moved overseas, I had never talked to someone who advocated the approach. As a young worker with three years of experience on the field (one with my family), I was eager to both hear the seminar leader's perspective and to set him straight. I went into the seminar ready to explain to him everything wrong with his ideas.

I came away from the seminar disappointed. I didn't get my questions and objections answered. The seminar leader didn't talk about persecution or syncretism or contextualization—all of the buzz words on my agenda. He didn't talk about believers going to the mosque or saying the Muslim creed. Instead he talked about social networks and the Gospel's spread through families. I remember reflecting with Michelle afterwards and almost fuming with frustration. Didn't he see what the *real identity* issues were?

Within eighteen months, I would come face-to-face with the issues he had described. Indeed, I would begin to see that my questions were back-burner issues. He, not I, understood the real issues at stake.

A Seeker in the Mosque

I had one close unbelieving friend in our host country named Hajji Akbar. Short and stocky, clean-shaven and cheerful, Hajji Akbar befriended me in his kitchen supply stall in the bazaar. While I was browsing through his odd assortment of carrot peelers and colanders, he asked me my name. When I said, "Yusuf" (the Central Asian equivalent for Joseph), he said, "Yusuf—son of Jacob, brother of Reuben, Judah, Levi . . ." He rattled off the names of the 12 sons of Jacob. The Quran contains small snippets of many familiar stories from the Old Testament. It has an extensive story on the prophet Joseph, even. But it doesn't tell the names of his brothers. The only way this Muslim could have known about Jacob's sons was to have read Genesis. I was taken aback.

Hajji Akbar invited me to lunch on the upcoming Sunday. I was both intrigued and concerned. I said I would try to make it. I went home and told Michelle that either I had met a seeker planted in my way by God or else I was being trapped for religious proselytizing by the local equivalent of the KGB. With prayer and local counsel, I decided to keep the lunch appointment.

I met Hajji Akbar at his stall in the bazaar and we walked together to his house. He fed me a lavish feast. He showed me his copy of the New Testament (known to Muslims as the *Injil*) and told me he had read it twice. The book had worn and marked pages. He explained that he really liked Jesus. And he said he was particularly in awe of Jesus' singular command: love your enemies. No other prophet had made that command. He longed to understand Jesus better in light of it.

I went home shocked. Nothing about the exchange looked like a KGB setup. And, it was not. Hajji Akbar was simply an earnest seeker who found the New Testament to be a precious resource and wanted to talk about it. For him, there was nothing wrong with this. The Quran told him to read the *Taurat* (Pentateuch), *Zabur* (Psalms), and *Injil* (Gospels). He was obeying the Quran.

Over the next six months, I went to Hajji Akbar's house for dinner once a week. We would watch TV together and discuss world events. We would talk about his questions from Scripture. He asked different questions than I did, like, how could Jesus be God if 1 Timothy 6:16 says that it's impossible to see God? And who is the prophet that John the Baptist denied being in John 1:21? (He thought it had to be Mohammad). He was fascinated by Jesus but had no interest in conversion. He saw himself as a Muslim and he wanted to understand Jesus and the New Testament from within his own system.

I gave him a Russian translation of the whole Bible with explanatory notes for Central Asian Muslims like Hajji Akbar. He read it and loved it. He not only read it, he quoted it and some of the explanatory materials in it to people at his mosque. Some people didn't like it. A few asked him questions about it.

It was this development that made me first reconsider the seminar I had attended. I wanted Hajji Akbar to come to faith. He had become like the older brother that I never had. He showed more kindness to me than I could repay. Sometimes we debated religious issues like Jesus' divinity and the Trinity, but he usually dismissed my arguments and affirmed his interest in Scripture in spite of disagreement.

As I considered the seminar and my experience with Hajji Akbar, I realized that the process of exposing himself and his mosque to Jesus and Scripture would be very different were he to become a "Christian" or "Jesus follower" and join one of the existing groups of Muslim background believers in the city.

"New-term" believers—those that created a distinctive Jesus identity for themselves without associating with Russians or Americans—didn't exist in my city anymore. Government oppression meant there were only "Christian" believers and those that called themselves "Muslim believers." The "Christian" believers attended church in Russian church buildings and associated with Russian believers. "Muslim" believers, a mystery to me, were largely dismissed by the "Christian" believers with whom I worked. That happy middle—the ones that retained local culture, but rejected Islamic religion, did not exist.

With all this in mind, I surmised that inviting Hajji Akbar to join a Russian church and follow Jesus as a "Christian" would stop the one beautiful thing I saw going on his life: reading the Old and New Testament and sharing about it with other Muslims at his mosque. As someone still in the Muslim community, his friends listened when he read from the Bible. Were he to declare himself an "outsider"—a Christian associated with Russians—he wouldn't be allowed through the front door.

I don't have any dramatic breakthrough to share about Hajji Akbar. My concerns about his ultimate social identity were hypothetical because he never professed faith in Jesus. Today I have to wonder if an invitation to follow Jesus while retaining his Muslim identity would have made any difference. But I never made that offer because I wasn't yet convinced that a believer could legitimately do that. As these thoughts were churning in my heart, I moved to a nearby country and lost touch with him. But the hundreds of hours that I spent with him created a benchmark in my life.

Hajji Akbar gave me new lenses and the awareness that I did not see some things clearly. The seminar planted the seed of an idea that identity had to do with relationships and the spread of the Gospel through those relationships. Hajji Akbar cultivated that seed.

Are you Muslim?

At this point we moved to a more conservative Muslim country, to a city with no resident Christian witness. We stayed in a neighboring town with friends, making daily trips, searching for a house. On our first trip to the city, Michelle walked around open-faced with a scarf over her head. She was the only woman dressed like this. The stares she got made her feel like she was wearing a bikini. The next time she walked around, she wore a burqa. Michelle didn't want to stand out, so she gladly conformed to the local standard. This decision prompted our new host community to view us in a positive light. This key unlocked unexpected doors.

Michelle's adorning of the burqa, unknown to us, signaled to the local population that we were Muslim. Though foreign women didn't live in the city, some visited humanitarian aid projects. When they did, they went around unveiled. Local Muslims associated these foreigners with Christianity—even though most were secular Europeans. My wife communicated modesty and religious earnestness that people respected and received. Neighbors said Michelle was a good woman married to a God-fearing husband. In other words, they said we were Muslim.

This caught us off-guard. Though I didn't necessarily call myself "Christian," I did emphasize my allegiance to Jesus my Lord. I was dogmatic that I, as a "Christian" with a "Christian heritage," should never call myself Muslim. I thought doing so would be deceptive and dangerous, wrongly communicating allegiance to Mohammad and the Quran, and most importantly, communicating a rejection of Jesus and Christian teaching.

Michelle found that neighbors, without asking her, were calling her Muslim. When we enter a room with a friend or acquaintance in Central Asia, that person will introduce us to others in the room. No one, however, asks us questions. They ask the one introducing us. We often have people talk for five to ten minutes about us without a single question directed to us. They are providing a credible witness to who we are.

During our first year in this small town, people kept introducing Michelle as a Muslim newcomer moved from a neighboring country. Rather than denying the identity others were giving her, Michelle found the doors for conversation opening up when she did not contradict their introduction.

I experienced something similar in my conversations. I never said "Yes" when people asked me if I was Muslim. But I found that denying that I was Muslim *when people assumed I was* usually closed off my opportunity to talk about Jesus. Their eyes glazed over and they ended the conversation.

This puzzled Michelle, me, and the others on our team. Again, we did not want to downplay Jesus' place in our lives. But we were having a hard time communicating our faith to people in a way they seemed to understand.

A number of people in our community saw the world in two categories. They assumed the world was made up of *Muslims* and *Kafirs*—the Muslim term for idolaters. Muslims are the people who believe in God, read his revealed Scriptures, trust the words of His prophets, and live holy and respectable lives. *Kafirs* are people from other countries who do not believe in God, live sexually licentious lives, and disregard God's revelation. In a flash conversation, which identity is preferable? We decided that in five-minute conversation, we would much rather be labelled Muslims than *Kafirs*. The assumptions about Muslims is closer to who we are in Christ than the assumptions about *Kafirs*.

We processed all of this information as a team. We talked about our desire to expand people's perspective to add a third category to their worldview. We wanted them to consider it viable for Central Asians to be submitted to God and reconciled to him and one another through Jesus' death and resurrection. We wanted a new term, like "followers of the Way" in the book of Acts. But we were finding it almost impossible to form that new category ourselves. We had just arrived, and their stereotypes had existed for centuries.

To create a new category for people, we found we had to start in a known category first. Awkward, confused, and a bit nervous, we started to accept the labels that other people gave us.

In taking this step, we found we were reckoning with rather normal human behavior. When humans are exposed to something they don't recognize, they tend to plug that new thing into a familiar category. In his book *Tipping Point*, Malcolm Gladwell calls this "leveling." [6] Leveling is when a person or community remembers or sees a situation through their own cultural lens and blocks out what is unfamiliar. Gladwell tells the story of a Chinese professor touring rural Maine in 1945. After his visit, a rumor spread that a Japanese spy had come to town and taken pictures of key sites. The Chinese professor had a camera and a guidebook. In the context of World War II, Americans saw an Asian, i.e. a Japanese man, spying out the land. They had no category for a Chinese tourist. This leveling process was something we were seeing repeatedly, especially as people encountered other religious identities.

Most of us have some experience of this in our lives. We meet someone dressed differently than we expect or prefer be it earrings and dyed hair for an older generation or tight-laced and clean cut for a younger generation. Then, we hear that this person comes from a church we recognize or is friends with a person we respect or graduated from the same college as we did. Instantly, our assessment of the person will change from suspicion to warmth. We begin to view the person generously, with a willingness to receive him or her and hear what he or she has to say.

We experienced leveling in other spheres as well. My teammate and I began a humanitarian aid project to treat tuberculosis (TB) patients in the area. Our local team would go to villages to diagnose TB patients and get their treatment started at a local clinic. On one occasion, my American teammate went out to a remote clinic to meet with doctors and explain the program. A rumor started that our program was focused on finding Muslim children, taking them to the US under the auspices of medical treatment, and converting them to Christianity. All this from a visit to a medical clinic! But the paradigms in existence about how foreigners related to the community and particularly its children were so speculative and hostile that even the seemingly innocent act of TB diagnosis came across to some as an attack on the community's central concerns.

An interesting thing happened the longer we lived in this town. After a couple of years, most people started saying that we were "Christians." None of us, after all, were declaring ourselves as "Muslims" and none of us were going to the mosques and, for sure, none of us were saying the Muslim creed that declares Mohammad as Allah's prophet. But we sensed that people respected us. They saw our generosity, especially to the poor, and they witnessed no blatant sins among us. Our wives covered their faces when they left the house, communicating respect and fear of God to the community. Some were troubled that we wouldn't say the Muslim creed, but in general, people tolerated and listened to us.

The response of the community reinforced our initial assumption that we could carve out a new identity for people in the community. But as it was all happening, it forced us to look at other options, to read the missiological literature and talk to people exploring the identity issues. These events took place over a period of years, not months, and nothing in the situation was black and white. My wife's burqa had given us new things to see. We had to take off our American-tinted assumptions and try on some Central Asian ones instead. From that new perspective, we started to ask, "If we struggle to define ourselves as godly, Scripture-loving people apart from the category of 'Muslim,' what would it look like for new believers to do so? Following Jesus is hard enough as it is. Does rejecting one's formal religious identity have to be part of it? Is it an essential part of the Gospel?"

Reflection Questions

1. Have you ever changed your mind on an issue? What contributed to your change of perspective?

2. Think of a time when you were stereotyped by others. What did you want to explain to the people stereotyping you?
3. How do you describe your faith to others within your own local community? What ways do you use to describe yourself with people from your church? How do you do this differently when you are with those outside of your faith community? With people hostile to your faith? With family members?

---

1. "Christian" is also used in the New Testament in Acts 11:26, where the name is first introduced, and Acts 26:28.
2. John Piper, "Minimizing the Bible?: Seeker-Driven Pastors and Radical Contextualization in Missions," *Mission Frontiers* (January-February, 2006): 16.
3. Timothy C. Tennent, "Followers of Jesus (Isa) in Islamic Mosques: A Closer Examination of C-5 'High Spectrum' Contextualization," *International Journal of Frontier Missions* 23, no. 3 (2006): 111.
4. Lingel, Josh, Jeff Morton, and Bill Nikkedes, eds. *Chrislam: How Missionaries Are Promoting an Islamized Gospel* (i2 ministries, 2012).
5. A. Scott Moreau, a professor at Wheaton College and respected evangelical missiologist, defines it this way, "Syncretism. Blending of one idea, practice, or attitude with another. Traditionally among Christians it has been used of the replacement or dilution of the essential truths of the gospel through the incorporation of non-Christian elements. . . . Syncretism of some form has been seen everywhere the church has existed. We are naïve to think that eliminating the negatives of syncretism is easily accomplished." (Scott Moreau, "Syncretism," in *Evangelical Dictionary of World Missions*, ed. A. Scott Moreau (Grand Rapids, MI: Baker, 2000), 924. To introduce the concepts of the C-Spectrum in the early 2000s, I define syncretism in common ways. My more recent chapter on this issue addressed some of the complications with this definition. See Joseph S. Williams (2021), "Two decades of the letter 'C'", in Nehrbass, Kenneth and Mark Williams (eds.), *The Life and Impact of Phil Parshall: Connecting with Muslims* (Littleton, CO: William Carey Publishing), 71-90.
6. Malcolm Gladwell, *The Tipping Point: How Little Things Can Make a Big Difference* (New York City, NY: Little, Brown and Company, 2006): 201-202.

2
―――

ALPHABETS AND IDENTITY: THE C-SPECTRUM RUCKUS IN THE MUSLIM WORLD

There are two basic ways to [do mission]. One is to make the missionary culture the inseparable carrier of the message. This we might call mission by *diffusion*. By it religion expands from its initial cultural base and is implanted in other societies primarily as a matter of cultural identity.... The other way is to make the recipient culture the true and final locus of the proclamation, so that the religion arrives without the presumption of cultural rejection. This we might call mission by *translation*. [1]

Lamin Sanneh

CAN MUSLIMS FOLLOW JESUS AND CALL THEMSELVES MUSLIMS? THIS QUESTION confronted me when I moved to Central Asia in 2004. Fresh out of seminary and on my way to work in the Muslim world, I answered the question with a firm "No." Social identity and heart allegiance had to be aligned. However, as I began to live, work, and learn in first one and then another country of Central Asia, my assumption was challenged. Increasingly, the nature of the question began to shift. Was this a question about "names" or "place"?

The C-Spectrum

In the previous chapter, I described how experience forced me to look at the issue of identity with new lenses. Hajji Akbar's enthusiasm for Scripture from *within Islam* forced me to pause. The favorable response of our conservative Muslim community to our team when the women on the team wore the burqa compelled us to look at things anew. My presuppositions about identity were challenged. Along with my teammates, I began to look again at the missiological discussions on the issue. That fresh look with new awareness of my blind spots and new perspectives on the actual experience of Muslims prompted new questions.

In this chapter, I will present a seminal yet controversial article on the identity of believers that has defined the on-going debate. In the next chapter, I will look at the biblical argument that pushed me toward flexibility. This overview of the key terms will be crucial for understanding the discussion.

Missionaries, missiologists, and theologians have been debating what is called the "C-Spectrum" for the past twenty-five years. In 1998, a missiologist and mission practitioner named John Jay Travis, currently an affiliate professor at Fuller Seminary, published an article in the premier missions magazine, Evangelical Missions Quarterly.[2] The article was short, just a couple of pages you can download and read in five minutes. Yet the concept it laid before the missions community has spurred hundreds of articles and thousands of hours of debate.

As with all attempts to categorize dynamic, changing people, Travis' scale has its limitations. But he provided a framework to the missions for discussing what was actually happening in the Muslim world.

Travis listed six ways that believers in Jesus from Muslim backgrounds *were currently* relating to dominant Christian culture, language, and identity. He called this the spectrum of "Christ-centered communities," hence the "C-Spectrum." People like me mistakenly took the letter "C" to mean "contextualization." Contextualization is a term referring to the way the message and practice of the Gospel takes form within a culture. What clothes do Christians wear? What songs do they sing? Even, what language do they speak? These are all contextualization questions. In America, we discuss contextualization in our debates over worship style. Can Christians use the style of popular music to sing praise to God? Today, most would say "Yes," but not so long ago the worship wars were tearing churches apart. It was a debate over "contextualization"—how the Gospel relates to and utilizes the culture around us.[3]

I took the C-Spectrum as a statement on how Muslim background believers, or MBBs, related to their own culture, i.e. how they contextualize the Gospel. In my mind, C1 meant "far from culture" and C5 or C6 meant so "close to culture" that it was almost indistinguishable from the existing culture.[4] Even though I and many others understood the scale this way, it was not actually what Travis described.

Rather, Travis described different expressions of how *gathered* believers from Muslim backgrounds worshipped Jesus as Lord.[5] You can find the original scale in any number of articles on this issue, but for the purposes of this book, the following page shows how I visualize the C-Spectrum.

[The space below intentionally left blank.]

The "C-Spectrum"
Christ-centered communities among Muslims and how they relate to language, culture, and identity

Category	C1	C2	C3	C4	C5	C6
Language	Non-native	Native	Native	Native	Native	C1-C5
Culture	Non-native	Non-native	Religiously "neutral."* Local culture retained.	Retain many religious forms but give them fresh biblical meaning.	Retain many religious forms but give them fresh biblical meaning.	C1-C5
Religious Identity	"Christian"	"Christian"	"Christian"	"Jesus Follower." "Usually not seen as Muslims by the Muslim community."***	"Legally and socially within the community of Islam."**	C1-C5

* Travis, "The C1 to C6 Spectrum: A Practical Tool."
** Ibid.
*** Ibid. Additionally, Travis argues that C5 believers "Meet regularly with other C5 believers" and "Unsaved Muslims may see C5 believers as theologically deviant and may eventually expel them from the community of Islam."

Alphabets and Identity: The C-Spectrum Ruckus in the Muslim World | 21

To understand the scale, start on the left side and imagine a group of Muslims that have come to follow Jesus. When they worship, they gather at a traditional church building: it might be an English-speaking church in America, it might be a Coptic church in Egypt, it might be a Russian Baptist church in Central Asia. Whatever church it is, these believers from a Muslim background go into the same church building as other Christians, worship in English or Coptic or Russian, and call themselves "Christian" or whatever the traditional term is for believers in Jesus. That's C1.

C2 describes nearly the same approach except that the former Muslims in the church speak their own language. In C1 they spoke the language of the historical Christian group in their community (e.g. Russian, Coptic). But in C2 they speak their own mother tongue. That said, the setting would be strangely comfortable for a Christian-background person from that historic church. It might have the same worship songs and three-point sermon style translated into a local language. If you attended a church like this based on an English-speaking church model, it would "feel" the same as most churches you've attended, except that you wouldn't understand the words.

In C3 a shift begins from what Westerners perceive as Christianity. A C3 gathering of believers would make Western Christians with no exposure to other cultures either uncomfortable or intrigued. The men and women might sit separately. All of the women might wear scarves. In general, C3 is defined as having local cultural elements, but no religious elements from the Islamic culture. For instance, Muslims usually open their hands with palms upward when they pray and then wipe their hands over their face as they say, "Amen." A C3 church probably wouldn't do this because of its association with Muslim prayers. Neither would anyone do Muslim-style prostrations in prayer or wear specifically Muslim clothing. These things would have too much association with the religious elements of their culture.

The next two points on the C-Spectrum are where discomfort can turn to controversy. C4 communities of believers, as Travis defined them, not only use local language and local culture, but they also infuse many of the Muslim rituals—prostrations, holidays, and customs—with new biblical meaning. They might fast or abstain from pork and alcohol or prostrate themselves when they pray. But they would explain all of these activities in terms of their allegiance to Jesus. Unlike C3, for instance, they don't automatically filter out something because of an assumed association with Islam. Significantly, they try to distinguish themselves from any existing Christian communities as well as from the Muslim community. They try to carve out for themselves a new kind of identity in the community.

Hopefully, the traces of what I experienced while in the former Soviet Union are clear from the above. Our host country had C1 and C2 believers. Some Muslim background believers (known as MBBs for short) attended a Russian Baptist Church or a Russian Pentecostal Church. In some cases, they met with the other Russian believers and spoke Russian during the meetings. This would be a C1 or C2 church. In other cases, they held their own services and spoke their local Kyrgiz, Kazakh or Tajik, but kept the pattern of worship set by the Russian church. These would be C2 churches.

There were also C3 believers in this country. The C3 churches, adapted some of their own culture to the context. They might use the Russian Baptist Church building, but still worship in a cultural style that would make ethnic Russians feel awkward. Though they met in Russian church buildings, they often integrated their own cultures into the actual meetings. They created worship songs using their own cultural instruments and divided up men and women in the meetings. They took on the "Christian" identity markers but they also retained their own cultural distinctives.

There were also C4 believers. These groups, before government restrictions hindered it, often met in homes. Indeed, they shunned the Russian church buildings. They didn't associate with a Christian identity, but instead tried to define themselves as those who were part of "Jesus' community." One of them still wore a religious prayer cap. He didn't call himself Muslim, but he retained some outward signs to indicate that he was closer to the Muslim community than the Christian one. These believers did not want to be associated with the Russian Pentecostals, the Russian Baptists or the Russian Orthodox around them. To do so made it look like they had abandoned their own ethnic community for the Russian community. So, they would pick a new name and try to carve out a culture that was distinct from both the Islamic culture around them and the Russian Christian minority culture. If someone asked if they were Muslim, they would hesitate and say something like, "We're in the community of Jesus." They would *not* say, "We're Christian." These are what I call "new-term" believers.

Alphabets and Identity: The C-Spectrum Ruckus in the Muslim World | 23

With these examples in mind, I will discuss the most controversial group of believers that Travis described: C5 believers. Here's what he wrote in 1998:

> C5 believers remain legally and socially within the community of Islam.... Aspects of Islamic theology which are incompatible with the Bible are rejected, or reinterpreted if possible ... C5 believers meet regularly with other C5 believers and share their faith with unsaved Muslims. Unsaved Muslims may see C5 believers as theologically deviant and may eventually expel them from the community of Islam. Where entire villages accept Christ, C5 may result in "Messianic mosques." C5 believers are viewed as Muslims by the Muslim community and refer to themselves as Muslims who follow Jesus the Messiah.[6]

Travis provided a highly nuanced description of these C5 believers, but that nuance can be easily missed if you've never seen first-hand what Travis describes. Before I explain the controversy, let me clarify what these C5 believers look like in comparison to C4 groups.

First and foremost, C5 believers tend to socially identify as "Muslim." They might say that they are "Muslims who follow Jesus." Or they might just call themselves "Muslim." In terms of how their community sees them, they are still part of the Muslim community. The C4 believers tend to carve out *for themselves* a position distinct from the Muslim community. They still adapt some Muslim practices, but members of their community would probably say that they had left Islam. C5 believers would not usually be described this way. At some point, their community might expel them for their strange theology (affirming Jesus' deity and death on the cross, for instance), but they wouldn't start off in a position of conflict with their community.

The final category, C6, is the hardest to pinpoint. When a scale moves progressively from one thing (foreign language and culture) to another thing (localized culture and language), it is easy to think that the extremes of the scale are just more of the previous category. C3, for instance, uses local culture. C4 uses more of it, like religiously-complex symbols. But C6, as Travis described it, really was not something *more*. It was something *different*. C6 believers are secret believers, largely unknown as believers to those around them, even other believers. In practice, or in how they perceive themselves, they could fall anywhere on the scale. For instance, they could primarily read the Bible in English. Or they could define themselves culturally as "Christian." They could even think of themselves as "Muslims who follow Jesus," but simply be too scared to even mention Jesus' name to others. I draw out this distinction, because many confuse C6 and C5. C5 believers, as described in Travis' definition, do talk about Jesus. C6 believers, because of the intense persecution around them, often do not.

C-Spectrum about local expressions, not Christian workers

At this point, I need to offer a clarification that will be important later in the book. The C-Spectrum was designed to describe existing Muslim background fellowships centered around Jesus. It was not designed to describe the missionaries who work among Muslims. This has not always been clear, particularly among critics of those working with C5 believers.[7]

As is clear in the previous chapter, how local people in Central Asia identify me is a challenging issue. Some perceive me as a secular American simply seeking money through US-sponsored development projects in Central Asia. Some see me as one who wants to take away their children and claim them as a religious prize. Some think I am a CIA agent. And some think that I am a convert to Islam who wanted to raise my family in a pure Muslim country. With these baseline perceptions, I have to figure out how to present myself: as a Christian? as a Muslim? as a new category follower of Jesus? But this was not the intent of the C-Spectrum and it is a mistake to read the debates about identity as pertaining to how foreigners portray themselves.[8]

In the last chapter, I described how we tried to negotiate the identity issue for ourselves. We were actually called "Muslim" by our community. But we didn't set out to identify as Muslim. We did not tell people we were Muslim when they asked us, nor did we say the Muslim creed when people encouraged us to do so. At the end of the day, we tried to present our identity as a new category —not "Christian" (because we wanted to avoid false stereotypes) and yet not "Muslim" either. We found this middle-ground difficult to maintain, but it's the one we set out to establish.

Defining Disciples in a Muslim context

In most publications, the topic of C5 believers has been called the issue of "insider" or "insider movements." The term "insider" has conjured up negative images in the minds of some evangelicals. As I will show in the next chapter, for some the term intimates so-called believers that retain ultimate allegiance to Mohammad and their local mosque while incorporating a diluted form of faith in Jesus. For others, the term is so distracting that I have decided to avoid it. I am more interested in how believers retain connections to their community than I am in the particular "name" or "identity" they choose for themselves. The C-Spectrum has always been recognized as an approximation used by outsiders to describe what they see people doing. Many now recognize that its categorization is too limiting. Some "C3" believers, for instance, can have robust and meaningful connections with their existing communities. Some "C5" believers can meet with traditional Christians and talk about their shared faith. Locals do not usually get asked, "What are you?" That's a question foreigners discuss. And some "C4" believers may actually shift back and forth between a "C3" and a "C5" identity depending on the circumstances of persecution, political climate, presence of foreigners and other factors.

I am most intent on promoting on-going connection within families and communities. That is why I ask in the introduction *where* the conversation with Jesus should happen. "Staying in the community" means learning to follow Jesus within one's birth community. The challenge to that happening is far more complex and difficult than most imagine.

The term I use to describe this phenomenon is "disciples of Jesus in Muslim contexts." Each word of this definition is important. First and foremost, the people I'm describing and envisioning do what is taught in Matt 28:18–20—they seek to obey all that Jesus commanded including the command to disciple others. I frequently shorten this part of the expression from "disciple of Jesus" to simply "disciple," but the point is the same throughout. Their loyalty is preeminently to Jesus. Second, these brothers and sisters live in their context or, to put it another way, their community. People can leave their context by migrating to another country or by isolating themselves from family, friends, and neighbors. In this case, I'm describing an effort to *stay*, not *leave*. Remaining in the community, though, does not mean disciples adhere to all the things or do all the things that their community does. It means that they are physically and socially present in that community. Thirdly, their context is Muslim. In a later chapter, we will discuss this term in detail. For now, it means what you likely presume it means: they live and follow Jesus in a place filled with people that call themselves Muslim, that ascribe authority to the Quran, and attend mosque.

In short, my definition of a "disciple of Jesus in a Muslim context" is:

- a person who is meaningfully engaged with his or her community of birth;
- does not renounce his/her birth community as part of confessing his allegiance to Jesus' lordship;
- consciously works to submit all of his/her life and convictions to the authority of the Old and New Testament as God's revelation; and
- actively seeks to communicate the Gospel of Jesus to his/her existing family and social networks.

As with every disciple of Jesus, they are on a discipleship journey. None of us is exactly where we want to be. These disciples, however, are on a journey towards submitting everything to Jesus as Lord.

Since this book describes my relationships with individual disciples, rather than groups of disciples, I focus this definition on the on-going relationship these disciples have with their broader community. My primary concern, as I noted in the introduction, is how their existing relationships are part of God's design to bridge into their communities for the sake of the Gospel. Therefore, my definition allows for individual believers, particularly in their initial following of Jesus. A fifth, and important addition to these four elements that incorporates the vision for church, would be relating to other believers in a way that forms local church. Part Two (chapters 4-6) will clarify this.

Back to that seminar...

The response to the C-Spectrum has been vibrant. Some people have come to embrace C5 believers and fellowships as valid expressions of biblical faith. Others have denounced the possibility of a C5 position as a devastating accommodation to Islam.

Basil Grafas, a long-time mission leader, heard the critiques of Roger Dixon, one of the most stringent critics of those supporting C5 disciples, and concluded that Islam is a "false religion" that immerses people in darkness and "reaps terrible consequences for them."[9] He drew the conclusion that the C5 approach "is the unconscionable exposure of human beings to a world of evil." C5 persists in maintaining Islamic ideas and practices that essentially enslave people in darkness. For Dixon, Grafas, and others, remaining "in the Muslim community" is simply too dangerous. It cannot facilitate faithful discipleship in Jesus.

When I first moved to Central Asia, I was skeptical about C5 believers, but I did not see things as black and white as Dixon saw them. Rather, I was concerned about communication and integrity. I could see, even during my seminary days, that calling oneself a "Christian" within a Muslim context could be a form of miscommunication. For many Muslims, the term "Christian" is deeply tied to their perception of the West and, particularly, Western licentiousness. To this day, Michelle and I have to explain to people that despite being "Christian," we do not get drunk or sleep around. In light of this misunderstanding of the term, we adjusted how we referred to ourselves.

I was concerned about similar miscommunication through the term "Muslim." If someone described himself as a Muslim within his Muslim community, would anyone know that there was anything different about him? Wouldn't they just assume he was like everyone else? Wouldn't they assume that he held to all Muslim teachings, that he revered Mohammad as above all other prophets, and that he saw the Quran as the culmination of God's revelation? And most importantly, would they not disconnect that person from any allegiance to Jesus? Would not such a person be in danger of Jesus' warnings against denying him (Matt 10:33)?[10] I trembled at the thought of people facing Jesus' rejection on the judgment day.

In the next few chapters, I will suggest answers that I found to these key questions. The answers have theological roots, but they forced me to see things in broader, and largely, more holistic categories. I was forced to wrestle with the wholeness of people—how they live and breathe within community, how God intended these communities to function in light of redemptive history, and how Scripture fully testifies to this. I was forced to wrestle with how I had made the world too narrow. I was also forced to listen more carefully to how my Muslim friends experienced the world and religion. I was forced to see the crucial questions as centering around *where* believers began their journey of following Jesus and *with whom* they shared it.

Reflection Questions

1. Have you ever visited a worship service in a language you didn't understand? What did it feel like? What did you like? What didn't you like?
2. What elements of your own worshipping community do you see as reflections of your culture? What elements of your worshipping community do you see as reflections of the Bible's influence?
3. What are the essential elements of being a faithful disciple of Jesus? What are some passages in Scripture that you would reference in making this definition?

---

1. Lamin Sanneh, *Translating the Message: The Missionary Impact on Culture* (Mary Knoll, NY: Orbis Books, 1996), 29.
2. John Travis, "The C1 to C6 Spectrum," *Evangelical Missions Quarterly* (October 1998).
3. Paul Hiebert provides a helpful history of the term and concept in "Critical Contextualization," *International Bulletin of Missionary Research* (1987): 104–12. An engaging and wide-ranging processing of the concept and history of contextualization is Andrew Walls' award-winning *The Missionary Movement in Christian History: Studies in the Transmission of Faith* (Maryknoll, NY: Orbis books, 1996).
4. This mistaken understanding has also created other confusing phrases like "high-end contextualization" or "extreme contextualization."
5. Travis notes this error as common in John Jay Travis, "The C1-C6 Spectrum After Fifteen Years: Misunderstandings, Limitations, and Recommendations," in *Understanding Insider Movements: Disciples of Jesus Within Diverse Religious Communities*, ed. Harley Talman, and John Jay Travis (Pasadena, CA: William Carey Library, 2015), 492.
6. John Travis, "The C1 to C6 Spectrum," *Evangelical Missions Quarterly* (October 1998).
7. Travis clarified this in the 2015 chapter cited above, "This actually has nothing whatsoever to do with the Spectrum, yet the idea of cross-cultural workers 'becoming C5' keeps resurfacing in Spectrum discussions." "The C1-C6 Spectrum After Fifteen Years," 492.
8. See Appendix B, which is a reprint of a chapter I previously published: Williams, Joseph S, "Two Decades of the Letter 'C'," in *The Life and Impact of Phil Parshall: Connecting With Muslims*, ed. Kenneth Nehrbass and Mark Williams (Littleton, CO: William Carey Publishing, 2021), 71–90. Republished by permission.
9. Basil Grafas, "A View from the Bridge: Insider Movement Critics Speak Out," *St Francis Magazine* 6, no. 6 (December, 2010): 936.
10. "Everyone who acknowledges me publicly here on earth, I will also acknowledge before my Father in heaven. But everyone who denies me here on earth, I will also deny before my Father in heaven" (Matt 10:32-33).

3

THE ACTS 15 CIRCUMCISION CONTROVERSY AND MUSLIM BELIEVERS

For too long we have read Scripture with nineteenth-century eyes and sixteenth-century questions. It's time to get back to reading with first-century eyes and twenty-first century questions.[1]

N. T. Wright

REEVALUATION APPLIED

I arrived in Central Asia opposed to the idea of disciples of Jesus identifying themselves as Muslims. Five years into my service, I was on the edge of embracing it.

What changed?

My experience mattered. But experience wasn't enough. Experience seen through the lens of Scripture caused me to see the issue differently. All people read the Bible through the lens of their experience. This is a glorious part of God's revelation of Himself in Jesus and Scripture. God affirms our limitations by putting the Bible into human language and sending Jesus into the world as a human being in the midst of a particular place, time, and culture. God must be comfortable with our limitations to take such risks with the most important realities in the universe.[2] Of course, the universal message of the Bible never changes. It is a rock-solid foundation upon which we should build our lives. Yet, because of our limitations, our convictions do and should change as we go through life. Admitting the changes in our perspective so we are more in line with the Bible is part building our lives on Scripture.

How did that happen for me? I assumed certain things about Muslims, about discipleship, about evangelism, and about how people change. As I encountered actual Muslims and sought to see the Gospel run across the bridges I was building, I realized that many of my assumptions had been wrong.

One of those assumptions was that the C4 category could be permanent and acceptable in every context. In the previous chapter, I showed how the C4 category started to disappear as the local government prohibited house gatherings. C4 believers were pushed into a C3 category. They shifted from a "follower of Jesus" identity into one that was explicitly linked with "Russian Christian."

My other assumption had to do with what happened when someone in Central Asia explicitly rejected his or her Muslim community. I had assumed believers could remain socially connected to their family and neighbors while rejecting the name "Muslim." Watching my friend Hajji Akbar and meeting people in Central Asia who could only recognize two kinds of people in the world (God-worshipping Muslims and idol-worshipping *Kafirs*) challenged that assumption. Though contexts varied, I discovered rejection of the name "Muslim" could also communicate false things about allegiance to Jesus. It could suggest "I'm now a foreign blasphemer," instead of "I'm transformed by the power of Jesus to serve God only."

Finally, my assumptions about Scripture changed. I started looking at the passages about Gentiles with new questions. I had always seen "Gentile" in purely ethnic terms. I'm of Irish descent. You might be of German or African descent. The New Testament said that people could not be excluded from God's kingdom on account of a particular ethnic background. I thought it referred to bloodlines.

Reading the New Testament in my new context, I noticed the *religious elements* of being a Gentile. Seeing this pushed me into deeper engagement with those criticizing the idea of believers identifying as "Muslim."

Must I be "Christian" to be saved?

One of these critiques came from D. A. Carson, a prominent New Testament scholar from Trinity Evangelical Divinity School and one of my favorite Bible commentators. In a 2009 recording Dr. Carson's exegesis of 1 Cor 9:19-23 addressed this issue. He stated that the context of the passage does not support what he understood as C5 or "insider" approach.[3]

First Corinthians 9:19-23 is a great missionary text. Paul describes how he adapts to different cultures to win people for the Gospel. For the Jew, he will act like a Jew. For the Gentile, he will act like a Gentile. The Gospel is so primary to him that he will abandon certain cultural scruples so as to win people from a variety of cultures.

The text begs the question: could one take this same approach with Muslims? For the Muslim, could one become or continue to be a Muslim?

To get at the answer, Carson looks at the context of 1 Cor 8-11 and shows how Paul is radically committed to Jesus' supremacy. Paul devotes everything to the cause of Christ. In particular, Carson addresses Paul's discussion of who can eat meat sacrificed to idols.

As Paul addresses this topic, he prioritizes Gospel convictions. In other words, he prioritizes what is necessary to explain the Good News of salvation through Jesus. Some people hope that by refraining from eating meat sacrificed to idols they will be saved; Paul pushes against those ideas with all his might. But for the sake of loving others and communicating the Gospel, Paul shows flexibility regarding cultural rules. He allows seeming pagan activities (eating meat sacrificed to idols at someone's house), if it means people hear the Gospel.

When Carson gets to his focus passage, he points to the reason Paul can maintain this flexibility. Paul has entered a "third category" of identity. He is no longer a "Jew" in the sense he once was, yet he has not become a Gentile. Rather, he is a "Christian"—a third category with distinctive loyalty to Jesus.

As Carson engages the issue of identity, he rejects the idea that Muslim background believers (MBBs) could "remain Muslim." He says,

> This is the important bit... If Paul is in this third position, then as a

> Christian he is trying to win these non-Christians to become like him. He is trying to win people to become Christians like him. If he wants them to become Christians like him, he does not wish to leave them where they are.[4]

They, like Paul, must enter this new category of "Christian" and, like Paul with his Judaism, abandon their previous category of "Muslim."

I resonated with Carson's beautiful argument for the Gospel's central focus on the person of Jesus. His exegesis of 1 Corinthians 8-9 was spot on. But what about his application of this to the issue of identity?

At this point, he offered a strong critique of C5 communities. Carson says,

> That is where the mistake of C5 is so desperately profound. It does not recognize that there are idols in every culture. And all of us—to become Christians—must leave those idols behind and come under the new covenant . . . Christ-centered community number 5. How is it a Christ-centered community anymore? It isn't a Christ-centered community. It's basically a Muslim community with a little bit of Christian gloss.[5]

These are strong accusations. Carson understands C5 believers to be those who stayed fully in the Islamic religious system, tacking on some "follower-of-Jesus" language. But, where did he get this idea? He inferred it, apparently, from the term "Muslim." Unfortunately, Carson never defines this term in his talk. He associates it with idolatry but never explains the idolatrous elements that he assumes are part of being Muslim. The *mere* label of these believers as "Muslim," not their activities or beliefs, means for Carson that their core relationship to the false idols of their culture, actions and beliefs must stay intact. But this is an assumption, an inference from a label made from his presuppositions and lack of context.[6]

Carson betrayed a disconnect between his assumptions about C5 communities and the arguments of those supporting them. The practitioners' description of C5 communities and Carson's accusations are not congruent. He imputes dynamics to those who retained connections to their Muslim communities that its own practitioners rejected.

At this point in my journey, I and my colleagues on the field had been in personal communication with John Travis, Kevin Higgins, and other practitioners wrestling with the issue of identity in Muslim communities. Travis and Higgins argued that changing one's formal religious identity not be a requirement of saving faith. They were clear that absolute allegiance to Jesus was necessary for true believers. They emphasized that believers, including those from Muslim backgrounds, should submit everything to the authority of the Bible. They insisted that disciples of Jesus in Muslim contexts not just tack Jesus onto Islam. These Muslim background believers were reorienting everything by Jesus—evaluating the Quran, Mohammad, marriage practices, family, daily routines, prayer, sickness—everything by what they learned from Jesus. With that, Travis and others were asking questions about religious identity and community that resonated with the tensions I felt in my host community. Indeed, they were doing the very thing that Carson prescribed in his talk.

At the end of his lecture, Carson says:

> The flexibility and accommodation envisaged in this passage are the flexibility of the messenger, not the message, and not the convert... Muslim converts would show that they've got this not by remaining indistinguishable from other Muslims except that they've tacked on a bit of follower-of-Jesus language but now by so identifying with the third position, with the Gospel, with Jesus, with the cross. They are Christians, but now they will have to flex to win their fellow Muslims.[7]

Apart from one phrase, this statement could have come from the mouths of those advocating C5. As I continued to read various descriptions of C5 communities; none of them advocated that these disciples remain "indistinguishable from other Muslims." Yet all of them said they didn't need the social label "Christian" to communicate their identification with the Gospel, with Jesus, and with the cross.[8]

I cannot speak for all writers on this topic, nor do I aim to defend anything and everything written by those Carson was critiquing. I speak only of those I was reading and with whom I was conversing. These articles,[9] particularly the ones by John Travis, Kevin Higgins, and Rebecca Lewis, testified that they were supremely concerned that believers maintain social networks for the sake of the Gospel. They too were concerned that believers not distort biblical truth. It was about learning to "flex to win their fellow Muslims," as Carson put it. I quoted Travis' definition of the C5 position in the last chapter. He said explicitly that "aspects of Islamic theology which are incompatible with the Bible are rejected or reinterpreted if possible." Others reinforce this crucial understanding.

Rebecca Lewis, missiologist, practitioner, and daughter of missions educator Ralph Winter, wrote,

> An insider movement is any movement to faith in Christ where the gospel flows through pre-existing communities and social networks, and where believing families, as valid expressions of faith in Christ, remain inside their socio-religious communities, retaining their identity as members of that community *while living under the lordship of Jesus Christ and the authority of the Bible.*[10]

Kevin Higgins, President of Frontier Ventures and another frequent contributor on the contextualization debates, defined these believers this way:

> A growing number of families, individuals, clans, and/or friendship-webs becoming *faithful* disciples of Jesus within the culture of their people group, including their religious culture. This faithful discipleship will express itself in culturally appropriate communities of believers who will also continue to live within as much of their culture, including the religious life of the culture, *as is biblically faithful. The Holy Spirit, through the Word and through His people will also begin to transform His people and their culture, religious life, and worldview.*[11]

One could take all these claims as inherently contradictory, like Roger Dixon did. Travis and others say, for instance, that these C5 believers live under Jesus' lordship within the Muslim community. They also talk about living "within the religious life of the culture." One could say that what Travis and others posit is an impossibility: living under Jesus' lordship within the religious life of an Islamic community. Islam is inherently against Jesus' lordship, so these practitioners and missiologists are deceived.

But this is not Carson's argument. Rather, he insists these believers are not transformed, that they are not different, that they only have a "Christian gloss" laid over their Muslim core. He denies, in fact, that they are being like Paul. He presumes that their identification with Jesus is only on the surface. He does not understand that, like Paul, allegiance to Jesus has reoriented their view of everything, including their birth identity.

When I listened to Carson, I had yet to meet mature disciples in Muslim contexts. Since then, I have. The ones I have met are passionate for Jesus. They are students of their own communities and intense students of the Scriptures. Eager to find creative ways to reach their communities, they know how to sidestep ways of talking that put people on the defensive and get labelled as "foreign." But they also, surprisingly, find ways to pinpoint the idols of their culture, boldly asserting Jesus' supremacy in ways that I could never have imagined or said without facing immediate rejection.

This level of transformation was what Travis and others were telling me about. Revisit the quotes above and you will see an emphasis on *changed people* within their existing social networks. These practitioner-missiologists were also arguing for the "third category." They insisted there could be *Muslims* with allegiance to Jesus, just as there could be *Gentiles* with allegiance to Jesus, and *Jews* with allegiance to Jesus. **Allegiance to Jesus put them** in the third category, not rejection of their birth identity.

I can understand why someone might look at articles on identity issues and assume Jesus was secondary. I had made my own assumptions about this. A big part of that assumption likely has to do with the term "religious." I suspect the use of that term implied to Carson and many readers full-scale agreement with all of the teachings of the Quran and Mohammad. This need not be the case, as I will discuss in chapter five, with a fuller discussion the appendix. "Religious" elements of a culture are tremendously difficult to pin-down and as I have increasingly come to see, these writers were simply grappling with the difficulty of distinguishing between seemingly neutral "culture" and "religious" elements of culture.

I was finding out firsthand that it was extremely difficult to separate "religion" (devotion to Mohammad) from culture. Moreover, I saw how difficult it was for my local friends to separate my foreign identity from my message about Jesus. They were hearing my invitation to Jesus as an invitation to join my foreign identity, indeed, as a requirement to change the "social location" where they talked to Jesus. I was seeing, how identification could be a hindrance to true understanding among Muslims. I was repeatedly experiencing how these labels *miscommunicated*. My Central Asian neighbors assumed I was a Christian. With that they assumed I slept with other women, drank frequently, and, interestingly, believed in three gods ("the Father," "Mary," and "Jesus.") Indeed, this is a common perspective for Muslims in many other parts of the Muslim world. The label "Christian" in this case distracted from the essentials of the Gospel. Was it necessary to invite Muslims to take on this label in order to be saved? Ironically, Carson convinced me that Paul would have agreed that believers had flexibility under the Gospel to discern how to relate to their birth identities.

Carson misunderstands how supporters of the C5 communities used the term "Christian." The terms identity, community and allegiance get intertwined, confusing people debating this issue. Those supporting C5 distinguish between perceived labels (like "Christian") that are associated with particular communities and identities, from heart-level allegiances and beliefs. Carson holds C5 believers as those who *do not* have ultimate allegiance to Jesus as Lord and Savior. The "C5" notion, under this reading, would be that one could add Jesus on as secondary to one's allegiance to Mohammad and Islam. If this were the argument, I would reject it.[12]

From all I have been able to discern, Travis and others have not advocated allegiance to Jesus as subordinate to allegiance to Mohammad or their community. Practitioner-missiologists distinguish between the social identity of "Christian"—someone born into a nominally "Christian context," be it the Bible Belt or Coptic Egypt, as well as devoted believers—and someone who consciously follows Jesus and submits everything to the teaching of the Old and New Testament. Must one identify under the social label "Christian" to belong to Christ?

Carson makes the radical point from his exegesis of Paul's writings that Paul refused to "jeopardize the exclusive sufficiency of Jesus' work as Savior and mediator." Hence, Carson in his talk begs the question: what must a Muslim do *in addition to faith in Christ* in order to be saved? Must he take on a new label, renounce an old label, or denounce his community? Even missionaries critical of these approaches to identity concede that the "Christian" label is not a requirement for salvation. But Carson wrongly understands disciples in

Muslim contexts to tack faith in Jesus onto a Muslim system like an extra arm on the human body. He does not see how these disciples could actually be doing what Paul advocated: making cultural adjustments so that their wholehearted devotion to Jesus might be passed along to others in their community.

Must one stop being Muslim (or Gentile or Jew) to be saved?

The other major critique I read at this time came from Dr. Timothy Tennent, President of Asbury Seminary and a highly respected missiologist with a degree in Islamics. Tennent's article from 2006 pinpointed the central issues for me. He addressed the potential parallel between circumcision in the early church and identity in the present debate.

Writers addressing identity issues draw parallels between the way some Jews, the Judaizers, wanted to require circumcision of new Gentile believers and missionary practice among Muslims. They insist Muslims take on a Christian identity in order to be recognized as bona fide believers in Jesus. Under this reading of Scripture, "identity" is a form of the circumcision controversy. Those forcing "Christian" identity onto new believers are acting like the Judaizers of the New Testament. They are adding requirements to the Gospel.

As Tennent assessed this claim, he came to the following conclusion:

> [It] would be Judaistic to pressure a new believer in the Muslim world to adopt all of our cultural accoutrements. But this does not provide much help in resolving the issue of Islamic religious identity, because from Paul's perspective the issue was not about 'staying in' Judaism or 'staying in' paganism, but about the recognition that both Jew and Gentile must together identify themselves as sinners in need of grace and together find their new identity in Jesus Christ ... *The only hope is to find a new identity together as the redeemed people of God, made up of both Jew and Gentile.*[13]

Tennent's argument is similar to Carson's. But Tennent brings into focus the key element of how a person relates to his or her past. Specifically, Tennent argues the controversy over circumcision had to do with forming a *new* identity rather than addressing concerns about one's *birth* identity.

Tennent's conclusion contains a wonderful insight. He says that identity in Jesus should not be a cultural category. It should be what we are as followers of Jesus—a category that both distinguishes from our culture of birth and unites us to people from other cultures of birth. He is right.

But Tennent's argument depends on an assumption he shares with Carson. Carson assumes that one has to reject one's past in order to be part of that new identity in Christ. He assumes that past associations have nothing to do with the process of acquiring a new identity. I struggled with this assumption. Did Gentiles, for instance, stop being Gentiles when they decided to follow Jesus? Did Jews stop being Jews? Tennent did not do justice to these questions. Was it really the case, as Carson and Tennent argue, that the apostles expected new believers to reject their community identity in order to take on a new identity in Jesus? Or was it possible that one could be a Jew or Gentile *and* a follower of Jesus? I came to believe that as the church sorted out how Gentiles and Jews were to be joined together in a new community, what we call the "church," they honored and renewed their birth cultures rather than rejecting them.

Acts 15 and the Gentile Inclusion

Two passages were pushing me in this direction, Acts 15 and Galatians 2.

Acts is the missionary handbook, the story of how Jesus' disciples spread the Gospel from Jerusalem to the uttermost parts of the world. At this point in my journey, I was seeing afresh how the Gospel's progress wasn't instantaneous. It faced geographical *and* sociological barriers of massive proportions.

Acts 15 is the turning point in Acts when the apostles decided that Gentiles were not required to be circumcised to be saved. If you follow the story of Acts from beginning to end, this was a big deal. From Acts 1-9, there weren't any "pure Gentile" converts. The Gentile believers were all Jewish proselytes, i.e. they had embraced Judaism so fully that they went through circumcision. By Acts 15, Cornelius, an uncircumcised Gentile, had come to faith (Acts 10-11), and Paul and Barnabas had planted numerous churches among non-proselyte Gentiles (Acts 13-14). When Paul and Barnabas returned to their multicultural sending body in Antioch, some expressed concern about the fruit they claimed.

Concerned teachers tried to set the record straight by telling those in Antioch that these new Gentile believers were *really* in the kingdom. New Gentile believers had to be circumcised, they said. Paul and Barnabas disagreed. Luke puts it softly by telling us that there was "no small dissension and debate" (Acts 15:2 ESV). They all met in Jerusalem to address the conflict.

I live in the Muslim world, where men have refused to shake my hand on the grounds that they would become ritually impure. I have experienced being sociologically outside society, being told to meet some external standard in order to be part of a community. I've stood outside my door at dusk and watched a crowd of men heading to the local mosque knowing that my entrance into their place of worship would be the cause of considerable controversy. I have sat before Muslims as they debate whether or not my monotheistic faith is sufficiently orthodox for them to drink tea with me. Most decide, at least in the moment, that my convictions are enough. Some reject me as a corrupting influence.

The conservative Jews in Acts 15 believed that Jesus was the long-awaited Messiah. Their doctrinal concerns were about the Gentile believers. They heard reports of non-circumcised Gentiles coming to believe in the Messiah. They knew that should they meet with them, they wouldn't be able to shake their hands. Some might not even associate with them. Moreover, these Jews were concerned that the Gentiles were taking a shortcut into the kingdom. The Jews reckoned themselves as the people of God. For them, the phrase "Uncircumcised Gentile members of God's people" would probably have been the height of impossibilities.[14]

The apostles sided with Paul and Barnabas on the circumcision question. Most Christians know this. But few pay attention to other parts of the decision. They are equally relevant. As James wrapped up his opinion on the issue, he added some seemingly cultural requirements, like prohibiting the eating of blood. I remember the tinge of conscience I felt on my first visit to England at age 19. In a little British cafe, I ate black pudding, or cooked blood, for breakfast. I was in a historically Christian country eating something that was explicitly prohibited by the early church! After saying these Gentiles didn't have to bear the burden of Moses' law from the Old Testament (Acts 15:10), did the apostles let Moses in the back door by requiring Old Testament food laws to be saved?

Dean Flemming, a New Testament professor at European Nazarene Seminary, helped me sort this out. In his book *Contextualization in the New Testament*, he points out the communal issues at stake for the early Christian church. If Gentiles were not circumcised and in submission to Moses' law, fastidious believing Jews wouldn't be able to meet with them. All these ritual purity issues would still be on the table. If Gentiles could be saved without circumcision, Jewish and Gentile believers could not be a community. There would not be any meaningful fellowship between the two groups. In Leviticus 17-18 there were instructions for "strangers who sojourned" among the Israelites. These Gentiles were allowed to live in the Jewish community, but while there, they were not allowed to eat meat sacrificed to idols, to eat meat with blood in it (Lev 17:8-12), nor to participate in sexual immorality (Lev 18). In other words, these Gentiles did not have to join the Jewish religion—they didn't have to be circumcised—the Jews could still be neighbors and not be ritually compromised.

Leviticus 17-18 provided the early church with a solution for its communal conundrum. They asked the new believers to follow these instructions so that the Jews could still associate with the new Gentile believers. There is a lot for us to learn from this profound decision.

In Acts 15, the early church addressed the social needs of the Jewish community as well as the Gentile one. Pause over this for a moment. We live in an age in which Jewish followers of Jesus are relatively rare. There was a time, however, when they were dominant members of the church. Those Jewish followers of Jesus also faced scrutiny from their family and neighbors as to whether or not they were being faithful to their community and the Old Testament laws. Had they associated with uncircumcised Gentiles, their own community would have marginalized their message. Novelist Chaim Potok provides this stark description of first century Jews in his popular history of the Jews, *Wanderings*:

> The Jews of Judea . . . spoke Aramaic and Greek. Pagans lived in their midst. Jews had little to do with them, would rarely enter their homes, would not drink their wine or milk, eat their bread, or purchase meat from their butcher shops. Three days before a pagan festival Jews would cease their business transactions with pagans; they wished to contribute in no way, directly or indirectly, to pagan rites. Many Jews would not enter a pagan city during a pagan festival, not even to pass through. Jewish workers would not participate in construction that was in any way connected to pagan worship . . . Resentful and uncom-

prehending pagans mocked the Jewish rite of circumcision, the observance of the Sabbath, the abstention from pork.[15]

Jews faced the same problem as Gentile believers. Gentiles who submitted to circumcision were seen as joining a foreign, Jewish community. On the other hand, Jews who associated with uncircumcised Gentiles risked being reckoned as Gentiles by fellow Jews for abandoning Jewish ceremonial purity. Each feared being labelled as a convert to the other's community: being reckoned as a cultural or ethnic traitor. Flemming writes, "Acts 15 describes a church on a journey to a deeper understanding of identity as the one people of God comprised of two distinct cultural groups who believe in Jesus. Neither group must *surrender* its cultural identity . . ."[16]

That conclusion is crucial and worth pondering: *Neither group had to surrender its cultural or social identity.* Jews could remain Jews. Gentiles could remain Gentiles. Yet both groups were remarkably changed by their allegiance to Jesus and found a way to fellowship together. This is a remarkable pattern for retaining past identity and prioritizing one's current and future identity in Jesus.

Tennent says the hope of Christian unity is found in all cultural backgrounds, Muslim, Hindu, Christian, and Jew, finding their unity in Jesus. I agree. But he and Carson overemphasize what that unity means for retaining one's past identity.

In 2009, a few sentences from Andrew Walls, missions historian, emphasized this relationship between identity and background. He wrote:

> Second-century Hellenistic Christians who wished to present Christ to those who shared the same cultural heritage had to consider the relationship of Christ to that heritage, to their past as Greeks. *No one can have a sense of identity without their past.*[17]

Walls writes about how Greco-Roman engagement shifted Christian theology in the second century. The Gospel came into a Hebrew context, but its expression adapted upon articulation to Greeks. First and second century Greeks had to wrestle with Jesus in light of their own cultural heritage. They had to reckon with their past. They could not ignore it.

The connection Walls makes between identity and the past was like lightning for me. Asking Muslims or Gentiles or Jews to renounce their birth identity so they could follow Jesus was akin to asking them to erase their past. On the surface it seemed to be a way of inviting them into all the riches of the Gospel. Yet it threatened to detach those riches from their community, from their history, and from their sense of identity. That, I recognized, was not required of new believers. Walls describes this process in Acts 15: "considering the relationship of Christ to [their] heritage."[18] Fundamentally, Acts 15 affirms the right of believers—from Jewish and Gentile backgrounds—to retain and renew the way of their own community. Neither group is required to make an absolute break with their community of birth, nor with their past history. They all retain, in some significant way, the identity of their birth.

Studying Acts 15, **I did not see a loss of past cultural identity as a prerequisite for unity in Christ.** The church allowed, and even encouraged believers to maintain their connections with their communities for the sake of Jesus. The apostles, by the Spirit's leading, recognized that following Jesus did not obliterate a community's past. James, Paul, Peter, and Barnabas did not tell the Jews in Acts 15 to accept the Gentiles *carte blanche*. There were stipulations within the relationship that the Gentiles were asked to consider. Put another way, they asked the Gentiles to accept the Jews *as Jews* by upholding the rules of Leviticus 17-18. And the apostles didn't ask the Gentiles to be circumcised. They knew circumcision would be a rejection of their own past and turn them into cultural Jews. Instead, they found a remarkable path forward that involved both retaining connections to the past and pursuing deeper fellowship with people outside of their community of birth. It was a beautiful, Holy Spirit inspired step forward in a long journey. It also provides a model of intentional accommodation for the sake of loving, Gospel-centered community.

But is this not religious accommodation?

At least one objection may remain, specifically, how the term "Gentile" is used in the New Testament. Is it an exclusively ethnic term? This is a key issue. In seminary, I learned that ethnic distinctions could not be required for salvation. Though there has been controversy over this in past centuries, the current controversy is over *religious* distinctions. Could the term "Gentile" have a "religious" meaning?

Paul addresses the concerns of Acts 15 by warning the Galatians (chapter 2) that they must turn a deaf ear to Jewish believers who are pressuring Gentile believers to be circumcised. To require this would be to abandon Jesus' exclusive role in their lives. This is unacceptable.

Paul gets into this debate. He explains how he stood up against the very "rock" of the church—the apostle Peter himself. Peter had been eating with Gentiles, possibly even eating non-kosher food. When Jewish believers came to Antioch, Peter separated himself from the Gentiles. Even Barnabas, Paul's ministry partner who had seen much fruit among the Gentiles, followed Peter's example. Paul was livid. Here's how he explains this controversy:

> When I saw that they were not acting in line with the truth of the gospel, I said to Peter in front of them all, "You are a Jew, yet you live like a Gentile and not like a Jew. How is it, then, that you force Gentiles to follow Jewish customs? We who are Jews by birth and not *'Gentile sinners'* know that a man is not justified by observing the law, but by faith in Jesus Christ . . . (Gal 2:14–16, NIV; emphasis added).

Every time I read this, I am shocked by what Paul calls the Gentiles. He calls them "Gentile sinners!" The label screams ethnocentrism—portraying one ethnic group as morally superior just because of its ethnicity. Paul contrasts these "sinners" with his own culture and ethnicity of birth: Jewishness. Paul indicates that in some sense, Gentile-*ness* had deep associations with sin. Perhaps Jews presumed that Gentiles participated in the grossest of human activities: idolatry, homosexuality, prostitution. This is what Carson has done concerning Muslims, presumed that they are naturally connected to sin. Whether by birth or by association, Gentiles were presumed to be sinners. Not only did Gentiles not have the promises of Abraham, but as a culture they were sin-soaked. Yet, the argument of this passage is that God accepts these Gentile sinners as they are, apart from any required departure from their "Gentile-*ness*" into Jewish-*ness*. The latter point is usually our point of emphasis. They did not have to become Jews to be saved. But does not Paul say even more? Is he not also saying that they did not have to stop being Gentiles? They, like Peter once did, could continue to "live like Gentiles" (Gal 2:14)![19]

The term Gentile was not a neutral one. It was loaded with connotations of idolatry and ungodly behavior (see, for example, Eph 2:11; 1 Thess 4:5; 1 Pet

4:3). Does Paul endorse that idolatry and ungodly behavior? By no means. But he and the early church were willing to take significant cultural and theological risks. If Gentiles stayed connected to their pagan communities and retained their identity as "Gentiles," people might still think they were pagans. They risked people saying they were participants in the evil elements of paganism. Worse, as will be seen in 1 Corinthians 8–10, some probably did participate in these evil elements because of the blurred lines. Why take such a risk? For only one reason: *to ensure that only allegiance to Jesus, not the presence or lack of particular identity labels, is the standard by which entrance into God's kingdom is judged.*

Risk for the sake of Jesus' exclusive sufficiency

The parallels to the Muslim world should be clear by now. The question I faced was the same one Paul and the early believers were facing. Was it not a form of *miscommunication* to allow Gentiles to stay Gentiles as they followed Jesus? Would it not proclaim they were still in relationship with darkness? It might. And on the other side of the equation, what might be required of me to faithfully disciple Muslims in light of well-meaning pressure from Christians for them to conform to a certain social identity—to do this and not do that? Galatians 2 had insights for both concerns.

I was confronted with a multitude of problems: association, identity, community and allegiance, questions the first century church had also faced. None of this was new. Yet I saw in the New Testament the powerful leading of the Spirit to help those devoted to his name sort out these messy controversies. Their worlds were swirling with risk and confusion and debate. Yet somehow, God led them forward into deeper truth.

So, the early church took those risks. And I was forced to ask if disciples of Jesus in Muslim contexts could handle those same risks. To put it in shockingly clear terms, I believe in the 21st century we must accept the risk that both Christians and Muslims might consider the on-going connection of disciples of Jesus with their Muslim contexts as ongoing participation in false religion. Dixon and many Western evangelicals today define Islam as inherently evil. They see this connection as inherently corrupting. Yet that accusation, I came to see, is the same one the early church faced in its embrace of Gentiles. The term Gentiles similarly held connotations of evil and heinously false worship to the Jews. Inclusion of these Gentiles, still somewhat connected to their Gentile communities, as full members of the people of God risked contaminating the purity of the Gospel for first century believers. Disciples in Muslim contexts present the same risks to the global church today that the Gentiles did to the predominantly Jewish believers of the first century. Yet we must take the same risks for the same reason: to ensure that allegiance to Jesus alone be the standard by which entrance into God's kingdom is judged. Or, to use Carson's words, to uphold the exclusive sufficiency of Jesus.

REFLECTION QUESTIONS

1. What are some issues of controversy among Christians today that you feel passionately about? How does experience influence those debates and controversies?
2. Have you ever changed your mind on a significant issue in your life? What factors played into your change of perspective? In what way did Scripture inform that change?
3. Think about one of your communities. How does your community describe itself? To what extent are these "labels" religious, social, or racial? In what ways do those different aspects of the labels intersect in your life and the life of your community?
4. As you reflect on your spiritual community, what are the barriers that prevent other people getting access to that community?

---

1. N. T. Wright, *Justification: God's Plan and Paul's Vision* (Downers Grove, IL: IVP Academic, 2009), 37.
2. See Tom A. Steffen, "Foundational Roles of Symbol and Narrative in the (Re)construction of Reality and Relationships," *Missiology: An International Review* 26, no. 4 (October, 1998): 485.
3. D. A. Carson, "That By All Means I Might Win Some: Faithfulness and Flexibility in Gospel Proclamation," The Gospel Coalition National Conference (2009). The transcript is now available at D. A. Carson, "That By All Means I Might Win Some: Faithfulness and Flexibility in Gospel Proclamation," (2017): accessed May 23, 2023, https://www.thegospelcoalition.org/conference_media/means-might-win/.
4. Carson, "That By All Means." Quotations are transcribed from the audio and may very slightly from the more recent print version.
5. Carson, "That By All Means."
6. Carson hints at that context at the beginning of his talk. He presumes, with some others, that an insider paradigm can be associated with the emergent church, an approach to ministry in the West that Carson had written a whole book critiquing. At least two key writers on

insider issues, Higgins and Travis, have denied any awareness let alone association with the emergent approach. (Travis said this to me in a phone conversation; Kevin Higgins published it in "Speaking the Truth About Insider Movements: Addressing the Criticisms of Bill Nikides and 'Phil' Relative to the Article 'Inside What?'," *St Francis Magazine* 5, no. 6 (December, 2009): 62.)

7. Carson, "That By All Means."
8. My adaptation of Carson's words would be like this: "The flexibility and accommodation in this passage encourage Muslim converts to identify themselves with the Gospel, with Jesus, and with the Cross. They are now people who express their allegiance to Jesus and under that allegiance they can flex about their social identity so as to win their fellow Muslims." Indeed, this wording is essentially the thesis of this book.
9. In addition to articles already referenced, some of the articles I was reading at the time were: John Travis, "Four Responses to Tennent," *International Journal of Frontier Missiology* (2006): 124–25; Kevin Higgins, "The Key to Insider Movements: The 'Devoted's' of Acts," *International Journal of Frontier Missions* 21, no. 4 (2004): 155–65; Kevin Higgins, "Acts 15 and Insider Movements Among Muslims: Questions, Process, and Conclusions," *International Journal of Frontier Missiology* 24, no. 1 (2007): 29–40; Kevin Higgins, "Inside What? Church, Culture, Religion and Insider Movements in Biblical Perspective," *St Francis Magazine* 5, no. 4 (August, 2009): 74–79; Rebecca Lewis, "Promoting Movements to Christ Within Natural Communities," *International Journal of Frontier Missiology* 24, no. 2 (2007): 75–76; Rebecca Lewis, "The Integrity of the Gospel and Insider Movements," *International Journal of Frontier Missiology* 27 (2010): 44–48; and Rick Brown, "Biblical Muslims," *International Journal of Frontier Missiology* 24, no. 2 (Summer 2007): 65–74.
10. Lewis, "Promoting Movements," 75–76; emphasis added.
11. Higgins, "Speaking the Truth," 74-79; emphasis added.
12. Carson's assumption that the label "Christian" is necessary for being in the third category he upholds would also rule out the C4 position on the C-Spectrum.
13. Tennent, "Followers of Jesus," 109; *emphasis added.*
14. There is considerable debate among scholars of the first centuries about how Jews viewed Gentiles. See D. R. de Lacey, "Gentiles," in *Dictionary of Paul and His Letters,* ed. Gerald F. Hawthorne and Ralph P. Martin (Dowers Grove, IL: InterVarsity Press, 1993) and John M Barclay, *Jews in the Mediterranean Diaspora: From Alexander to Trajan (323 Bce–117 Ce)* (Edinburgh, Scotland: T&T Clark, 1999).
15. Chaim Potok, *Wanderings: Chaim Potok's History of the Jews* (New York, NY: Alfred A. Knopf, 1978), 203-204.
16. Dean Flemming, *Contextualization in the New Testament: Patterns for Theology and Mission* (Downers Grove, IL: InterVarsity Press, 2005), 52, emphasis added.
17. Walls, *The Missionary Movement*, 97.
18. Walls, *The Missionary Movement*, 97.
19. One of the greatest difficulties in this discussion is that the clear boundaries we think we have in the 21st century between "ethnicity," "religion," and "culture" turn out to be post-Enlightenment concepts that many historians of religion and social scientists today simply do not believe existed in the first century. For further details on this issue, please read the Appendix on "A Discussion of Religion, Culture, Ethnicity, Gentiles, Muslims, and Jews." For a thorough discussion of the issue, see Brent Nongbri, *Before Religion* (New Haven, CT: Yale University Press, 2013).

PART II

THE VISION EXPANDS

Missing in Mesoamerica on the part of missionaries was the sensitivity to see that God had been present and speaking for centuries before the arrival of the Spaniards, and that now a new opportunity was being given in this place to pursue life through the death and resurrection—the self-sacrifice of Christ. Rather, these missionaries insisted the people leave all that they knew about God and how he worked. But this was to ask them to lose their identity—to stop being who they knew they were.[1]

William Dyrness and Oscar Garcia-Johnson

---

1. William A. Dyrness, and Osca García-Johnson, *Theology Without Borders: An Introduction to Global Conversations* (Grand Rapids, MI: Baker Academic, Kindle, 2015), 1701.

4

AN EXPANSIVE VISION OF CHRIST IN MISSION

[As] the gospel has been translated into Chinese, Indian, African, Korean, and other cultures, we gain more and more insights into the beauty and reality of Jesus Christ. I have referred to this phenomenon as the 'ontic expansion of God in Jesus Christ.' This expression, of course, does not refer to any ontological change in the nature of Jesus Christ himself, but rather, to how our own understanding and insight into the full nature and work of God in and through Jesus Christ is continually expanding as more and more people groups come to the feet of Jesus.[1]

Timothy Tennent

RISKS AND REWARD IN PERSPECTIVE

Risk. We participate in risk on a daily basis. We go in one direction; we turn from others. One choice may lead to disaster; another opens a bright future. Risk is integral to being human, to being finite.

I took a risk when I moved my family to Central Asia. Most Americans and many Central Asians look at me like I am crazy. Isn't it risky? It is risky to live anywhere in this sin-fallen world. Some risks in Central Asia are higher. There are suicide bombers. There is warfare. We have heard bombs and gunfire. We have had friends kidnapped and gunned down. We have risked, and in some cases, we have suffered.

But other risks are reduced. My children know diverse cultures, have experienced a global world, and speak multiple languages. Living in Central Asia has sheltered them from much of the cultural decay that Christians in America battle. In Central Asia our children learn respect for parents and respect for guests. They share our family's mission to see the Gospel break into and transform communities. We have seen miracles. We have felt the immeasurable privilege of watching tears in the eyes of Muslims as they hear about God's love through Jesus for the first time. These gifts are ours because of the risks we have been willing to take. I would not trade that joy for the cost any day.

Making decisions about discipleship and identity issues in ministry has been no different for me. Discipleship in Muslim contexts involves risk. The threat of faith in Jesus being corrupted by false religion seems great. Mixing orthodox faith in Jesus with something foreign to Scripture, what is commonly called syncretism, presents danger. We could potentially be promoting allegiance to a rival to Jesus. We could be changing the core of biblical faith. We could divide our hearts or undermine Jesus' supremacy.

But the risk of contextualization is more like a bridge than a cliff. When we walk along a cliff, the farther we get from the edge the better. Some people see contextualization and identity issues that way. The closer believers adhere to a Muslim context, the closer, it is said, they are to the edge of a cliff. But bringing the Gospel to a new culture is a lot more like a bridge. It is possible to fear stepping off one side of the bridge *so much that you end up falling off the other side.*

Falling off the bridge can happen in a variety of ways. For one, it can impact whether a young church endures. I have seen gathered believers, who left their community identity, show initial signs of success but not last beyond the presence of the foreigner who initiated the gathering of the believers. Once the foreigner leaves, gatherings fall apart, along with the interpersonal relationships among the believers. Our team served a church in Central Asia that had five appointed local Muslim background elders with one hundred participants. We provided the elders' salaries. We taught them theology from our sending church's statement of faith. That church no longer exists. Our model for ministry was too foreign, too dependent on us. The church died soon after our team left.

We can also fall off the bridge by failing to bring reproducible transformation to the core of people's lives. New believers may copy the foreigner's practice and identity, because it seems the "Christian" way, but this might not involve lasting internal change. Young disciples have affirmed what I say to them simply because I say it, not because they understand or believe it. I have watched others seemingly build a fellowship of believers with a non-Muslim identity, only to find out that none of them share about Jesus with their families, not truly understanding the Gospel for themselves. New believers may conform, yet internally their thoughts, desires, and allegiances remain untouched. They aren't transformed. Syncretism can result through external conformity to standards professed by the missionary, while a person's internal convictions and desires remain unchanged.[2]

What about discipling within an existing context and identity? This approach can still teach the "faith once for all delivered to the saints" (Jude 3, ESV) *within* their life and community. This approach can emphasize Jesus' supremacy and build dependency on the Scriptures and the Holy Spirit, allowing community members more access to the Gospel. Like the parable at the beginning of this book, seekers of Jesus often think they have to leave their community when they come to faith. Hearing that they can stay in that community as a follower of Jesus opens the possibility for personal and community transformation.

I risk extraction by encouraging new believers to reject their Muslim identity. I risk missing what God might do in and through their community. I risk imposing my blinders on Central Asians. The lesson from the burqa illustrates this. I risk assuming that I have complete vision *outside of the burqa*. I risk missing the theological truths Central Asians can show us about God and his work in this world. The spread of the Gospel is arrested when my culture is presented as *the* Christian culture.

Encouraging believers to reject their identity as Muslim risks undermining God's intention to magnify his own splendor through every culture on earth.

Risk is unavoidable. Could it be that squashing God's purposes is the greater risk?

Expanding Vision in the Biblical Storyline

God is supremely interested in revealing his own character and glory as more people groups "glorify God for his mercy" (Romans 15:9, ESV). God's mission in redeeming more kinds of people from sin is to show off how one sliver of humanity cannot come even close to understanding and proclaiming his divine revelation sufficiently. God's words to the servant in Isaiah apply broadly, "It is too small a thing" for God to reveal himself to one nation, let alone to reveal himself *through* one nation (Isa 49:6).

My foreign experience of the gospel is not luggage to be carried from my home in America to Central Asia and dropped off into the homes of Muslims. I cannot simply unpack doctrines I learned in seminary from my suitcase and expect Muslims to take that same suitcase to other homes and people.

Missions requires something greater than the task of a baggage handler at the airport. It involves whole-self engagement with a community of people created in God's image, yet in need of transformative hope. New believers will be powerfully endowed with gifts to be enjoyed, savored, and explored.

There is a telescopic element to the missional task. By entering into the complex and broken world of another community, we are also invited to see anew. A telescope, though difficult to position and focus, offers the possibility of expansive vision into the heavens every time I set it up: from every location that I use it. From each spot on the globe different angles and constellations come into focus. From the new vantage point of Asian Muslims, I discover angles I have never considered, never even tried to see. They are the same heavens. God and his revelation are objective. I, however, am the finite one—unable to see all that God has for me to see.

This is not a position of universalism or inclusivism, as though all paths or religions lead us to a right relationship with God. The Bible teaches an exclusivity to Jesus, his claims, and Scripture's authority. I believe that conscious faith is necessary to find salvation; apart from faith, all people face God's judgment and wrath. But this exclusivism does not require us to articulate all truth through a singular cultural lens. In Christ, there is an expansive way of knowing and explaining God's grandeur and purposes. The story of that expanding vision begins in Genesis.

In Genesis 1:26 we hear God's vision for his creation of man and woman:

> Then God said, "Let us make human beings in our image, to be like us. They will reign over the fish in the sea, the birds in the sky, the livestock, all the wild animals on the earth, and the small animals that scurry along the ground."

Past theologians have emphasized the "moral aspects" of God as the meaning of this phrase "image of God." Humans make decisions, are intelligent beings, do creative things, and so reflect God. This skews the focus of the passage. As many biblical theologians argue today, the passage likely refers to humanity's role as representatives of God's leadership over the earth. The second half of verse 26 talks about people *reigning* over the fish. Wheaton Old Testament professor John Walton states, "In Genesis, people represent God to the rest of creation."[3] It is the role of an ambassador. When you talk to an ambassador, you are talking to the person charged to do and say what the king himself would do or say.

Here's the interesting part. The command given to these divine representatives in verse 28 is to "be fruitful and multiply and fill the earth and subdue it." God's plan from the beginning of creation is to have the world filled with his representatives, employing his ways "on earth, as it is in heaven" (Matt 6:10).

Though not initially obvious, God's plan is not for monocultural expressions of himself to expand throughout the world. His plan is for diverse expressions. Ten chapters later in the story of Babel, we get hints of this crucial development.

In Genesis 11, the author describes people gathering together and building a tower that reaches up into heaven for the sake of their own reputation. God interrupts their plans. He confuses their languages and forces them to spread out (echoing God's command to *fill* the earth). God's intervention here catalyzes greater diversification of culture through diversification of language.

Anyone who travels to another country or enters a different part of a major Western city these days is immersed in a confusion of languages. This confusion extends beyond the individual terms people use for bread, water, and toilet. Languages represent whole complexes of thought, complete paradigms making sense of life. Confusion between peoples happens because of the way we intuit understanding, infer meaning, and follow the most easily assumed path of meaning.

With the extent of confusion possible through diversified languages, we could take the story of Babel as proof that cultural diversity is a curse from God for human pride. It's akin to the weeds of the Fall in this perspective. Adam sinned and God sent weeds as punishment. The town of Babel sinned and God sent different languages as punishment. With redemption, God will take away the weeds, right? And he'll take away the diversity of the world and replace it with uniformity . . . right?

Wrong. That's not the direction salvation history takes. Indeed, immediately following Babel we get an indication of the direction God intends to take this: Abram is told that "all the families" (i.e. all those diverse groups now catalyzed by the diversification of languages) will be blessed through Abram (Gen 12:1–3).

Abram becomes Abraham, "the father of many nations." Abraham's children become Israel. Israel (Jacob) has twelve sons who become an enslaved people in Egypt, freed by Moses, and eventually planted in Canaan. God gives this people His law—a highly detailed and culturally specific law—a law designed for a farming community in the Middle East. They don't keep this law; the economic justice required by the law is hard enough, but they especially disobey the commands to worship God only. God sends them into exile, forced to live among other cultures and prone to assimilate when they are supposed to stand out. Returned at last to their land, they still *feel* themselves in exile—ruled by foreigners (pagan idol-worshippers) whose cultures radiate blasphemy to the holy people of God.

Jesus comes into this context. He is born to a virgin. He grows up. He says amazing things about himself. But he is specific about his calling to the people of Israel. When a Canaanite woman asks for his help, he tells her he has "come only to the lost sheep of Israel" and implies that, as a Gentile woman, she is no better than a dog in comparison to the "children" of Israel (Matt 15:24–26). Is his mission for just that one people, that one culture? And does God's self-revelation as a Jewish carpenter mean that first century Judaism is the pinnacle of cultural purity and beauty? That Gentiles are vastly inferior? Is this what we are to know of God?

My Muslim friends compare themselves to others in this way. Much of the conflict in the Muslim world these days—sadly spilling all over the globe—is about the extent to which God's revelation to Mohammad in the seventh century Arabian desert applies to the modern world. Do we need to dress like Mohammad, eat like him, wear a beard like him and treat our women like he did to know God? Is that God's best? Ask the question of the seventh century Arab world or first century Palestine and the root issue is the same. Does God privilege one culture as the fundamental expression of who he is? Is God *essentially* Jewish or *essentially* Arab or Greek or American? How do we understand the use God makes of a culture to explain himself?

I have indicated part of my answer in the previous chapter. In the Gospels and the book of Acts, there's an explosive outreach from Israel to the diverse communities of the world. "Go to all nations," Jesus says at the end of the Gospel of Matthew. The Spirit blows on the first apostles and they give their message in many languages. Gentiles start following Jesus. The early church makes radical decisions: "No" to circumcision for all and "Yes" to varied, pagan-associated members of God's kingdom. This opens the floodgates. So much so that we think of Christianity today in Greco-Roman categories, too often forgetting the Jewish context in which the story came.

When we come to Revelation, we find images that blow open the category of monoculturalism. Genesis is fulfilled in a way no Hebrew, Jew, or even first century Gentile could have expected. Diversity becomes a central part of the very worship of God. The Apostle John sees "all tribes and peoples and languages standing before the throne and before the Lamb" (Rev 7:9). At the end of history, we find Genesis 1 fulfilled. Humanity has been fruitful and multiplied. They have filled the earth. Now, from those diverse contexts, cultures, and languages, they bow to worship together.

A few years ago, a part of Revelation helped me see this worship in deeper tones. Most of my readers are likely comfortable with the image of people praising God in multiple languages. In a post-Vatican II world the Roman Catholic church holds to colloquial languages in worship now. Evangelicals and Protestants have held to this basic principle since the days of Luther. But the link between language and culture has been more deeply understood over recent decades and Revelation draws that out. Reference the C-Spectrum: On the far left, C1, new believers gather to worship in a language not their own. This happens today. God is honored in it. C2, though, is a subtle shift. The worship is linguistically native, but culturally foreign. It is possible to worship God with your mother language but adopt foreign culture in the process. Have you ever heard a Chris Tomlin song in Spanish or another language? The words are translated, but the cultural meaning may be lost to those from another culture. The rhythm and tune of the song are American even if the words come from another language. God is honored in this. But it does not represent the fullness of his intention.

The apostle John foresees the kings of the earth entering into the New Jerusalem "in all their glory," and the nations bringing their "glory and honor into the city" (Rev 21:24-26). Andy Crouch, an editor at Christianity Today, and Richard Mouw, former president of Fuller seminary and a respected New Testament scholar, helped me see the connection between this passage and Isaiah 60. The Apostle John is writing about the fulfillment of Isaiah 60, and its shocking message.

Isaiah 60 describes Israel's enemies marching into Jerusalem to worship. But God declares that these very enemies from distant lands will come to bow before Him and fill out the worship by making his temple glorious. Here's a sampling of the stunning vision as the Lord speaks promise to the city of Jerusalem:

> Vast caravans of camels will converge on you, the camels of Midian and Ephah. The people of Sheba will bring gold and frankincense and will come worshiping the LORD. The flocks of Kedar will be given to you, and the rams of Nebaioth will be brought for my altars. I will accept their offerings, and I will make my Temple glorious (Isa 60:6-7).

The nations bring their prizes—camels from Midian and gold from Sheba. In these strange details, we see a connection between culture and the way people spread throughout the earth.

Crouch defines culture simply, but helpfully, as "what we make of the world."[4] Kenneth Nehrbass, a missiology professor, writes that culture is "everything we think, do, or have as members of a society."[5] Significantly, the things we "think, do, and have" change based on where we live. Camels are important along the dry steppes of Central Asia, but they prove unnecessary in Minnesota's land of lakes. Spreading throughout the world means that humans learn ice fishing and invent snowmobiles in addition to using camel caravans and 4Runners. The spreading of the nations throughout the globe, even through sinful means, has increased the cultural production of the peoples.

In keeping with John's vision at the end of the age, the more places people live, the more types of things they will "think, do, and have." Mouw notes,

> Indeed, linguistic, racial, and national boundaries have provided the framework for a variety of cultural and social experiments involving the human spirit. When the end of history arrives, then, there is something to be gathered in. Diverse cultural riches will be brought into the Heavenly City. That which has been parceled out in human history must now be collected for the glory of the Creator.[6]

Put another way, the very diversity forced upon the world through Babel becomes a source of greater worship to God.

That is what Revelation 21 indicates. These different nations and kings do not just bring their languages to worship God. They bring their *caravans of splendor* that are particularly their own. The New Living Translation puts it even more dramatically—"the kings of the world will enter the city in all their glory" (21:24). Glory for pagan nations? For idolaters? For people not from the monotheistic, special people of God—Israel? Yes, John says. Glory that God designed through centuries and millennia to come from even them.

This idea is reinforced by the Apostle Paul in Ephesians 3. Paul's proclamation of the Gospel to the Gentiles is linked to God's eternal purpose "to use the church to display his wisdom in its rich variety to all the unseen rulers and authorities in the heavenly places" (v. 10). God shows off, in short, by redeeming all these different people, different cultures, different languages and making their "glory" his own. This variety, this diversity, this expansive possibility is part of God's universal purpose. *Now that is stunning.*

This expansive vision has altered the way that I see my work among Muslims. I have taken Mouw's words to heart:

> No one human individual or group . . . can fully bear or manifest all that is involved in the image of God . . . The image of God is, as it were, parceled out among the peoples of the earth. By looking at different individuals and groups we get glimpses of different aspects of the full image of God.[7]

Revelation 21 brings us full circle to Genesis 1. God creates two image bearers in Adam and Eve. And yet, those two image bearers eventually become billions. I think that exponential increase is significant. It shows us there is more to see and know—more to reflect and represent of God than any one culture, let alone any individual person, can manage. It is a lot like the difference between a hand-mirror and the sun. The sun is far too bright and powerful to be reflected in a single hand-mirror. It would take millions, if not billions, to reflect the sun's splendor. That is how stunning God's own brilliance is in comparison to human culture.

Fear and stereotyping

We began this chapter by reflecting on risk. In closing, consider how fearful many are that we will lose the core of Christianity. In the West there is a feeling of being under assault, of losing what is most important to us—our freedoms, our financial security, or our religion. That protective and fearful posture prompts us to relate to Muslims in a certain way. We tend to see them in attack mode, making an assault on Christian culture, perhaps on Christian theology. I suggest this perspective is based in unbiblical fear rather than the confident hopefulness that Scripture radiates. God is intent on putting himself on full display through all cultures, even Muslim ones. We should approach mission with expectation not fear.

Fear tends to close down possibilities. It loves to pigeon-hole people defining them in order to protect us from emotional, physical, and spiritual vulnerability. God calls us to love, not fear (1 John 4:18).

God placed Muslims in the world. Paul says this clearly in Acts 17:26: "From one man he created all nations throughout the whole earth. He decided beforehand when they should rise and fall, and he determined their boundaries." Part of God's purpose in placing nations where he did and permitting them to develop culturally and religiously as they do is that they might bring forth fresh cultural riches as they are redeemed. These would not have been possible had those people developed as they did through history. All peoples must repent (Acts 17:30). And all cultures are woven with sin. But they are also intertwined with glory that God alone can sort out. Missions is a pursuit of that glory.

As cultural beings, we can be blind to cultural glory and confuse it for sin, simply because it is different than our experience and upbringing. The vision of this book treads sensitively in the crossing of cultures. It is far too easy to crush culture. It takes the power and mercy of God to refine it and redeem it. God calls us to be vessels of that power unleashed in the Muslim world.

This is the strongest argument for discipling *within* Muslim contexts. To honor the supremacy of Jesus in all things, we must position ourselves as those in pursuit of that supremacy. Part of pursuing his supremacy means humbly recognizing our own cultural blindspots. In the coming pages, I will draw parallels between presumed Islamic sins and hidden Western ones. Believers from all cultural backgrounds have been changed by grace, but none are complete, including those from mature Christian communities. We do and say and see many things incorrectly. If we are to see Jesus' splendor, we must recognize the plank in our eye before we critique the specks in Muslim eyes (Matt 7:3–5).

This means calling Muslims first and foremost to the throne of Jesus—not to culturally defined Christianity. Some reject the idea that these two things can be distinguished. But I have seen the distinction make sense to my Muslim friends. With Jesus as Lord, transformation from the inside-out is possible. Deep cultural riches that God has prepared for his own worship will stream into the heavenly throne room as a result. I don't want to crush those riches. I want to mine them out.

In the next chapter I take on our tendency to pigeon-hole Muslims. My resistance to discipleship in Muslim contexts had a lot to do with *who* I thought Muslims were and *what* I considered their fundamental problem. If that issue can be addressed, perhaps a door will open to disciples functioning within their local identity.

REFLECTION QUESTIONS

1. How have you understood the task and goal of missions?
2. What aspects of your own culture can you envision being brought in worship to God on "caravans of splendor" into the New Jerusalem?
3. What aspects of others' cultures can you envision being brought in worship to God on "caravans of splendor" into the New Jerusalem?

---

1. Timothy C. Tennent, *Theology in the Context of World Christianity: How the Global Church is Influencing the Way We Think About and Discuss Theology* (Grand Rapids, MI: Zondervan, 2007), 111.
2. See Robert Priest, "Missionary Elenctics: Conscience and Culture," *Missiology: An International Review* 22, no. 3 (July, 1994): 305.
3. John H. Walton, *The Lost World of Genesis One: Ancient Cosmology and the Origins Debate* (Downers Grove, IL: InterVarsity Press, 2010): 68. cf. G. K. Beale, *The Temple and the Church's Mission: A Biblical Theology of the Dwelling Place of God* (Downers Grove, IL: IVP Academic, 2004); Henry R. Van Til, *The Calvinistic Concept of Culture [With a New Foreword]* (Grand Rapids, MI: Baker Academic, 1972), 1688, Kindle; N. T. Wright, *How God Became King: The Forgotten Story of the Gospels* (New York, NY: HarperOne, 2011).
4. Andy Crouch, *Culture Making: Recovering Our Creative Calling* (Downers Grove, IL: IVP Books, 2008), 25.
5. Kenneth Robert Nehrbass, *Advanced Missiology: How to Study Missions in Credible and Useful Ways* (Eugene, OR: Cascade Books, 2021), 111.
6. Richard J. Mouw, *When the Kings Come Marching in: Isaiah and the New Jerusalem* (Grand Rapids, MI: William B. Eerdmans Publishing Company, 2002), 743, Kindle.
7. Mouw, *When the Kings*, 743.

5

LOVING PEOPLE MORE THAN CATEGORIES

After spending forty-seven years in the Arab world, and after acquiring the ability to lecture in four kinds of Arabic, I never said to my Arabic-speaking friends, "We Arabs." Knowing where that un-crossable line is drawn is a critical piece of acquired awareness... [The Apostle Paul] knows that he cannot become a Gentile [in 1 Corinthians 9:21], and he plays no games with his readers. Only when we are deeply rooted in our own culture can we risk reaching out across a cultural chasm to people on the other side. A bridge must be securely anchored at each end. Only then can the bridge be completed and only then is travel across the bridge possible. [1]

Kenneth Bailey

LOOKING FOR LOGS BEFORE STUDYING SPECKS

What does it mean to be an American?

Living in Muslim countries for twenty years, I thought about that question a lot. It comes up in some form in almost daily conversation with my Central Asian friends.

We can answer the question from a variety of vantage points. An American is someone born in America. But that is not the entire answer. One of my sons was born in former Soviet Central Asia, yet he's still American because he has two American parents. There are also naturalized citizens—people born in another country that have lived long enough in America and have expressed sufficient loyalty to the American constitution to be reckoned political citizens.

We have other ways of talking about being American. We sometimes call a war hero or respected leader a "true American." What we usually mean by this is that they uphold American ideals. What are those ideals? Some would say they are individual liberty, representative government, capitalism, respect for political rights, entrepreneurial spirit, and so on. African Americans and Indigenous Peoples question some of these portrayals. Though they might embrace the ideals, some question that Americans have lived up to them. We bear 200 years of a slavery tradition, a history of land seizures, a century of explicit legal racism and all sorts of other indications that respect for "life, liberty, and the pursuit of happiness" has been a distant reality.

Perhaps we could ask non-Americans to define an American. Europeans might talk about how loud we are, how strange our politics are or how we love our guns and big cars. Pakistanis might talk about how interventionist we are, how we think we control the world, and gladly violate other nations' sovereignty when it serves our own interests. Latin Americans might reflect on our hypocrisy—using Latin labor for cheap products and then blaming immigration for all our problems.

Most of my Central Asian friends buy into the American dream from afar. They imagine our country, if not our people, to be void of war and full of unlimited possibility. They also think we are all rich, without any constraints on our financial resources. Most think we are sexually licentious, picturing Hollywood portrayals of casual sex to be part of our daily lives.

What can we say on a spiritual level? A majority of Americans claim to be Christian.[2] As many as 24% even claim to be evangelical Christian.[3] Many have attended church at one time or another. Christian influence is constantly debated in the political sphere. Some want more of it. Some want it expelled from the discussion.

Then there are other spiritual influences on our national character. We love sports, malls, and restaurants. We are known for workaholism and obesity. All these things consume our affection—it is hard to be crystal clear about who or what we fundamentally worship.

So, what does it mean to be American? Can we pick one of these characteristics and make it the essential American quality? Of course not.

Americans are some of these things, none of these things, and all of these things. You cannot define Americans as one quality. If you try, you will surely find exceptions and offend a large segment of Americans in the process.

The same is true for Muslims.

Learning what it means to be Muslim from a Muslim

Azizullah is a good friend of mine from Central Asia. He worked for over ten years at an aid office that I directed. Partially literate, Azizullah was a hardworking farmer, father of eight, and devout Muslim. When I say devout, I mean that he prayed five times a day and rigorously kept the fast during the month of Ramadan. He also served as one of my best cultural informants.

I remember the day Azizullah made a landscaping proposal to me. Central Asians love to tell stories. He took me out to the office compound—a big open space used to park two vehicles, a Toyota minivan and Toyota 4Runner, used by our office to find and treat Tuberculosis patients. He told me how the property had been when our humanitarian aid office first took it over. It was filled with large and lush fruit trees. Now it was a brown and dusty parking lot. Then he said to me, "With spring just around the corner, wouldn't it be nice if we planted some trees around the perimeter? Then, someday, when those trees are nice and big and green, *some Muslim might sit under them and find shade.*"

At the end of the day, Azizullah wanted me to allocate office money to pay for saplings. I did so. But that one phrase stuck with me: "some Muslim." He used the term for "Muslim" as we might say, "somebody." *Someone* might sit under that tree *someday*. But why assume a "Muslim" would sit under that tree?

I was not a Muslim. Was he trying to exclude me from this future possibility? Not at all. He was just using a local expression, but a local expression that gave insight into how his community viewed religious identity. It intrigued me that he said it to me. He did not curb his language because he was talking to an American Christian. Nor did he assume religion was the main issue. He asked me to do a kind thing so that a kind, but unknown, person in the future might benefit.

This was my introduction to the linguistic complexity of religious identity, at the heart of identity issues. Most people rejecting the idea of disciples of Jesus identifying as Muslim assume a sharp distinction between ethnicity, culture, and religion. They assume that these things can be parsed out within a person and community without miscommunicating the free offer of the Gospel to all, regardless of ethnic or cultural background.

But Azizullah used the term "Muslim" in an ambiguous way. Was he referring to his ethnicity? Was he referring to his culture? Or was he referring to his religion? Most definitely, all three were mixed together as he used this common phrase.

This tension, over the distinction possible between religion, ethnicity and culture, extends to how we understand what it means to be a true follower of Jesus[4] and what it means to be a Muslim. When we assume certain things about other people based on our own context, we project onto others contradictions or conflicts that may or may not exist. These assumed contradictions are often heightened when communities are not in contact with each other or when there has been significant conflict or war.

A true follower of Jesus could be defined as someone who believes that God is three persons in one essence (Trinity) and that Jesus died on the cross for their sins. Or a Muslim could be defined as someone who denies Jesus' death on the cross and holds to strict unitarianism (i.e. denies the possibility of God as Trinity). Can a Muslim, then, by these definitions, be a true follower of Jesus? Of course not. The two are opposite. They are mutually exclusive.

It is also possible to assume that a true follower of Jesus is one who goes to a church, reads only the Old and New Testament as divinely inspired text, or identifies with the international body of Christ including all of those that call themselves "Christian." It is also possible to consider Muslims as those who go to a mosque, read the Quran, and do not identify themselves as "Christian." Again, the two are in opposition.

The problem, of course, is that the definitions on both sides of the equation are rather arbitrary. The definition of a "true follower" of Jesus above depends on post-biblical concepts of true discipleship, as the New Testament does include church buildings. The words used to describe an "orthodox Christian" have changed throughout history depending on where a person lived. In my community, "evangelical" is most common. A few decades ago, the more commonly accepted moniker was "born again Christian." Other times and places have used a variety of terms to emphasize their differences from some other kind label.[5] "Christian" itself is a term hardly mentioned in the New Testament. On the other side of the equation, the assumptions about what it means to be Muslim are only assumptions at best and far too external at worst.

I have already described how people assumed I was Muslim based upon how I spoke and what I wore. But looking at Azizullah's words again, there is more to observe. He assumes someone is "Muslim" based upon *where the person lives*, without reference to convictions at all.

Another aspect of Azizullah's life provides an additional example of the difficulty in pinning down Muslim identity. Azizullah, more than any others at my office, prayed five times per day and kept the fast during the month of Ramadan. He was also wildly superstitious. He went to see pseudo-mullahs that many purist Muslims denounce as pagan for their practice of black and white magic.[6] He sacrificed a chicken and received Quranic recitations to get his headaches cured. He engaged in folk magic practices that some Muslims would consider heretical.

Was Azizullah still "Muslim?" Of course. Could other Muslims consider his behavior heretical and even say that he was not truly Muslim because of his actions? Of course.

Muslims, like people, are not all the same

Most Americans associate suicide bombers and gross acts of terrorism with Muslims. The collapse of the Twin Towers tells many of us: "That's what it means to be Muslim." Few in the West have heard Central Asians repeatedly denounce those who do such acts as worse than *Kafirs* (idol-worshippers). They tell me in no uncertain terms, "Those people aren't Muslim. They use Islam for their own lust for power." Yet that isn't the only definition of Islam in the community. Jihadists preach at the village mosques that people who work for the US-supported governments or international aid offices, like the one at which Azizullah served, are likewise *Kafirs*, people who have abandoned Islam for foreign religion and power. Just as we saw with definitions of American, the definition of "Muslim" varies significantly when real people are examined.

I push against any type of fixed definition of what it means to be Muslim and even more so when a fixed definition is determined by an outsider of the community. I want to argue against a purely *doctrinal* or *cognitive* definition, such as the ones described above: "Muslims believe x, y, and z." There are cognitive and doctrinal elements to Islam as a religion. The way these elements are lived out by individuals and communities is so varied that Muslims quickly defy stereotypes.

My family has experienced this over and over in our community. After living near us and watching us for a season, many of our friends will testify to us that we are "good Muslims." Indeed, some will say that we are "better Muslims" than they are. When they say this, they are not referring to any doctrinal shift on our part. We have not denied Jesus or affirmed the Quran. One of my friends told me what a good Muslim I was after I shed tears in front of him while I talked about Jesus' importance in my life. This friend said, "You really love Jesus, Joseph. You are a good Muslim." Within my Central Asian community the definition of Muslim is determined by more than cognitive beliefs.

Within a Muslim community, there is generally tacit agreement as to who is and who is not Muslim. There is also a general understanding of what a Muslim believes and what a Muslim is obliged to do. Yet, there are strange exceptions to this general pattern, so much so that I have learned to accept that variation is almost always possible. I have Muslim friends that confess to me they are atheists. One friend admitted this while thumbing his Muslim prayer beads. I have other friends that invite me to drink vodka with them (something prohibited by Islam) and comment, "I'm no mullah." [7] Admittedly, these friends don't vocalize their convictions or behaviors broadly, but they still identify as Muslims and others still recognize them as such. They find space, within their community to believe and act differently than what some would define as crucial elements of the term "Muslim." In this sense "identity" has very much to do with being physically and socially present in a particular "community."

There are five fundamental "pillars" to Islam. My Muslim neighbors all recite them off hand, like most Christians say the Lord's prayer:

1. Reciting the creed that there is only one God and Mohammad is his messenger,
2. Praying five times a day,
3. Fasting for the Muslim month of Ramadan,
4. Giving a percentage of the value of one's assets once a year as alms, and
5. Going on a pilgrimage to Mecca

I do not deny the centrality of these commitments for a Muslim community. But do these *define* what is Muslim? Even these "pillars" are not lived out by all Muslims. Few actually make the pilgrimage to Mecca. And in my community, many criticize the stinginess of those that do. They note that generosity towards the poor would have been more consistent with their understanding of Islam than external adherence to the pillars. There can be a gap between stated conviction and action. There can also be various interpretations of what each of these pillars *mean*. Due to this variance between individuals and communities, I find myself asking questions: What is the role of these pillars in the life of *these* Muslims? What effect do these things have on their identification *as Muslim*?

How a person feels about his identity matters

In social science literature, the process of simplifying and reducing complex phenomena, such as individuals, groups, or cultures, to a few essential characteristics or traits, is known as essentializing. It involves treating these entities as if they possess inherent, fixed, and universal qualities that define their identity and behavior. When Muslims are defined by the pillars of Islam, it is a form of essentializing. Anthropologists caution against defining whole ethnic groups or even individuals based upon limited attributes, particularly attributes defined by outsiders. As believers, this is an issue of love. No one likes to be stereotyped. Surely an effort to avoid stereotyping falls into Jesus' command to love others as we love ourselves (Luke 10:27). We all want to be honored as unique human beings. We don't want to be pigeon-holed. And we particularly do not want to be defined in a certain way by a skeptic or a potential enemy. To get some sense of what it feels like to be defined by an unsympathetic critic, consider your emotional response to how an unsympathetic critic might represent evangelicals in the media. An effort to love includes understanding people on their own terms.

Anthropologist Gabriel Marrinci helped me with this process in his book, *An Anthropology of Islam*.[8] He notes, for instance, that there are generally two kinds of identity: (1) the perceived identity of outsiders and (2) the community's understanding of its own identity. To avoid essentializing, though, it is necessary to consider a person's "autobiographical self." It is important to ask, how do these people feel about themselves?

In my context, the way people describe themselves "as Muslim" is often quite different than I expect. Many emphasize the centrality of the Quran and their allegiance to Mohammad, but not all of them. Others describe the essentials of "Islam" as integrity, worship of God, and generosity. They have a saying in our community, "Build a road and tear down the mosque." This means it is more faithful to the ideals of Islam to serve the greater good of the community than to faithfully attend the mosque. Others will talk about being Muslim as obeying what they know of God's teachings. They highlight submission to God's authority in their lives, the true meaning of the word "Islam." In these contexts people get most confused about my identity. They describe me as "Muslim" in those moments, not because I say their creed or attend their mosques, but because I live out their ideal of what it means to be "Muslim." Significantly, many recognize their own and their community's failure to live up to these ideals. Many want to be "this kind of people." Many recognize that they are not.

I have seen how this feeling of "being Muslim" can integrate with a person who has committed themselves to Jesus as Lord by reading what disciples in Muslim contexts say about themselves. One such disciple, resilient in both his allegiance to Jesus and self-identification as a Muslim, is Mazhar Mallouhi. Mallouhi, born in Syria, has been exiled from his homeland for several years. His biography is beautifully told by Paul-Gordon Chandler in *Pilgrims of Christ on the Muslim Road*.[9] Mallouhi has cogently described his own experience as a Muslim for a Western audience in his own words. Some years ago, here's what he said about his "autobiographical experience":

Here is something that most people in the West don't understand: I was born into a confessional home. Islam is the blanket with which my mother wrapped me when she nursed me and sang to me and prayed over me. *I imbibed aspects of Islam with my mother's milk.* I inherited Islam from my parents, and it was the cradle which held me until I found Christ. Islam is my mother. You don't engage a person by telling them their mother is ugly. No matter how hideous your friend's mother may be, you don't say to him, "Your mother is ugly." Even if he knows she is, his initial reaction will certainly be to fight you. For me being an insider means that I have an emotional attachment to my culture which I imbibed along with my mother's milk. Islam is MY mother too.

However, although I am born a Muslim, I am not obligated to practice it, nor am I obligated to believe all of it. But the day I reject it outright, I disavow myself of my family, my community and my people. There are many ways to bring the gospel into this confessional home, and the words I use to describe a life-changing relationship with God through Christ will determine how the community understands and reacts to my journey.[10]

It seems fair to say that Mallouhi *feels* Muslim. This is significant. Some that come to faith reject Islam so wholeheartedly that they no longer "feel Muslim." But they are not the whole or only story. There are many, like Mallouhi who continue to feel Islam as their heritage. Mallouhi pleads with us to respect these deep attachments.

Furthermore, Mallouhi's words demonstrate the connection between past and identity. Like many disciples of Jesus in Muslim contexts, Mallouhi sees the issue as tied intricately to his attitude towards his past. Must he reject his past, his heritage? Must he embrace it? Mallouhi's answer is nuanced—he recognizes the flaws in his heritage, just as all of us recognize the flaws in our own parents. But he refuses to outright reject them.

Mallouhi's refusal resonates with Walls' observations: disciples never start out with a blank slate. In coming to Christ, they do not automatically lose the history that formed them. Quite the opposite. Healthy disciples integrate their past with their present allegiance to Jesus. I believe Mallouhi and others like him are finding a healthy path forward as they carve out space within a Muslim identity.

Mallouhi's experience is not unique.

I decided to disciple with an awareness of community and identity about a year after my friend Hajji Odam had come to faith. Our interactions in Central Asia had pushed my wife and team into exploring how these ideas worked out practically, particularly because of our experience relating to Hajji Odam.

When Hajji Odam first expressed his allegiance to Jesus, he started exploring a new creed. The Quran calls Jesus the "Word of God." Hajji Odam started practicing the creed with this confession: "I believe in the one and only God and Jesus the Word of God." He shared these words with people in our NGO office to see how they would respond. They gave him a strange look which did not stop him from the exploration process.

A year and a half into discussing things of Jesus with him, I invited him to my home to talk more about identity. We met in the rooms where Central Asians host guests, like a hosting room. We read through Acts 15 together. We read parts of Galatians and Romans. I told him some of the things I had been learning. Then I told him I didn't want him to be socially identified as a "Western Christian." I wanted him to be a follower of Jesus and serve him with wholehearted allegiance.

Hajji Odam responded with words a lot like Mazhar Mallouhi. "Thank you. That's what I'll do. I'm Muslim and you can't take that from me. Being Muslim is like the skin on my body. You can't tear it away from who I am."

Hajji Odam was honored by this invitation. It resonated with his being, with his sense of who he was in his community and with who he was in Christ. It did not negate the internal transformation going on in his life. Hajji Odam believed Jesus had died on the cross for his sins. He expressed whole-hearted loyalty to the person of Jesus. That loyalty to Jesus was not fundamentally at odds with his feeling of "being Muslim."

Continue to live in whatever situation the Lord has placed you

A growing number of interviews and descriptions of disciples in Muslim contexts tell stories like that of Hajji Odam over and over. These disciples are finding space to stay as they are and follow Jesus.[11] The Apostle Paul describes this as a biblical pattern. In his discussion of singleness and marriage, he inserts some seemingly out of place comments about circumcision:

> Each of you should continue to live in whatever situation the Lord has placed you, and remain as you were when God first called you. This is my rule for all the churches. For instance, a man who was circumcised before he became a believer should not try to reverse it. And the man who was uncircumcised when he became a believer should not be circumcised now. For it makes no difference whether or not a man has been circumcised. The important thing is to keep God's commandments (1 Cor 7:17–19).

Whether or not one was circumcised influenced one's social, ethnic, and religious status[12] in the first century. Paul battled hard to keep circumcision from becoming influential in defining one as a disciple of Jesus. Paul's insistence on this is relevant today. It seems a legitimate application of verse 17 is to allow Muslims to "continue to live in whatever situation the Lord has placed them" as they follow Jesus. As Mallouhi explains, the "only thing that is required of me to stay inside is to not be against my Islamic heritage." Accepting his past, Mallouhi argues, is the thing he must do to heed Paul's command.

As Paul tells people to "stay as they are," he also calls them to "keep God's commandments." In the next chapter, we will push deeper into this issue of relating to the past and social relationships. We turn to examine how evangelism and discipleship can heed the command to "stay as you are" and "keep God's commandments" rather than be a way of pulling people out of their community.

REFLECTION QUESTIONS

1. Prior to reading this chapter, how would you have defined a "Muslim"? How would you define a "Christian"?
2. How do you understand Azizullah's use of the term "Muslim"? What surprises you about this story? What resonates with you?
3. Reflect on Mazhar Mallouhi's statement, "Islam is my mother. You don't engage a person by telling them their mother is ugly." What

might this statement mean for how followers of Jesus talk about other religions?

---

1. Kenneth Bailey, *Paul Through Mediterranean Eyes: Cultural Studies in 1 Corinthians* (Downers Grove, IL: IVP Academic, 2011), 256.
2. Jeffrey M. Jones, "How Religious Are Americans?" *Gallup* (2021), https://news.gallup.com/poll/358364/religious-americans.aspx.
3. There has been a significant decline in Americans identifying as evangelical over the past ten years. Gregory A. Smith, "About Three-in-ten U.S. Adults Are Now Religiously Unaffiliated." *Pew Research Center* (2021), https://www.pewresearch.org/religion/2021/12/14/about-three-in-ten-u-s-adults-are-now-religiously-unaffiliated/.
4. Most of my readers will likely associate the description of a true follower of Jesus with the term "Christian."
5. David and Paul Watson call this "Branded Christianity" and argue it is a major hinderance to the spread of the Gospel in new communities. David Watson and Paul Watson, *Contagious Disciple Making: Leading Others on a Journey of Discovery* (Nashville, TN: Thomas Nelson, 2014).
6. Mullah is an honorific term given to Sunni and Shia clergy or the leader of a local mosque. It is derived from Persian so is more common in the eastern part of the Muslim world.
7. I do not accept their invitations.
8. Gabrielle Marranci, *The Anthropology of Islam* (New York, NY: Berg Publishers, 2008), 2546, Kindle.
9. Paul-Gordon Chandler, *Pilgrims of Christ on the Muslim Road: Exploring a New Path Between Two Faiths* (Lanham, MD: Rowman & Littlefield Publishers, 2007).
10. Mazhar Mallouhi, "Comments on the Insider Movement," *St Francis Magazine* 5, no. 5 (October, 2009), 6.
11. There is a growing list of published accounts that give insider's own perspective on their calling and theology. In addition to Chandler's account of Mallouhi, Chandler, *Pilgrims of Christ*, see also: Henk Prenger. "Muslim Insider Christ Followers: A Grounded Theory Research," (DMiss diss., Biola University, March 2014); Jens Barnett, "Living a Pun: Cultural Hybridity Among Arab Followers of Christ," in *Longing for Community: Church, Ummah, or Somewhere in Between*, ed. David H. Greenlee (Pasadena, CA: William Carey Library, 2013); Jens Barnett, "Refusing the Choose: Multiple Belonging Among Arab Followers of Christ," in *Longing for Community: Church, Ummah, or Somewhere in Between* (Pasadena, CA: William Carey Library, 2013); Usman Kadir and Daniel Roberts, *Seeing the World Through New Eyes: A Journey From Extremism to Love* (Fremantle, Australia: Vivid Publishing, 2013), Kindle; Darren T. Duerksen, and William A. Dyrness, *Seeking Church* (Carol Streams, IL: InterVarsity Press, 2019); and Darren T. Duerksen, *Christ-Followers in Other Religions* (Fortress Press, 2023).
12. See the appendix for a fuller description of how "religion" as a distinct concept is an idea of recent history, foreign, in fact, to the New Testament.

6

WHOSE STORY DO THEY JOIN?

The most successful answer to ostracism is the conversion of chains of families. The lone convert is particularly susceptible to boycott. But after the first big groups have accepted Christ, ostracism becomes difficult.[1]

Donald McGavran

To recognize a community you have to ask yourself and others a few questions: If a man is part of a vital action taking place, either performing that action himself, or having it done to him, whom does this action affect in the same vital way it affects him? If a man were to kill or be killed, on whom does the effect of this action fall? Or, if a man were approached to become a Christian, who would be affected by his conversion, his baptism, his living out of his Christian convictions? His tribe? Hardly. His clan? No again. But there are people who would be vitally affected by an action of his, like conversion. And you could actually put your hand on those people if you get to know them even a little. That is his real community, certainly and infallibly. To find out what this community is, is necessary to this kind of work. Without finding it, and working within it, there is no possibility of evangelizing the Masai.[2]

Vincent J. Donovan

Learning from failure[3]

Hajji Odam worked for me in the small town where Michelle began wearing the burqa. He helped out with odd jobs. He often stayed at my house at night to provide an extra level of security. He watched out lives closely for two years and heard us talk a lot about Jesus. I began discipling him and this influenced how I processed these new insights.

At Easter one year we invited Hajji Odam to go through a contextualized version of a Passover Seder. We read through a number of Old Testament passages using food items and other symbols to explain salvation history. When we read from Isaiah 53 together, his eyes lit up. Hajji Odam had listened to some audios of the Scriptures. He had watched a movie about the life of Jesus in his language. He had heard Isaiah's portrayal of the Suffering Servant as a familiar tale:

"He was oppressed and treated harshly, yet he never said a word. He was led like a lamb to the slaughter. And as a sheep is silent before the shearers, he did not open his mouth" (Isa 53:7).

Hajji Odam saw the connection between the passage and what he had learned about Jesus. The next day he pleaded with me to tell him more about this Suffering Servant.

For two months Hajji Odam and I met every few days to read through the Gospel of Luke together. It was invigorating. He loved all that Jesus said and did. About half-way through the Gospel of Luke—chapters 11 or 12—Hajji Odam told me he wanted to devote himself to Jesus. This Jesus who exposed hypocrisy, healed the sick, cast out demons—who spoke like no one else—he would follow him anywhere.

We left for an eight-month furlough and our teammate discipled Hajji Odam while we were gone. When we returned I continued the discipling relationship. Despite all of our team's efforts Hajji Odam never led anyone to faith. We talked about it a lot, but we never seemed to get traction. Over a period of five years, Hajji Odam and I continued to meet. When we moved to a city an hour away, security problems made Hajji Odam's city unsafe for my family. He no longer worked for me which cut down our interaction and time together. We still read the Word at times, but his enthusiasm waned.

Eventually, I told him that I couldn't talk with him about the Scriptures alone, that we needed another person to join us or he needed to provide a concrete plan to explain the teaching to others. I had become convicted that I needed to teach truth to those who would pass it onto others (2 Tim 2:2). Our one-on-one approach was not reproducing. He did not have any ideas on how to share with others so that was the last time we studied together.

My experience with Hajji Odam is my greatest disappointment in my efforts in discipleship. I have wept over the experience multiple times, repenting of my mistakes and asking God over and over where I went wrong. I still talk to Hajji Odam on the phone occasionally. But I feel I let him down. How so?

While working with Hajji Odam my teammate and I were beginning to consider how identity issues related to discipleship. We never encouraged Hajji Odam to identify himself as a "Christian" or to renounce his community. We talked openly with him about retaining a local identity. But concurrently, we were influenced by Roland Müller's book *The Messenger, the Message, and the Community*.[4] Müller, who served as a missionary in Arab countries for decades, has a wealth of experience and many helpful insights. He says one thing, however, that I believe led us astray.

Müller rightly argues that followers of Jesus need community. The Muslim community is a strong one. So, to solidify discipleship in Jesus, the cross-cultural discipler needs to offer an alternative community. Müller goes on to suggest that the cross-cultural discipler himself, along with his family and team, can provide that community. He writes, "So when seekers start exploring your Christian community, share it with them . . . Allow them to come to your meetings and bask in the love of Christ."[5] That is what we tried to do.

My teammate and I met with Hajji Odam as a threesome. There were some limitations because of gender rules, but we also tried to invite his family to our house with limited success. I visited his home as often as I could. I did so despite sensing distinct coldness during and before my visits.

On one occasion we had an American visitor who had written local worship music. We tried to teach Hajji Odam songs based on the Psalms—the four of us together (three Americans and Hajji). Those are the times when I remember the greatest confusion on Hajji Odam's part. He appeared awkward and out of place. That event and the visits to his house led to greater distance on his part. We were not able to provide him the community he needed.

We also confused him in the process. During my five years working with Hajji Odam, he fell into some family disputes that landed him in jail. Hajji Odam was probably innocent of any wrongdoing, apart from self-defense. But in the midst of the disputes, one of his nephews killed a policeman. In keeping with the Central Asian justice system, the whole family was jailed. Bribes and legal fees sank his family financially. He came asking me to tap into "my community"—the community that I had tried to get him to join—for financial help. The request hit me at a particularly difficult time. I was struggling intensely with dependency issues—questions about "rice Christians."[6] My own relief and development projects had financial difficulties. I rejected his request. I can see now how my message was mixed. Was I not inviting him into a community, where real needs were met?

This is a sticky issue. But I believe now it was a mistake to try to be his community. I believe I stifled his spiritual growth and hindered the spread of the Gospel. I regret it all deeply.

Where did I go wrong? What are the alternatives?

People make sense of the world in groups

I found answers to these questions in the social sciences. This may prove problematic for some, thinking, "Stick to the Bible, please." I want my life to be fully submitted to the authority of God's revealed Word.

I hold dear Jesus' command to "love your neighbor as yourself" (Matt 22:39). Cross-cultural work, marriage, parenting, and interaction with any other human being has taught me—even as I banged my head against walls of missed expectations and confusion—it is hard to love someone when you do not understand them. The social sciences (anthropology and sociology, in particular) have helped me understand others, especially those from another culture. As I dip into sociology to explain how I failed Hajji Odam, please see love, not secular accommodation or brash expediency, as the goal. Ask with me: How can I best love Muslims with the Good News? As we submit to Scripture, we will see these ideas corresponding with biblical testimony.

Nearly fifty years ago, sociologists Peter Berger and Thomas Luckmann wrote *The Social Construction of Reality*,[7] describing the impact community has on the individual. For a person to hold convictions that transform his or her life, he must have his convictions reinforced by a community. Communities, from the family unit to nation states, reinforce ideas and concepts by causing them to be internalized.

Most of us know this experience from our time in middle school. If you make a blunder, do something different than the way others do it, peers laugh at you. The group reinforces the cultural norm by making the alternative seem absurd. I experienced this as a single man teaching English in the former Soviet Union. I had my students over for pizza and a student laughed at me for cutting the onion up and down instead of crosswise. She had never seen an onion cut that way. For her, it was wrong. Her communal experience defined the "right" way to cut onions. We all have thousands of experiences like this. We internalize the way our community does things and the way we talk about them. We rarely know about alternatives until those experiences are challenged.

Berger and Luckmann point out that people can step out of this "social plausibility structure" for a time, but they cannot stay outside of all community groups indefinitely. If they stay in an in-between-zone, they get disoriented as humans. Eventually, they will go back to their former community, go insane, leave their community completely and join another community, or end their life. Social plausibility structures are serious things.

In a follow-up book, Berger wrote a few sentences that helped make sense of my experience with Hajji Odam.

> [The] individual who wishes to convert, and (*more importantly*) to '*stay converted*' must engineer his social life in accordance with this purpose. Thus he must dissociate himself from those individuals or groups that constituted the plausibility structure of his past religious reality, and associate himself all the more intensively and (if possible) exclusively with those who serve to maintain his new one. *Put succinctly, migration*

between religious worlds implies migration between their respective plausibility structures.[8]

Don't get lost in the sociology jargon. His point is crucial. To make a real change, a real conversion from one religion to another, a person has to abandon the old structure (and people) and fully operate within the community of the new religion. This did not happen for Hajji Odam. He lived between two communities. We tried to form a new community with him, but it was small and thin compared the robust and thick community from which he came. It did not work.

Moreover, this tension between the two communities explains why Hajji Odam was so cold towards me when we tried to mix worlds. When I visited his home, unbeknownst to me, I raised the issue of his local identity for him in front of his whole village. My direct association with him—going into his home, meeting with him publicly—made others ask if he had rejected his community identity and joined *my community and religious identity*. When he met with us to sing, something he had never done before in his life, he likely wondered about the community we were inviting him to join. These two dynamics forced on him the "disorientation" that Berger predicted. He felt the tension between these plausibility structures. Our structure was incomplete for him, and when we tried to enter his structure, we presented a threat not a help.

Roland Müller was right. Hajji Odam needed a community. The question that Berger forced me to grapple with, was this: Was I supposed to help Hajji Odam create a new community with me or might it be possible that he could stay in his own community and bring a pattern of change from within?

The difficulty I was observing in our host country was that very few local believers were actually bringing others into the new Christian community they were joining. Other expatriates in our host country, were also seeing people come to faith in small numbers, but these local believers usually followed one of two patterns. Some were secret about their faith. They could study the Bible with a foreigner but would never let anyone else know about it. This is the position that Hajji Odam moved towards. Some, on the other hand, were more vocal about their faith. They led a few others to faith. They started to form secretive groups to study the Scriptures. But then some kind of exposure happened and the leaders of the groups left. They didn't just stop meeting. Many of them left the country and sought asylum in Western countries.

This led to a disturbing perspective for us. Our local believing friends began to act and talk like it was impossible to follow Jesus on their own country's soil. This was consistent with Berger's paradigm: they were separating themselves from their old religion and fully immersing themselves in the context of their new religion in Europe or America or India. Though this made sociological sense, it was not what we believed God intended for his kingdom in Central Asia.

Berger's writing and Hajji Odam's experience, forced me to see that this identity issue was not *just* about *names*. The word "Muslim" and the word "Christian" were not the fundamental issue. Rather, the internal sense of community and identity—that strange connection between our past and our present experience of wholeness—were the real issue. We told Hajji Odam he could keep his "name." But we did not know how to envision his discipleship within that community. We provided a hybrid model that left him confused and disoriented.

The question Berger forced me to ask lingers. How can I disciple people within their community? Is there a way to disciple *in their community* and not just individuals? Discipling individuals seemed to lead towards extraction. Believers ended up leaving or being forced away from their homes and land. What was the alternative?

A vision for discipling within God's story

The alternative was to disciple them within God's story. To illustrate this possibility, we return to our discussion of God's endorsement of diversity in redemptive history. I prefer to use "story" instead of the technical phrase, "social plausibility structure."[9] We all live within a story. We have personal stories—our ancestors (close, distant, past), our siblings, our neighbors, our friends. We have our national story—Washington, Lincoln, immigration, as examples. We all have a place in God's story, whether we recognize it or not. Indeed, his story is the overarching story, touching every human being and each human community. The central question is the role God's story has in our lives.

Even the most Christian community or society has elements to its own story that are out of alignment with what God wants for the world. It can be systemic—like slavery and racism that have plagued America since its founding. Or it can be subtle, like preferring personal prosperity over the good of a brother. It can be private—family conflicts and deep-hidden bitterness. However it is described, this world in all contexts falls short of God's calling.

Yet just as each community is out of alignment with God's story, each community has some element in which God's truth and intentions still shine through. We may be scarred image bearers, but we still bear God's image as communities. Even the most corrupt and dysfunctional community has elements that reflect and integrate God's redemptive story. I've spent hours in Central Asian government offices paying taxes, getting registration papers signed, and securing visas. It is time-consuming and annoying. But this waiting is social. Unlike the impersonal three hours I spent on the phone in America to correct an internet bill, in Central Asia I drink tea to solve disputes. There is an undeniable element of friendliness in the negotiation process. However time-consuming it is for me as a get-it-done American, there can even be elements of neighborly love and respect in the process. Sometimes I even get invited to a meal at the end of it all.

Communities, even ones that have not heard the Gospel, have means of caring for the poor, reconciling after disputes, addressing injustice, and expressing neighborly and family love. God has not left himself without a witness—anywhere in the world.

Visualize, then, God's story as a big circle [see Figure 1].

This is the redemptive, transforming story that God is writing for the world. It is trans-cultural. Though it interacts with culture, it ultimately transcends it.

Now we need to add cultures to the picture. We have all sorts of community stories that interact with the overarching story God is telling. Those stories align in some places with God's purposes.

Whose Story Do They Join? | 81

Figure 1. God's story depicted as a single, big circle

In other cases, they fall outside of God's design. Many like to debate the degree to which certain cultures align with God's purposes. I leave that to another book. We can assume that some cultures align with God's designs more and some less. But all of them have a mix of both good and bad. It looks something like this [see Figure 2].

Figure 2. God's story and human communities

Now I return to the issue of social plausibility and conversion. I described my experience with Hajji Odam as him moving from his existing community into mine. My aim was for him to move deeper into God's story. But by inviting him into my community, I asked him to take a roundabout route to get there, something like Figure 3.

Figure 3. Seeker engages God's story

I invited Hajji Odam into my community's story as a way of engaging in God's story, making it a complex process. I wanted him to reach his own community. I wanted him to stay Central Asian and witness to his community. But by seeking to be his community, I invited a move out of his community and into mine. We understood our goal as creating a new community, distinct from the Muslim community around him yet different from our American community. But this goal wasn't viable. It forced Hajji Odam and others out of their community and into mine.

The alternative? The alternative is for the person to stay *in* his community and work with others within that same community to move towards God's story. It looks something like Figure 4.

Figure 4. Seeker engages God's story with his or her own community

How can this happen? It happens when I intentionally refuse to create a new community with Hajji Odam and do everything I can to help him lead his existing community into God's story, not mine.

Does this sound too good to be true? The journey to see this is part of an expanded vision, a crucial element in my journey to embrace Jesus' supremacy at the edges of the kingdom.

Defining God's story as the Good News of Jesus' Reign

I want to diverge slightly here to address a crucial assumption in the paradigm described. I have assumed a lot in distinguishing God's story from human expressions of that story. Part of what frees me to do this is my perspective on the Gospel: the Good News that Jesus and his disciples proclaimed.

Paul's definition for the Good News in 1 Corinthians 15 is foundational to this issue of discipleship. He writes,

> Let me now remind you, dear brothers and sisters, of the Good News I preached to you before. You welcomed it then, and you still stand firm in it. It is this Good News that saves you if you continue to believe the message I told you—unless, of course, you believed something that was never true in the first place. I passed on to you what was most important and what had also been passed on to me. Christ died for our sins, just as the Scriptures said. He was buried, and he was raised from the dead on the third day, just as the Scriptures said (1 Cor 15:1-4).

The Gospel, as Paul defines it, is (1) Jesus died for our sins, (2) was buried, (3) was raised from the dead and (4) that all of this was in keeping with the story of the Old Testament. That is an extremely compressed version of the Gospel.

Point four, of course, allows for us to put a lot on the meat of this barebone Gospel. What does it mean, after all, that Jesus' death, burial, and resurrection are in keeping with the story of the Old Testament?

Narratives about Jesus in Matthew, Mark, Luke, and John (the Gospels) are intent on showing how Jesus' life and ministry are a fulfillment of the Old Testament. All these writers make this explicit. Matthew uses the word "fulfill" dozens of times in detailing Jesus' life and words. Luke tells about Jesus explaining to the pair walking to Emmaus how all the prophets pointed to himself (Luke 24:27). The writers of the Gospels and Paul are unified that the declaration of Good News in Jesus is tied to what he fulfills of the Old Testament.

That fulfillment has to include humanity's role as God's image bearers as discussed in chapter 4. People were supposed to enact God's rule in the world as his royal representatives. They did not. But Jesus comes in fulfillment of this initial purpose. New Testament scholar N. T. Wright helpfully describes the Gospel and the Gospels' story to be "how God became king."[10] In Jesus, God declares his reign and rule and shows us what his leadership looks like.

Wright's book *How God Became King* urges readers not to treat Good News like a cloak without a man by ignoring the *context* of the Gospels and what they tell us about Jesus.[11] We cannot jump from Matthew 2 to Matthew 25 or Luke 2 to Luke 22. We cannot go from his birth to his death without regard for who Jesus was and what he did. This is why point four is important. All that Jesus did, said and experienced was "according to the Scriptures." He himself claimed to proclaim the "Good News about the kingdom" *before* he died and rose again (Matt 4:23). Jesus' proclamation of the Good News was not independent of his cross, resurrection, and the gift of the Holy Spirit. Rather, his acts and words indicated that God's saving sovereignty was let loose in a radical new way. Nothing would ever be the same again. This is the Good News of the kingdom: Jesus' work in the world means God's rule can be known and experienced as blessing. That kingdom or rulership includes things like reconciled relationships, bold compassion, fierce justice, and sacrificial love. These things happen when God rules our lives, our families, and our communities.

This perspective on the Gospel explains for me the moments when Hajji Odam and another man, Ahmad, confessed their allegiance to Jesus. Hajji Odam, as I wrote in an earlier chapter, said he would follow Jesus anywhere after reading Luke 1 to Luke 11. Luke 11 doesn't talk about the reasons for Jesus' death. It doesn't even talk about forgiveness. This is how Luke 11 ends: "What sorrow awaits you experts in religious law! For you remove the key to knowledge from the people. You don't enter the Kingdom yourselves, and you prevent others from entering" (Luke 11:52). Luke 11 ends with a description of hypocrisy by those of the religious class. This hypocrisy had been on full display for Hajji Odam to see for 30 years. He had seen wars and killing perpetuated by those claiming to know God's ways. Here he heard Jesus proclaiming something different. He heard Jesus exposing hypocrisy, forgiving offenses, and healing sick people. He saw him giving himself, rather than taking, so Hajji Odam said, "I'll follow him anywhere." He saw and heard Jesus declaring God's way of ruling the world as different than the way those around him were doing it. This was good news to him.

Ahmad was the same way. He defines his moment of converted loyalty to Jesus as Matthew 6. It was the middle of Ramadan, when some people are fasting and a lot of people are pretending to fast. He read the words of Jesus on fasting and was blown away:

> And when you fast, don't make it obvious, as the hypocrites do, for they try to look miserable and disheveled so people will admire them for their fasting. I tell you the truth, that is the only reward they will ever get. But when you fast, comb your hair and wash your face. Then no one will notice that you are fasting, except your Father, who knows

what you do in private. And your Father, who sees everything, will reward you (Matt 6:16–18).

What impressed Ahmad was not the cross—not yet! He had not read about it yet. What impressed him was the kingdom Jesus proclaimed. Jesus described what living under God's rule looked like. Ahmad responded, with all his heart, "Yes. That's the king I want to be under." Both Hajji Odam and Ahmad came to embrace the forgiveness of God through Jesus' cross. But they embraced Jesus because of what he showed them about God's rule in the world.

Defining the Good News as God's reign over the world as revealed by Jesus need not undermine any of the precious doctrines we tend to emphasize when we proclaim "the Gospel." The way God rules the world is to accept those asking for forgiveness. The way God rules the world is as a loving father that embraces prodigal sons who have splurged their inheritance and come back home. The way God rules the world is by pouring love and joy on those that once scorned him. The way God rules the world is by sending Jesus into the world to be scorned and beaten unjustly and then raising him miraculously from the dead. The way God rules the world is by giving His Spirit to his children so they can follow in the pattern of love, forgiveness, compassion, and joy as Jesus did. The way God rules the world is by welcoming back those that swore they would do everything for Jesus always and then deny knowing him twelve hours later. This is what it means to be under the rule of God as Jesus proclaimed it.

This is how Paul's words in 1 Corinthians 15 connect with the whole of the New Testament and the whole of the Old Testament. Jesus died for our sins, went into the tomb, and was raised from the dead to bring about God's rule over all the earth. Jesus' death is crucial to that progression. Without it, there is no peace with God. From that crucial moment in history flow all the rich benefits of what it means to be under God's authority, under God as our king. But the stuff of the middle, the bulk of the Gospel's testimony to Jesus' actions and words, are not incidental. United to his purpose in the cross, they too explain God's kingdom, the kingdom to which I invite Central Asians.

Muslims challenged by the Gospel of the Kingdom

As Muslims engage this story, God's story, they are deeply challenged. There are apparent interpretative conflicts—like Jesus' crucifixion. Most Muslims in my community, for instance, deny that Jesus actually died. They argue that Judas or Barabbas was miraculously substituted for Jesus on the cross and that Jesus was taken up into heaven. But their understanding of this does not come directly from reading the Quran. It comes from their tradition and a traditional interpretation of one passage in the Quran. Even some Muslim scholars admit that the Quran nowhere denies Jesus' death.[12]

In my experience, this has rarely been a point of contention with a genuine seeker. Both Ahmad and Hajji Odam expressed allegiance to Jesus before they discussed the implications of the cross. Once they accepted Jesus—accepted his authority and rule over their lives and good intentions for their souls—they accepted the cross readily. Jesus won their allegiance so dramatically that this stumbling block became a non-issue. None of these brothers saw their embrace of Jesus' death as fundamentally at odds with "being Muslim." They obviously feel the tension with their community over this issue. But they have not verbalized any contradiction to me between "believing in Jesus' death for their sins" and considering themselves "Muslim." This has always been quite different than my expectations.

The nature of the kingdom challenges how they live and think. This challenge, rather than concern with religious externals, becomes the heart of discipleship for them. Muslim communities do not formally oppose living with integrity, showing compassion to the poor, or being honest. But like most communities, when someone begins to insist on integrity, compassion, and honesty at the cost of financial or personal gain, they face plenty of practical opposition. Muslim communities, like most communities in the world, have plenty of hypocrisy, greed, selfishness, and other sins. A person who lives under the reign of God through Jesus will challenge people at the heart level, not necessarily at the formal religious level. That is a remarkable power unleashed by the Gospel. Disciples who maintain their connection to their community unleash that power within their communities. They challenge the status quo. Eventually, they may be ostracized because of it. But they start, as Mazhar Mallouhi indicated, by bringing the power of Jesus' Good News into the heart of the community.

Discipling within existing identity structures, then, is not a way of embracing Islam or endorsing a false religious system. Rebecca Lewis puts this in wonderfully stark terms:

> Let me make clear . . . that I think Islam is every bit as demonic as any worldview or religion that promises salvation apart from Christ . . . I take the position I do out of . . . great optimism about the power of the Gospel to bring light, whether in cannibalistic tribes, Christo-pagan religions, the Greek pantheon, or our own mammon-steeped American culture (without having to remove believers from their families or community context).[13]

My confidence in God's story is exactly that, a confidence in God's power and intent to break through lies and demonic power of this world for the sake of his glory. Summoning whole groups into that glorious power is not a call for people to remain unchanged. Rather, it's a bold statement of faith in God.

With that faith, I have great hopes for my host community that the miracles of the New Testament era are possible today. If you feel doubtful about my fundamental argument that a group of disciples can pledge allegiance to Jesus and remain in relationship with their Muslim community, consider the extraordinary story we find in Acts 19. Paul spent two years working in Ephesus, proclaiming the Good News about Jesus. As a result, a dramatic drop in silver sales prompted one of the idol makers to lead a mob protest against the discipleship movement Paul was leading. As the mob got to a fiery pitch, the mayor of the town told them to go home. He was not ready to deny the central role of the god Artemis in the city. He was also unwilling to concede that Paul had done anything wrong. He simply said, "You have brought these men here, but they have stolen nothing from the temple and have not spoken against our goddess" (Acts 19:37). Two years in the city preaching and celebrating the lordship of Jesus and the mayor did not see Paul as speaking "against [their] goddess." Is this not remarkable?

I believe it is a testimony to the way Paul operated in his proclamation of the Gospel. It spread through networks of people in powerful ways. Profoundly, Paul did not feel a need to speak in way that denounced the religious institutions of the community or at least was not perceived as doing so. Nevertheless, as people came to Jesus, they were changed. People confessed sins. They burned sorcery books. They stopped buying idols. This is the power of the Gospel unleashed on a whole community.

I have only scratched the surface of this issue. To lay out the alternative requires more space. In part three I will go into the implications of this expanded vision, for discipleship, for controversial cultural issues, and for the global church. In the next chapter, I will outline how I envision the discipleship process to happen from *within one's existing identity structures*. How does it look to encourage someone to stay in their community as a disciple of Jesus? It is slower process. It means starting where people are (with devotion to the Quran) and then sifting through *everything* to see how it lines up with the testimony of Jesus. That is a process that involves experimentation and even failure. It is a process that I have committed to walk with people.

REFLECTION QUESTIONS

1. Have you ever made mistakes that you regret? What did you learn from those experiences?
2. Reflect on someone you led to the Lord or saw come to faith. What was that person's community before he or she came to faith? How did this new believer relate to his or her old community?
3. If you are currently discipling someone, consider the community of that disciple. What ways is that disciple able to maintain his or her relationships with the community? What ways do you think the Scriptures compel her to distinguish herself?
4. What would it look like in your community if the announcement that God has revealed his kingdom through Jesus influenced family and social networks?

---

1. Donald Anderson McGavran, *The Bridges of God: A Study in the Strategy of Missions* (Eugene, OR: Wipf and Stock Publishers, 2005), 20.
2. Vincent J. Donovan, *Christianity Rediscovered: An Epistle From the Masai* (London, UK: SCM Press, 1982), 1637, Kindle.
3. The substance of this chapter was originally published in J. S. Williams, "Whose Story to Join? The Problem of Social Plausibility, Social Mission Stations, and Their Relationship to Church Planting Movements," *Great Commission Research Journal* 7, no. 2 (Winter 2016): 213–29.
4. Roland Muller, *The Messenger, the Message, the Community: Three Critical Issues for the Cross-Cultural Church-Planter* (CanBooks, 2006).
5. Muller, *The Messenger*, 329.
6. "Rice Christians" is the idea that people profess faith because of the financial benefits or "rice" that comes to them.
7. Peter L. Berger and Thomas Luckman, *The Social Construction of Reality: A Treatise in the Sociology of Knowledge* (New York, NY: Anchor Books, 1967).

8. Peter L. Berger, *The Sacred Canopy: Elements of a Sociological Theory of Religion* (New York, NY: Doubleday, 1969), 50-51, emphasis added.
9. Steffen, "Foundational Roles," 477-494.
10. Wright, *How God Became King*.
11. Wright, *How God Became King*.
12. Abdullah Saeed, *Reading the Qur'an in the Twenty-First Century: A Contextualist Approach* (London, UK: Routledge, 2013), 143-144; see also Joseph L Cumming, "Did Jesus Die on the Cross? The History of Reflection on the End of His Earthly Life in Sunni Tafsir Literature" (Yale University, 2001).
13. Rebecca Lewis, "Comment," on Jeff Morton, "Insider Movements and the Historical Approach,'" *Biblical Missiology*, http://biblicalmissiology.org/2011/02/08/insider-movements-and-the-historical-approach/.

PART III

APPLYING THE VISION

Through faith one must "depart" from one's culture because the ultimate allegiance is given to God and God's Messiah who transcend every culture. And yet precisely because of the ultimate allegiance to God of all cultures and to Christ who offers his "body" as a home for all people, Christian children of Abraham can "depart" from their culture without having to leave it (in contrast to Abraham himself who had to leave his "country" and "kindred"). *Departure is no longer a spatial category; it can take place within the cultural space one inhabits.*[1]

Miroslav Volf

---

1. Miroslav Volf, *Exclusion and Embrace: A Theological Exploration of Identity, Otherness, and Reconciliation* (Nashville, TN: Abingdon Press, 1996), 49, emphasis added.

7

A VISION FOR DISCIPLESHIP WITHIN MUSLIM CONTEXTS

We are human, but we don't wage war as humans do. We use God's mighty weapons, not worldly weapons, to knock down the strongholds of human reasoning and to destroy false arguments. We destroy every proud obstacle that keeps people from knowing God. We capture their rebellious thoughts and teach them to obey Christ.

2 Cor 12:3-5

Please note that it requires no faith to learn something. It requires no faith to teach or to train someone else. But discipleship requires faith: the faith to be a believer in and a follower of Christ, and the faith to do what Christ commands—the faith to say to others, "If you want to be a disciple of Christ, copy my life" (see 1 Corinthians 4: 16; Philippians 4: 9; and 1 Timothy 4: 12). Learning does not require faith, just intellect. Obedience requires faith. It is a faith that, when acted out, says to others, "I will obey all the commands of Christ regardless of the circumstances in which I find myself or the consequences of any actions I must take or the consequences of any words I must say in order to be obedient to Christ in all matters, public and private."[1]

David and Paul Watson

94 | CARAVANS OF SPLENDOR

SHOULD I PRAY AT THE MOSQUE?

When Ahmad came to me, his first burning question was about the daily prostrations. Every day, five times a day, devout Muslims go through a set of ritual prayers in Arabic. In the midst of these prayers, they bow repeatedly, putting their forehead against a prayer rug laid on the ground with an arrow pointing towards Mecca. Muslims can do this alone or at a mosque. In our community, men consider it particularly important to do these prayers together at 1:00 pm on Fridays. Friday is the Muslim holy day. Doing prayers together before a weekly sermon maintains community pride and cohesion. Ahmad wanted to know what I thought about him participating in the Friday prayers.

Ahmad knew very little about Jesus. He decided to follow Jesus when he read Jesus' words about fasting. He discovered this teaching after his English teacher gave him an electronic copy of Matthew's Gospel in a local language. Ahmad read portions of it and was blown away by Jesus. One afternoon, he called his teacher, my friend, on the phone and declared in English, "I want to join your religion." Jesus wooed him. All Ahmad knew to do was declare his allegiance to the religion he associated with Jesus. Ahmad was ready to leave Islam.

His teacher, away on an extended leave, had given Ahmad my phone number. We arranged to meet and this was his first question: "My father wants me to do the Friday prayers. I don't want to. What should I do?"

I refused to answer him.

I had decided after my experience with Hajji Odam to stick to a few key principles in discipleship. First, I would only do chronological Bible study. I would start in Genesis and work to Jesus. We would build the redemptive story and let that structure inform how he should see Jesus. Second, I would ask good questions focused on application. I would not explain every text, nor would I give answers to big questions. Third, I would ask every week if he shared the story with someone else.

When Ahmad shared this question, I offered an invitation to walk through redemptive history, to obey what he read, and to share what he learned with others. He accepted.

We began the journey. We worked through the world's creation and the story of Adam and Eve, Cain and Abel, Noah, Abraham, Joseph and Moses. At each step Ahmad's responses reflected deep thought.

After the creation story, Ahmad commented, "God loves us like a father." When we read about Cain's movement away from God and his increasing distance from Eden, Ahmad said, "Wow. This is who we are. We've moved away from God." When we read about Noah, Abraham, and Joseph, "This life has a lot of suffering. I know suffering. But God cares for us."

We got to Moses and the Ten Commandments; Ahmad's question about prayer came up again. His dad was still pressuring him to participate in Friday prayers. What should he do? We now had context to consider the question.

I turned it back to Ahmad: "What have we read over our two months together that answers your question?" He gave me an instinctual, "I don't know."

I paused and waited.

He was thoughtfully quiet. Then, "Honor your father and mother."

"Okay, that's one answer. Does anything we've read say you shouldn't do what your father says?"

Ahmad reflected on the first three commandments to worship God alone. He noted, there was no inherent contradiction between this call to worship and attendance at the mosque. Islamic mosques do not have any images. In his mind, the prayers are focused on reverence for God.

He paused. Then he turned the tables and asked questions about images of Jesus and Mary in churches he had seen in movies. This puzzled him. Representations of Christian worship on satellite television seemed to contradict Moses. That was a problem. But he could not find anything in the first two books of the Bible that prohibited mosque attendance.

This conversation taught me what it meant to be Scripture-centered in the discipleship process. I am called to teach people to obey what they know. When I disregard religious externals and focus on responsiveness to God's redemptive story, the immediate heart issues become prominent. Disciples deal with God's leadership of them in that moment. I do not think Ahmad has done the Friday prayers as his father asked him. Something at the heart level has prevented him. It may be an issue of conscience. It may have to do with his ongoing conflict with his father. A significant part of discipleship was to find the path of forgiveness and love. Jesus' calling reoriented his faith towards submission to God in love for a father who had hurt him. That lesson proved far more crucial in Ahmad's life than deciphering the truth or falsehood of the mosque institution.

It may be that as Ahmad matures and others join him in following Jesus they will find Friday prayers problematic. But early on, for Ahmad, the fundamental question was honoring his father. Getting at those fundamental questions is essential in discipleship. I want to move towards actual, concrete, lived-out allegiance to Jesus in response to biblical content.

Being a disciple

Discipleship is the crucial work. Discipleship has to include awareness of how disciples wrestle with their own identity and their relationship to their community. But wrestling with identity, without obedience to the living Christ, could turn into religious pluralism. It could suggest "all roads lead to God" and "it doesn't really matter what you believe or do."

This is not what it means for disciples to retain local identities. In suggesting disciples can retain their connections to the community and their birth identity, I am not suggesting they should stay completely the same. All people and all disciples desperately need transformation. It all has to do with the process of that transformation.

In coming to Jesus, do we start as blank slates? No, we have relationships and past hurts—stuff and junk—in our lives. The process of transformation is to see Jesus realign all we bring with himself at the center. Muslims, like all people, need radical transformation—radical reorientation of their lives and communities in terms of Jesus' reign over the universe. But where does that process begin? From within their current context or from without? I have been challenged over the years to see that this process best begins from within. Jesus begins talking to people in the setting he finds them.

Disciples are as distinct as people—different for each context. As one called to declare the Gospel among Muslims in a particular Central Asian context, I am called to reflect intentionally on how I am call people to act and believe. I've sought to do that during my dozen years on the field.

I myself am first and foremost a disciple of Jesus. My personal journey, described here, is a pilgrimage—learning to follow and obey Jesus in every sphere of my life, as a disciple of Jesus the Messiah. I seek to learn from Jesus and do what he says, as Paul says in Ephesians 4:20. In ministry, I seek to teach others to do the same (Matt 28:18–20). A change in religious labels is not necessary to that process, but what do I aim for in discipleship. If a follower of Jesus is not a "Christian," so to speak, what is he? What does he believe? What does he know? What does he do? And how do I, a foreign outsider, catalyze those things?

Discipling

The redemptive story dominates my approach to discipleship. Jesus' death and resurrection and the introduction of the kingdom as Good News make best sense when seen in the light of the Old Testament context.

For Muslims, this approach taps into an existing paradigm. Most Muslims respect the prophets God has chosen throughout history. Stories deeply transform systematic thought even though they do not necessarily confront systematic theology head-on.[2] This invites Central Asians to apply the Gospel to their context without having to journey through my wide array of Western cultural development. It is their journey with God's story.

I believe engaging God's story is best done in community and, in many ways, as a discipleship of the community. I do not disciple Ahmad, or anyone else, in a vacuum. Indeed, I disciple him with a view towards his whole community.

While I encourage disciples like Ahmad to stay connected with their family and community, I simultaneously disciple him to abandon practices and beliefs at odds with God's kingdom. That process is complex. There is no magic bullet or instantaneous program. In what follows, I provide an outline of the process in which we are engaged as catalysts in our community.

My framework comes from the perspective of a team sent to engage a community with the Gospel. Though I lay things out sequentially, I find cross-cultural ministry, like everything involving human beings, is messy. Nothing goes according to plan and there are false starts, restarts, failures, and surprises along the way. This outline is what I have come to aim for in light of thoughtful consideration of community and identity issues.

I have utmost respect for anyone doing the labor and love-intensive work of discipleship, whether as one who sees the retention of community identity as viable or as one using more traditional categories of religious identity. In discipleship, disciplers are all different. <u>This "plan"</u> is one I continue to develop and test. In no sense is this the *only* approach to discipleship.

<u>(1) The search for local apostles and how I am not like Paul</u>

When I first lived overseas, I saw myself as following the Pauline pattern of missions. My first inspiration for missions was John Piper's *Let the Nations be Glad*. In it, Piper describes two types of missionaries: Paul and Timothy. He says that Timothy missionaries reinforce existing work, as Timothy did in Ephesus. He went to train and appoint elders *after* the Gospel had broken through. Paul, on the other hand, was a pioneer missionary. As Paul described, he aimed to preach the Gospel where "the name of Christ has never been heard" (Rom 15:20).

That is how I thought of myself—going where there had not been a breakthrough of the kingdom. I wanted to be the first to preach Christ there and plant a church—just like Paul.

But could I really be like Paul? As I started to interact with my host community and continued to read the New Testament, I realized how different I was from Paul. I was trying to learn new languages. I was oblivious to cultural differences between myself and the Muslim world. There was a chasm between me and those I was trying to reach. I was, frankly, an outsider.

What about Paul? Paul already spoke the language everywhere he successfully planted a church. This is a stunning fact. Paul knew Greek. He knew Hebrew. He probably knew Aramaic. The one time we see Paul at work when he did not know the language (Acts 14), people nearly sacrificed animals to him. He left no believers behind in Lystra.

Paul grew up as a Jew in a Greco-Roman city. Despite crossing religious and ethnic boundaries to preach the Gospel to Gentiles, he was a cultural insider. He knew Jewish culture inside and out. He likely had Gentile neighbors growing up. He was a near-culture missionary[3] to the Gentiles.

Methodologically, Paul operated as one working within an existing framework familiar to him. When Paul arrived in a new city, he went first to the synagogue. Even as the "apostle to the Gentiles," he operated strategically in light of his cultural comfort zones. Paul preached on Mars Hill in Acts 17, but this was the exception, not the norm. He was arguably less effective in that setting. It is not until late in his ministry that we find him branching out into Gentile meeting contexts meeting in a Gentile lecture hall (Acts 19:9). Paul always *starts* in a familiar setting, namely the synagogue. He moves to the Gentile lecture hall only after a core group has embraced the Gospel, a core group that he met in the synagogue.

A few years ago, it hit me that I could not be a Pauline missionary in the sense I am describing. I would always be an outsider—never a Pauline insider.

Though I found myself on strange ground in that realization, I also recognized I had a calling . . . to find a Central Asian Paul.

Many missionaries reflect on a concept Jesus gives us in Matthew 10 and Luke 10. Jesus instructs his disciples to go out into neighboring villages, enter a home, and declare a blessing of "peace" on that home. If the people there are "peaceful," that blessing will stick and the disciples should stay there. If the people are not peaceful, the disciples should leave.

In the missions community, this is called the "person of peace." For many, it has taken on meaning beyond the context of Matthew 10 and Luke 10 to describe a pattern found throughout the New Testament. A person of peace is a gatekeeper or door opener or bold evangelist. He or she is the kind of person that receives those carrying the message of the Gospel and opens the door for others to hear that message. Some will define a person of peace as someone who actively spreads the Gospel in his or her community. Some expand the definition to include those that may not even believe themselves but open up the door for the messenger.

The Bible doesn't give a precise definition for a person of peace. In the Gospels and the book of Acts, there are many of these people—people God providentially puts in the way of his messengers to give traction to the Gospel in a new community. This is seen in the demoniac who had a legion of demons in him—he went back to his community to tell them the "great things Jesus had done for him" (Luke 8:39). The Ethiopian eunuch who continued with the message that Phillip gave him (Acts 8:39) is another example. Lydia, who opened up her home to Paul in Philippi and led her household to faith (Acts 16:15), provides more evidence. And the Roman Centurion, who searched out Peter and brought his whole household together to hear what Peter had to say

(Acts 10–11) demonstrates another person of peace. Ananias in Damascus, who was told to pray over his enemy Saul (Acts 9:10–18), is a person of peace.

This is a biblical pattern of God providing a person who becomes a gateway for the Gospel into a new community. Often through these means the Holy Spirit overcomes the chasm between one culture and community and another culture and community. He uses willing people, like Peter, Phillip, and Ananias, people with sufficient influence to make the Gospel accessible to others, like Cornelius, the Ethiopian eunuch, Lydia, and Saul. David Watson has seen thousands of churches planted by finding local apostles. He puts it this way:

> I have learned that God has prepared men and women in every culture who can meet those who love Jesus from another [foreign] culture, learn to love Jesus from them, strip away the cultural baggage attached (which we can minimize), and present Jesus to their own culture in a loving and caring way that results in lives changed and the Kingdom enlarged.[4]

I have increasingly come to see myself as more like Peter, Phillip, or Ananias —the one from whom those prepared by God to carry the message into their community can learn. I am a pioneer, but my role is to clumsily cross a culture and find the person (or persons) God has appointed to spread his Good News. How is that done?

Others have helpfully described what the process looks like. Jerry Trousdale's *Miraculous Movements*[5] describe this process in beautiful stories. He tells of African believers going to nearby villages with tremendous faith in what God will do spontaneously. And God does things in matters of days and months, not years. The pattern Jesus describes in the Gospels happens today. I believe the closer one is to being a cultural insider, the more one can follow the direct pattern found in Matthew 10 or Luke 10 and see rapid multiplication. In those passages, the disciples go to a new village and simply look for those willing to host them.

The more culturally distant the messenger, the longer that process takes. For us, it meant leaving our home in America, finding a place to live, learning a language, living in three cities, starting a business, building trust, making lots of mistakes, and persisting anyway. It has meant speaking explicitly about Jesus, but also paying attention to ways our words about Jesus miscommunicate. It has meant prioritizing prayer and sacrificial acts of love over explicit words so people observe our intent as for their good.

It has meant prayerfully keeping our eyes open. That is how we found Ahmad. Ahmad came to a colleague's English classes. He started pestering him after class. He got a copy of Matthew's Gospel and was blown away by Jesus' integrity. We did not find Ahmad. He found us. We were simply willing to be near him.

We do not know if Ahmad is the Paul we have been looking for. But he has shown key signs—he has received us (even into his home, including letting Michelle share the Gospel with his mothers, sisters, and aunt) and he has expressed his desire to get this message to his family and community. It has not happened yet. As we walk through the discipleship process with him, we continue to hope and pray for fundamental breakthrough.

(2) Discipleship on day one

In popular American parlance, a preacher or missionary does evangelism first and then, once someone makes a profession of faith, he or she begins the work of discipling. Unfortunately, this perspective creates a divide between the proclamation of the Gospel (evangelism) and the actual process of following Jesus (discipleship). The Bible does not seem to divide them. The Gospels themselves are vague about when the first disciples made concrete decisions of faith. Was it when they first began to follow Jesus? Was it when they confessed Jesus as Messiah? Was it after the resurrection? Acts emphasizes that they were with Jesus all along (Acts 4:13). The first act of discipleship in the Gospels could be seen as that first encounter with Jesus. This is where the story begins.

In this sense, discipleship begins on day one. "Discipleship" comes from the word Jesus uses in Matthew 28:19—"make disciples." But the root word, *matheteo* in Greek, is "teach." We gained a great insight living overseas: we are always teaching. We teach from our first step into a community. People are watching. We are teaching.

When we moved to our second country in Central Asia, Hajji Odam watched me. He observed my mistakes, especially with language and culture. He saw how I dealt with those mistakes as well.

One day I blew up at a manual laborer who was repairing well. The project had been a disaster—miscommunication, deceit, and delayed results. In anger I refused to pay for his services and sent the laborer away empty-handed.

After he left, and with my head cooled down, I asked Hajji Odam about the situation. I learned that culturally I was the wrongful one—I had wronged the laborer. With the Holy Spirit at work in my heart, I asked Hajji Odam to take me to the man's house. I sat on his dirt floor in the tiny hovel of a home. I paid him and asked him to forgive me.

A year later, Hajji Odam asked about the incident. Hajji Odam was in conflict with his brother. He wanted to know about forgiveness. It was my first opportunity to talk about the practical impact of the Gospel, but the discipleship process had already begun.

This aspect of discipleship—the "telling" of words and life—is constant. But a significant element is often lost: the response. If discipleship begins on day one, it means seekers can become disciples, followers of Jesus—before they make a full-fledged commitment. This happens in several ways.

With Ahmad, it began the first time we sat down together. I told him we would not simply read the Bible for information. We would read it with the intent to respond in obedience. We would ask the question, "If God said this, what does it require of me?" He did not need to know the whole Bible story—he simply needed to acknowledge some level of authority in the text and apply what he learned to his daily life.

This application of the Scriptures can even happen in casual conversation. My friend, Zahid, told me about his struggle with worry as we stood chatting on a dusty road. I shared Jesus' words about worry in Matthew 6, "God takes care of birds and flowers; we can trust him with our problems." I then offered to pray for his worry. That act of prayer together is a step of obedience. It is discipleship, even though this man had not made any commitment to Jesus.

This model allows the gradual movement of an individual or group into God's active and living story. Neither Ahmad nor Zahid need to entertain a change in religious identity to ask forgiveness from an offended friend or entrust worry to God the Creator. They do need God's Spirit to work in them these acts of obedience. They begin the transformation process without identity or community issues getting in the way. As they obey, others in their community will notice. Jesus is behind the transformation they are experiencing—this will become increasingly evident as they continue to obey. These tiny steps of discipleship trigger curiosity in others. Disciples beget disciples.

(3) What to do when a seeker wants to know more

You have been living a life of integrity. You have been telling stories. You have begun to understand the language and culture. Now someone, like Hajji Odam or Ahmad, says, "**I want to know more.**" What do you do?

That is a question I think about more than any other. It keeps me awake at night. It drives my study of the Bible. It frames my conversations and relationships. I have relived this question multiple times as I reflect on my experience with Hajji Odam. I have faced this opportunity only a few times. When it happens again, I want to be ready. Five steps have become important to me for this process.

First, identify the group.

The first issue is to extend this question beyond the individual asking it. When Hajji Odam stated, "I want to learn more." I invited him to meet with me in our private hosting room for a study of Luke's Gospel. I would now insist that he bring someone with him. His son? His father? A close friend? Meeting with him individually increases the likelihood of pulling him into my story, my social plausibility structure, rather than inviting him to see his own story and group transformed.

Even better, I would ask to meet in his home rather than mine. Location matters. Meeting on my turf implies movement into my sphere. Movement to his turf says Jesus is coming to his sphere. A reciprocal invitation could sound like, "Sure. Is there a way that I could come and share with your family?" This follows the model in Acts 10. When Cornelius wanted to know more, and Peter went to Cornelius' house to share with him. A whole household hears and processes God's story together.

I have yet to have a man accept my invitation to share in his own context. As a foreigner from another religious setting, I am seen as a threat. Michelle, however, has had multiple opportunities to go through Old and New Testament stories in Central Asian living rooms. Women come in and out. Children cry and play. Throughout, they engage God's story together.

Though it goes against my ideal, I have been willing to meet individually in my home with men. With Ahmad, I have done so under the condition that our conversations have his family and friends in view. We always talk about his experiences sharing the biblical stories. We discuss with whom he will share biblical stories that week and with whom he shared them the previous week. Our times together are often filled with a discussion of how others responded to his stories. We celebrate when someone engages and responds with prayer or obedience. We reflect when he gets pushback or, at times, hostility. I aim to keep him from engaging God's story in isolation with me alone. It is not ideal, but it is a direction we have been willing to take in a tough environment.

SECOND, EXPLAIN THAT THIS IS GOD'S STORY, NOT MINE.

I've talked to Hajji Odam and Ahmad explicitly about community identity. In this initial conversation with Hajji Odam I wrestled with whether this conversation was actually necessary. Was I imposing a paradigm on seekers, and even violating my own principle for an inductive, discovery-oriented approach?

I don't think so. To the contrary, I am presenting an option for seekers that they simply do not know is available to them. Most people in today's world assume they have to change their self-identification label to know Jesus. My local friends describe this: Jesus is for Christians. Mohammad is for Muslims. And Moses is for Jews. I believe, based on the Scriptures, that Jesus is for all peoples (Romans 3:29–30). He didn't *just* come for Jews, or Americans, or Europeans, or any ethnic group in the world. He came to give blessing to all, just as Abraham was told millennia ago.

When I told Hajji Odam he could follow Jesus *without renouncing his community identity*—remain attached to the label "Muslim"—I validated him as a person. I validated the place where he was born. I emphasized that he could enter directly into God's story without taking a detour through mine. I respected his heritage, his past. I honored his very birth.

Michelle and I now have these conversations with friends and acquaintances early on in our relationships. It has given us great freedom in talking about Jesus. How people relate to their community and identify with them is a front-burner issue for almost everyone I talk to. It is on their minds from the moment they shake my hand. When I assure people I am not interested in having them change religious identities, it removes a stumbling block to conversations. People visibly relax and start to listen. Taking "identity" issues off the table allows us to talk openly and forthrightly. Others realize we can keep talking where we are. They do not have to commit to a new location to begin the conversation. This allows us to shift the issue on the front-burner from identity to allegiance.

This approach to religious identity frees me to be the blessing I want to be to the community. It pulls down defenses. In my city, I operate openly. I am not a proselytizing "missionary," a term connotes colonialism and cultural imperialism. I am openly a follower of Jesus who aims to show mercy because of the mercy God has shown me. I talk with people about Jesus in public places consistently tying my very presence there to Jesus' call on my life.

When I spoke with Zahid about what Jesus had to say about worry, another shopkeeper interrupted our conversation. "Oh, Zahid, here you are talking to our local missionary," was his comment.

Zahid responded, "No, not at all. He's not a missionary. This is my good friend, Joseph. Today, we are discussing Jesus and what he has to say about worry."

For Zahid it made perfect sense. He denied I was a missionary but admitted to discussing Jesus. In a Western context, it makes no sense at all. I had built trust with Zahid and removed any threat from our relationship. We could talk freely. Talking freely did not mean there was no meat to our discussion.

Zahid and I first met when I was debating a mullah in his business partner's carpet shop. The mullah was quizzing me about Christian beliefs, and I was pressing him to embrace the relevancy of the New Testament for his community. Zahid knew I was loyal to Jesus and believed Jesus had significance for his life. But the misconceptions of religious conversion did not have to stigmatize our relationship or hinder him from hearing what Jesus had to say. All this shifts the entrance point of the conversation from *my story* for this community to *God's story*.

> THIRD, GO THROUGH REDEMPTIVE HISTORY WITH A VIEW TO CONCRETE RESPONSE.

Our current strategy for content is to do chronological Bible storying. This approach was introduced 40 years ago, and is far from novel. It simply means walking through the story of the whole Bible.

There are numerous ways to do chronological storying. We have favored tapping into the common ground found in the Quran by going through the lives of biblical characters and prophets that Muslims have already heard about and believe in. These include Adam, Noah, Abraham, Joseph, Moses, David, Solomon, and Jonah, then culminate with the person of Jesus. In the process, I try to show the progression of the redemptive storyline. Muslims in our context often think of God's revelation as a simple series in a long chain—dots on a paper without any necessary historical or chronological connection between them. Many of my Muslim friends do not know the time setting of different prophets and biblical characters. My colleagues and I emphasize that God revealed things progressively to Moses, David, and Isaiah and direct the conversation towards something, or rather Someone (Luke 24:44).

Others find help in this process through "Quranic bridging." They read passages from the Quran about each prophet being described. To the surprise of many Christians, these passages usually reinforce the biblical story and often draw out redemptive themes for a Muslim audience. The Quran is not readily available in the common local language where we have not adopted this approach. Those working in Arab contexts report significant fruit from this approach.

Within this framework, we have specific content aims for disciples. At the most basic level, we aim for disciples to understand and internalize these steps in salvation history:

- the goodness of God's creation and God's fundamental love for people and the world
- the devastating effects of Adam and Eve's sin in the Garden of Eden and how it separated us from God's design
- the boldness of God's promise to Abraham to bless all the families of the world through his heir
- the selection of Israel and its failure to live out God's purposes

- the exile of Israel—and fundamentally all mankind—from God's good purposes
- the principle that God's prophets and God's people go through suffering but God persistently cares for them
- Jesus' earth-shattering entrance into the world and proclamation that God's kingdom has come now
- the call to love, radical forgiveness, integrity in all of life, and God-dependency as embodied expressions of God's kingdom today
- the unleashed power for such kingdom relationships given by Jesus' atoning death and death-conquering resurrection
- the gift of the Holy Spirit that comes through Jesus' death and our reconciled relationship with the Father
- the power Jesus gives to destroy the works of the devil, including demonic oppression, abusive relationships, and disease
- Jesus' promised return for which we prepare as disciples by spreading his kingdom from heart to heart, family to family

As disciples of Jesus, Michelle and I have internalized certain themes as we walk through the Scriptures. We emphasize the priority of God's movement towards us—prior to our movement towards him. This comes out in stories from Adam to Jesus. We often hear of this from seekers. Hajji Odam told me, as a child his mother told him stories of Jesus that engaged his heart. Ahmad talked of his deep longing for God starting when he was ten years old. Disciples often tell stories of dreams and visions God gave them. God's initiative shines through.

We emphasize the priority of God's acceptance and happiness with us through Jesus our mediator. Muslims often view life as a perpetual test to pass or fail, putting God in the position of test-giver—constantly evaluating us. As we walk together, we reinforce God's overarching love through the biblical storyline. This fundamental acceptance by God, apart from my performance and success, has been one of the hardest realities for me to internalize as a disciple of Jesus. It gives me patience as new disciples encounter these aspects of God's love.

Finally, we emphasize hope and God-dependency. Ninety percent of my conversations with Central Asians are about the future, and usually include fear of what the future holds. Following Jesus' pattern in Matthew 6, we emphasize repeatedly, God's willingness to answer our prayers as we cry out to him. Hope destroys despair, sin, shame, and the world's system. With each trial a disciple faces, we point to the unmatchable goodness God has in store for those who trust in him.

Our aim is not to pass on information. We constantly ask about the relevance of the stories for our lives, encouraging the seeker in how they will apply what the text says. This is what James tells us we are to do: "[Don't] just listen to God's word. You must do what it says" (Jas 1:22). This is where the discovery element of our times together is seen. I find that asking disciples what their response should be to the Scriptures we study is more powerful than my instruction. They *own* their response. Scripture becomes the authority in their lives. I am not the authority. I have to trust the Holy Spirit to lead them in this process. He is quite worthy of that trust and far more effective than I am.

What about when someone completely misses one of these themes or infers a heresy from a passage? We keep reading. I'm willing to correct when something is so egregious that there is no time for processing. For instance, I had one disciple consider helping a woman divorce her husband so she could run away with him. He justified his intentions as an expression of love and concern for her loneliness. I expressed disapproval, prayed, and the issue disappeared. Faithful discipleship includes the willingness to rebuke when necessary. But we use this cautiously and rarely.

FOURTH, DISCERN AND BE WILLING TO PULL BACK.

One of the tougher aspects of this process is discerning if the seeker is a "person of peace" that we are looking for in the community. Michelle and I are actively watching to see if a seeker continues to receive us and our message, to obey what he or she hears or reads, and to share that message with others. As we see these signs, we invest more energy in the relationship in keeping with 2 Timothy 2:2, "Now teach these truths to other trustworthy people who will be able to pass them on to others." If we don't see these signs, we invest less. For me, that primarily means not initiating communication. Though Ahmad has not seen others grab onto his stories, he has continued to obey and share. He has also persistently asked to keep meeting with me. Those have been signs that provoke more investment on my part.

This is a shift from how I related to Hajji Odam. In the latter years of our relationship, I was the one who called him. I missed the signs that his interest was lagging, along with his obedience and efforts to share. As a result, I wrongfully invested energy to prop up the relationship. I say it was wrong because the mental and emotional energy I invested in waiting for him to come to my house took away from the on-going pursuit of others in our community. I now believe it was a misapplication of the time and energy resources that God had given me.

We must be willing to allow a relationship to lag or drop in order to catalyze, rather than force, others to engage with the Gospel. The Spirit's work to drive someone forward in transformation is absolutely essential. If I act as the continual prompter, I am usually imposing my foreign paradigm and unintentionally trying to take the role of the Holy Spirit.

Fifth, pay attention to the demonic.

Westerners have been quick to overlook demonic activity in a community because of our largely secularized worldview. This is to our shame. It is incumbent on us to bring up these issues.[6] We help people pray for healing of emotional wounds. We declare Jesus' authority over demons. We invite believers and unbelievers alike to address issues of bitterness and demonic oppression in Jesus' name. Surprisingly, these practices are welcomed. They resonate with people who are desperate to deal with demonic oppression. Most local people deal with oppression by visiting pseudo-mullahs that often charge extravagant fees for reciting Quranic verses, creating talismans, or conducting animal sacrifices. We show the free offer Jesus gives to overcome the works of the evil one—a crucial testimony. We often address these issues early in the relationship. Michelle has found women open to praying about such things even when they are resistant to talking about Jesus or the things of God in other circumstance. This, then, can be seen as the discipleship process that we aim to initiate from the very beginning of a relationship.

(4) What to do when there are groups

I wait with deep expectation for the day when we see fellowship groups form or expand. I have gleaned thoughts and culled wisdom about the process of group development from those who have engaged them. I offer these as one way of imagining the implications of what I have argued for thus far into future relationships.

First, develop leaders.

As groups form, certain disciples will stand out as particularly gifted in teaching and leadership. Those working with these groups are wise to watch and provide some form of scalable leadership training. A growing group experiences new dynamics requiring specific leadership development. One example is for leaders of different house groups to meet together to discuss discipleship issues. They talk about what they are studying together. They address issues of identity. They pray for one another. They deal with conflict.

Second, do the hard work of submitting everything to Jesus' Lordship.

As groups form, disciples will deal with cultural issues in light of the the Scriptures. The Apostle Paul demonstrates the processing of cultural experiences in light of the Gospel over a myriad of issues big and small in I Corinthians. Some practitioners adapt the process of late missiologist Paul Hiebert, called "critical contextualization."[7]

Under Hiebert's paradigm, groups of disciples go through a process of exegeting their culture, exegeting the the Scriptures, critically evaluating their culture in light of the Scriptures, and finally implementing new practices in light of their analysis. All the steps are important, for them to open-handedly evaluate the good and bad of their cultural norms. It is absolutely essential that they study the Scriptures to see what they say about an issue. Significantly, Hiebert emphasizes that the study of the Scriptures has to break cultural boundaries. The Scriptures will have a counter-cultural message for both the cross-cultural worker and the recipient culture. Both parties need to pursue the original intent of the biblical authors and seek to remove cultural blinders they might have that undermine the intent of the Scriptures. Finally, if there is no integration and application, the exercise is fruitless. The local disciples have to discern concrete ways to apply what the Scriptures teach them within their own context. This process makes clear the authority of the Scriptures over the community.

Critical contextualization, however, can be an extremely long process requiring patience from the cross-cultural worker. One practitioner described taking seven years for a group to discern what to do with plural wives. However long it may be, it is preferable for those in the community to come to a conclusion for themselves on how to address the issue than to have an outsider dictating a solution which may have unintended and destructive consequences.

THIRD, FRAME BAPTISM AND THE LORD'S SUPPER WITHIN COMMUNITY.

I have come to see baptism and the Lord's Supper as important biblical expressions of faith within a developing believing community rather than in individual isolation. So many of my stories are about individuals. Baptism can often indicate within the Muslim world a *separation* from one's community and can be a trigger for violent persecution. Grappling with how, *not if*, to baptize and celebrate communion should be part of the critical contextualization process described above.[8] For readers from a sacramental tradition, Vincent Donovan's story of the Masai coming to Christ as a community and their participation in the Eucharist is a powerful example of how the sacrament's importance can be upheld while also heeding the principles this book describes.[9]

FOURTH, KEEP GROWING.

One exciting thing happening in the Muslim world currently is a group of disciples beginning to dream about seeing God's kingdom spread to new communities. Jerry Trousdale and David Garrison are documenting these developments.[10] Some groups are sending their own people across geographical boundaries to see the Gospel spread. These disciples feel the burden for the Muslim world more intensely than I or others from a different background. This step is crucial to the fulfillment of the Great Commission and is an exciting thing to see. I continue to hope and pray for this within Central Asia.

(5) What about persecution?

Persecution happens. The Bible does not tell us to pursue or avoid persecution. It tells us the world will oppose those who follow Jesus and we can expect persecution (Matt 5:10-12; 2 Tim 3:12; 1 Pet 4:12). These are two very different perspectives. Disciples who maintain their relationships with their family and community can do so in biblical ways. At the same time, the world is rife with injustice and idolatry. I expect disciples of Jesus will confront injustice and idolatry with their lives and witness. When this happens, there will be opposition. That opposition can lead to disciples being expelled from their community. Our experience of walking with believers through persecution they have faced "in the name of religion" is often tied to interpersonal relationships. One friend attempted to get an elected position as village representative. A jealous relative wanted the same position and accused him of converting to American Christianity because of his relationship with us. This was a form of persecution.

Another friend had promised their daughter to a relative in marriage (a common practice). The young man to whom she was engaged turned out to be potentially abusive, and they broke off the engagement. The scorned fiancé accused the girl of religious conversion to avoid public embarrassment. In these cases, the persecution was linked to other issues. These conflicts could be addressed without any denial of one's loyalty to Jesus. Indeed, Jesus' roadmap to peace (love your enemies, turn the other cheek) provided powerful action steps to resolve the situations. I have heard stories of disciples in Muslim contexts facing ferocious opposition explicitly for their loyalty to Jesus. Some have suffered deeply because of this, including loss of life and property. Cultivating meaningful relationships within the community, as I advocate in this book, can delay this kind of opposition but those deeper relationships may not prevent opposition and persecution.

(6) Finally, expect the unexpected

We have often been surprised. We were surprised by how Muslims saw the world. We were surprised by how the concerns about identity meshed with the Scriptures and reality. We were surprised by how some of our discipleship and evangelistic approaches were counterproductive. In discipleship, expect to be surprised.

I have learned best practices from others and seen how these cohere with my experience. Patterns and practices need the Spirit's empowerment. The Spirit may work in new and surprising ways completely outside of what I have described. Church history, especially as demonstrated in the book of Acts, shows that the Spirit moves in gloriously unpredictable ways. He put Philip next to the Ethiopian eunuch and then beamed him back to Samaria. He used a Jewish jihadist to spread the gospel to Gentiles.

My journey has led me to be open-ended on how new disciples define their identity. The Spirit leads believers in context and may lead in ways the foreign disciple-maker neither desires nor expects. New or mature believers may prefer a foreign identity in order to describe their new faith—some may prefer to call themselves "Christian" to emphasize their new allegiance. This seems to be happening today in some countries where there have been particularly oppressive regimes that function in the name of Islam. A number of field practitioners believed that they should plant C5, local identity churches in their community, but the believers themselves used the foreign Christian name to describe their faith. Significantly, in such cases, the disciples found a way to communicate their message and follow forms of obedience in ways that could be reproduced within their communities. That is the aim. The foreign disciple-maker, like myself, must be sensitive to the Spirit, listen well to the local disciples, and repeatedly teach reliance on Jesus and the Scriptures. God will lead the way through these efforts.

God's methods surprise and shock. We make our plans to be faithful to what we know. We do not presume. Nor do we propose any of this approach as a magic key to unlock a people movement. We should be skeptical of anyone making such a claim. Yet, we anticipate, expect, and hope in God to do radical things to bring Muslims into alignment with his redemptive story in Jesus for his glory.

REFLECTION QUESTIONS

1. When you became a believer, what were your first steps of concrete obedience to the Lord?
2. For those working cross-culturally, what do you imagine are the crucial steps in discipling people towards the Kingdom of God?
3. Describe a situation when you have seen God work outside of your expectations in bringing change to people's lives.

---

1. Watson and Watson, *Contagious Disciple Making*, 49.

2. Missiologist Tom Steffen has written extensively on the way biblical narrative can be a more effective way of bringing transformation in church-planting efforts: Tom A. Steffen, *Reconnecting God's Story to Ministry: Cross-Cultural Storytelling At Home and Abroad* (La Habra, CA: Center for Organizational & Ministry Development, 1996); Tom A. Steffen, *Passing the Baton: Church-Planting That Empowers* (La Habra, CA: Center for Organizational & Ministry Development, 1997); Steffen, "Foundational Roles," 477–94; Tom A. Steffen, *The Facilitator Era: Beyond Pioneer Church Multiplication* (Eugene, OR: Wipf & Stock, 2011).
3. "**Near-culture** missions involve reaching unreached people groups who are geographically, culturally, and linguistically proximate to you. It involves sharing the Good News with the unreached people in your own country or region." "What Are Near, Far and Same Culture Mission Workers?" Operation Mobilization USA, accessed 25 July 2023, https://www.o-musa.org/what-are-near-far-and-same-culture-mission-workers/
4. Watson and Watson, *Contagious Disciple Making*, 12.
5. Jerry Trousdale, *Miraculous Movements: How Hundreds of Thousands of Muslims are Falling in Love with Jesus* (Nashville, TN: Thomas Nelson, 2012). Trousdale describes finding people of peace in chapter 5 of the book, 83-95. David and Paul Watson also give principles for finding people of peace in *Contagious Disciple Making*.
6. See Anna Travis, "Spiritual Power, World Religions, and the Demonic," in *Understanding Insider Movements*, ed. Harley Talman and John Jay Travis (Pasadena, CA: William Carey Library, 2015) 521–36; and Paul G. Hiebert, "The Flaw of the Excluded Middle," *Missiology: An International Review* 10, no. 1 (1982): 35–47.
7. Hiebert, "Critical Contextualization."
8. For an example of this process see Kevin Higgins, "Speaking the Truth About Insider Movements: Addressing the Criticisms of Bill Nikides and 'Phil' Relative to the Article 'Inside What?'," *St Francis Magazine* 5, no. 6 (2009), 67-68. Darren Duerkson notes how the translation for "baptism" can contribute to how whether the Scripture and the ritual are foreign to the community: Darren T. Duerkson, *Christ-Followers in Other Religions: The Global Witness of Insider Movements* (Oxford, UK: Regnum Books International, 2022), 2427, Kindle. Relatedly, translation plays a role as to whether or not baptism communicates separation from the community. It is possible, for instance, to tap into existing practices of purification rituals for communicating the truth of baptism without alienating one's community. The meaning may be changed or expanded, just as John the Baptist expanded and changed the meaning of the cleansing rites for proselytes when he baptized people at the Jordan River. Though Commentator R. T. France, for instance, calls John's baptism an "innovation" he describes its potential connection to the Qumran community and Gentile converts. Jesus steps into the meaning that John made from this ritual. And then Jesus and his disciples give new meaning to the act as well. R. T. France, *Matthew: An Introduction and Commentary* (Downers Grove, IL: InterVarsity Press, 1985), 98-99.
9. Vincent J. Donovan, *Christianity Rediscovered: An Epistle From the Masai* (London, UK: SCM Press, 1982). Chapter 7 particularly tells the role of the eucharist and baptism in the community.
10. Trousdale, *Miraculous Movements*; David Garrison, *A Wind in the House of Islam: How God is Drawing Muslims Around the World to Faith in Jesus Christ* (Monument, CO: Wigtake Resources LLC, 2014).

8

DEMONS, MEAT, AND THE DISCIPLESHIP OF CULTURAL DISCERNMENT

In Christ God accepts us together with our group relations, with that cultural conditioning that makes us feel at home in one part of human society and less at home in another. But if he takes us with our group relations, then surely it follows that he takes us with our "dis-relations" also; those predispositions, prejudices, suspicions, and hostilities, whether justified or not, which mark the group to which we belong. He does not wait to tidy up our ideas any more than he waits to tidy up our behavior before he accepts us sinners into his family.[1]

Andrew Walls

Artifacts of Worship

The sacrifice of animals conducted during the Muslim holiday of *Eid-i-Qurban* was one of the initial issues confronting us on our arrive in Central Asia. Each year Muslims remember Abraham's attempted sacrifice of his son.[2] They commemorate the substitution of a ram for the son by sacrificing a sheep, camel, or cow and then share that meat with their neighbors, guests, and the poor. In our country of Central Asia, the holiday lasts three days.

Beginning at about 11:00 am that first day and through most of the second day, there is someone knocking on our gate. The poor of the community walk the neighborhood asking for the meat they have been allotted for the holiday.

When we arrived, we wanted to make sure we gave something. The holiday was a reminder to be generous, particularly to the poor. But we did not want to communicate that we had participated in the animal sacrifices done around us. There is only one sacrifice that matters today, that of Jesus our Lord (Hebrews 10:12). We did not want any association with what we considered false worship. So, we bought flour and sugar and tea and other supplies we thought the poor would need and appreciate.

The poor did not appreciate our gifts. They looked at what we had given them as a cheap substitute for the meat they had come to get. The poor cannot afford to buy meat. They can afford flour. They thought we were holding back. Our house was painted and in a middle-class style. Surely, they thought, we had the money to slaughter an animal. If we were not giving them meat, we must have been hoarding it for ourselves or our rich neighbors.

In recent years, we have purchased meat before the holiday to give to the poor. We buy multiple pounds and wrap a half pound in plastic bags. When the poor come, we bless them and hand them the meat. They thank God for our gift and move on to the next house.

We do not explain to them the nature of true sacrifice in this case. But we do communicate love in terms they understand. I believe this approach is faithful to Paul's concern in 1 Corinthians 8-10.

Is association with false worship the issue?

Our first concern when we went overseas was to make sure we did not miscommunicate through false association. We resisted the idea of serving meat because we wanted to mark out our Christian distinctives with people. This approach has benefits. It provokes questions. It gives opportunity to explain truth.

But as I study Paul's letter to the Corinthians, I see my focus on *dissociation* with false worship can often be a distraction and a form of miscommunication. It distracts from love.

Love and truth are not at odds. It can be loving to tell someone they are wrong. Love does not "rejoice about injustice [including falsehood] but rejoices whenever the truth wins out" (1 Cor 13:6). I have experienced how my intentions for truth were at times ineffective. The way Michelle and I initially treated the meat *for Eid-i-Qurban* miscommunicated. It is one example of how our fears about the meaning of something associated with religion led us to communicate stinginess and disregard for the poor—the opposite of the Gospel message.

I believe American Christians live in a context far more similar to the worship-soaked culture of first century Greco-Roman world than they realize. In I Corinthians 8-10 Paul is concerned with meat being sacrificed to pagan idols. Few in the west deal with that issue. But worship issues abound. Issues of association with false worship are relevant.

What do I mean by this claim? By worship, I do not mean prostrations, songs, or rituals. I mean things or beings that people adore. I mean ideas and items which provide comfort and security. I mean places in which individuals put their hope and longings. In this sense, worship is everywhere. It happens at churches, mosques and synagogues, but also in shopping malls, bars, coffeeshops, sport stadiums, voting booths, and Disneyland.

Paul was dealing with genuine followers of Jesus from Gentile backgrounds living in a Gentile world filled with worship. Must they completely dissociate with every false idea present? The context and question are not so far from our own.

In his commentary on 1 Corinthians, Richard B. Hays discusses this point well. The absence of physical idols carved from stone or wood in our culture does not spare us the danger of idolatry.[3] Indeed, as Hays notes, "the exclusive lordship of Jesus stands as a challenge to many arrangements that we take for granted." Hays includes the dangers in our churches of patriotism and materialism: "the most insidious form of idolatry."[4] The latter makes sense. The Apostle Paul defines covetousness as idolatry (Col 3:5). Materialism at its core seems to be cultivating ways to covet.

These are two potential forms of idolatry in our culture. We can add reverence for sports and entertainment as well. These potential forms of idolatry confront us every day. Just as places listed above contain acts of worship, so the daily events of our lives bump up against false worship. Cheering a beloved sports team. Voting in an election. Saying the Pledge of Allegiance. Singing the latest pop song. Searching the internet. Playing games on an Xbox. All of these rituals can be acts of participation in American worship. Or, they can be submitted to Jesus' lordship and used for innocent pleasure and love of others.

Forgetting this, it can be extremely easy for Western Christians to critique the way Islamic forms dominate the lives of Muslims. Our definition of religious expression and worship is so narrow we do not see the multitude of rival spiritual influences in our lives. On one hand, we tend to think of worship in categories of formal religion: Judaism, Hinduism, Catholicism, or Islam. But what is worship? Can worship be fundamental commitments to ideas, activities, or things? I submit they can. We can worship sports teams, possessions, status, government, and money. Any of these aspects of our culture can function like a religion. I have been forced to ask myself, how does my association with these worship acts impact my submission to Jesus as Lord?

These questions help make better sense of my context in Muslim Central Asia. In understanding other cultures, analogies help make sense of things. Most people I talk to about the Muslim world assume that a person coming to faith in Jesus in a Muslim context involves complete dissociation with Islam because they presume Islam is a dominating religion. How could anyone maintain any connection, any association, with such an all-encompassing religion? Some of the strongest critics of disciples retaining their identity of birth speak about it as a type of cruelty—disciples forced to stay connected with false worship to the destruction of their nascent faith.[5]

I have come to see Western religions—materialism, entertainment, patriotism—as similarly all-consuming. How do you extract yourself from their control over your life as a believer? Westerners deal with no less of a dominant religious context. We do not face immediate martyrdom for separating ourselves from that context as Muslims might, but we similarly face the social questions of how to live in the world and have relationships with family and friends. If Christians in the West would completely opt out of those cultural domains (voting, social media, sports, shopping for pleasure), life would look dramatically different from current practice. Self-reflection of one's cultural milieu can lead to a greater understanding of the social environment of a Muslim who decides to devote himself to Jesus' lordship. The reasons for maintaining connections with his or her community are in fact biblically possible.

This brings me to 1 Corinthians 8–10. This passage examines the crucial question: does faithful discipleship require complete dissociation with false worship?

The Jerusalem Council and the Context of Meat

Paul's discussion in chapters 8–10 of 1 Corinthians is a case study in apostolic engagement with culture and religion. As noted Paul was a bicultural missionary. I consider myself a *cross*-cultural missionary. I did not know the language or culture before I went to Central Asia. Paul knew both the language and culture of the Greek world even though he came from a Jewish context. This gave Paul a tremendous advantage in addressing the issues of discipleship for a particular setting. He could speak directly into the activities of his Jewish-Gentile audience as a cultural insider. This background to the passage leads to the premise that Paul spoke authoritatively both because he was an apostle and because he knew the setting. He was conversant with Greek philosophy and the Jewish Scriptures and he knew the context of pagan temples. He could speak authoritatively on the use of meat.

Central to studying Paul's response on the issue of meat is understanding Paul's broader context. Meat was often consumed at temples after being sacrificed to an idol. It was also sold in the marketplace after those rituals.[6] The issue would have been front and center for Gentiles seeking to orient their lives around Jesus' lordship. Commentator Gordon Fee summarizes the Corinthian context this way:

> In the Corinth of Paul's time, such meals [at the temples] were still the regular practice both at state festivals and private celebrations of various kinds. There were three parts to these meals: the preparation, the sacrifice proper, and the feast. The meat of the sacrifices apparently was divided into three portions: that burned before the god, that apportioned to the worshipers, and that placed on the "table of the god," which was tended by cultic ministrants but also eaten by the worshipers. The significance of these meals has been much debated, but most likely they involved a combination of religious and social factors. The gods were thought to be present, since the meals were held

in their honor and sacrifices were made; nonetheless, the meals were also intensely social occasions for the participants. For the most part, the Gentiles who had become believers in Corinth had probably attended such meals all their lives; indeed such meals served as the basic "restaurants" in antiquity, and every kind of occasion was celebrated in this fashion.[7]

In a way similar to the clash of American religious experiences with materialism, patriotism and entertainment, New Testament culture was charged with worship issues. Was it okay to eat meat that might have been prepared in the service of a false deity? Does one eat meat at all if there's a chance it had to do with idol worship? Can one eat meat at the temple during a ritual sacrifice? These are Paul's questions. They are tough questions.

In our case study, the early church had already ruled on this issue. The Jerusalem Council decided to ask the Gentiles coming to faith in Jesus to avoid meat sacrificed to idols (Acts 15:29). They did so out of respect for the Jewish community, to enable Jewish believers to stay connected with other Jews even if they had table fellowship with Gentiles. As commentator Richard Hays notes, "We might expect Paul to give a simple and clear-cut answer to this problem, for elsewhere in the New Testament there is a flat prohibition against eating such idol meat [referring to Acts 15]." [8] But Paul does not give a simple and clear-cut answer. He seems to decide the issue in a completely different way.

We are left with a list of questions to address. How does Paul deal with association with false worship? How does Paul draw lines about cultural and religious practices? And who makes the decision about these issues? Insights from Paul's answer to these crucial questions have proved deeply challenging for me.

First, it is not about association

Consider opening a Bible and reading I Corinthians 8-10. Read it a second time. It is a challenging passage of Scripture in its logical development. Paul is quoting from a letter the Corinthians wrote him. No copy survived. Most translations, using quotation marks, speculate what Paul wrote as quotes from the Corinthains. Commentators often point out that other statements may have been quotations and not Paul's assertions, which makes understanding the passage more difficult.

The Corinthian context is unique—creating another difficulty. It is not known exactly what the different believers in Corinth were doing. Pagan worship ceremonies are not clearly defined or understood, though the quote from Fee above provides some insight. This is instructive and impacts my conclusions. For now, it is simply helpful to note the complexity of Paul's argument.

Fee also helps clarify the argument of the passage. Based on the flow of the Greek text, Fee states Paul's arguments in chapter 8 and the first half of chapter 10 concern participation in pagan sacrificial ceremonies. When Paul writes "eating meat sacrificed to idols" in 8:1, 8:4, and 8:10, he is referring to eating in the temple, not consuming meat bought at the bazaar. The latter issue, which concerned Jews and pagans alike, is addressed in 10:23-11:1.[9]

What is striking about both sections is Paul does not instruct on Corinthian behavior based solely on how they may be associated with idols. Paul repeatedly affirms that ultimate truth about idols trumps false ideas about those idols. Paul's logic is pretty stunning:

> Well, we all know that an idol is not really a god and that there is only one God. There may be so-called gods both in heaven and on earth, and some people actually worship many gods and many lords. But we know that there is only one God, the Father, who created everything, and we live for him (I Cor 8:4-6).

He reiterates a similar point in chapter ten, "Am I saying that food offered to idols has some significance, or that idols are real gods? No, not at all" (1 Cor 10:19–20).

The point is highlighted further when Paul addresses the issue of eating meat sacrificed to idols outside the temple ceremonies. Lest you think I am proof-texting, the next sentence indicates that the sacrifices done at the temple "are offered to demons" (1 Cor 10:20). Ultimately, Paul argues against participation in ritual sacrifices. Paul's statement reinforces the shock of his answer later in the chapter, where he permits eating meat that had been sacrificed to what he describes as demons. Believers should be concerned about demons.[10]

Demons are a big deal. They exert spiritual power over people. They influence for evil. If there is any association between a ritual or a material item and demons, I expect Paul would tell us to avoid those material items completely.

But Paul does not. He argues against direct participation in the worship of demons, yet clearly permits eating the meat produced by those same ceremonies. We can understand why the Corinthians would ask about this. They likely noticed Paul ate meat when he was with them. Paul had to defend his own practice. He argues it is permissible to eat meat from the marketplace without worrying about its origins. By saying this, Paul contradicted the standard Jewish teaching[11] and the Jerusalem Council. This is probably why Paul gives an explanation of his apostolic strategy in chapter nine, where Paul declares boldly: "I have become all things to all people, that by all means I might save some. I do it all for the sake of the gospel, that I may share with them in its blessings." (1 Cor 9:22–23, ESV). Paul has the flexibility to violate Jewish cultural norms for the sake of seeing Gentiles come into the kingdom, even if it means doing something different in Corinth than was done in Jerusalem. Paul prioritizes the Gospel and people over cultural norms. He is not afraid of doing things that could associate him with false worship.

This passage deserves deep study. Few commentators dwell on this but careful reading of the passages and commentators suggests many of the Corinthians still visited the pagan temple compounds. This comes out in 8:10: "For if others see you . . . eating in the temple of an idol won't they be encouraged to violate their conscience . . .?" Fee asks, "[How] could they 'see' it if they were not present?"[12] This is a puzzling question. Is it possible that the "weak" believers were present at the temple and saw the "strong" eating in the midst of a sacrificial meal? That seems to be the case. Why does Paul not denounce the weak for going to a temple? On this point, Paul is silent.

I do not want to press this too far. The central point is clear: Paul ate meat sacrificed to idols or at least did not regard it an issue worth worrying one's conscience over (1 Cor 10:23). That clear position indicates that association with false worship was not a problem for Paul. Paul regards everything, idol food included, to be the Lord's and therefore available for constructive use (1 Cor 10:26).

One last concern remains: the association pagan Gentiles might make if a Christian Gentile or Jew ate meat sacrificed to an idol while a guest. On this point Paul says,

> If someone who isn't a believer asks you home for dinner, accept the invitation if you want to. Eat whatever is offered to you without raising questions of conscience. (But suppose someone tells you, "This meat was offered to an idol." Don't eat it, out of consideration for the conscience of the one who told you. It might not be a matter of conscience for you, but it is for the other person) (1 Cor 10:27–29).

Here Fee draws out the nuance of Paul's thought that I have been observing:

> The one who has pointed out the sacrificial origins of this meat to a believer has done so out of a sense of moral obligation to them, believing that Christians, like Jews, would not eat such food. So as not to offend that person, nor their moral expectations of a follower of Christ, and precisely because it is not a matter of a believer's moral consciousness, one should forbear under these circumstances.[13]

Paul's concern is for the heart of the unbeliever and their expectation of a believer. He is less focused on actions of the believer. I expect the unbeliever might think something like, "I think this person doesn't believe in idols. I'd better warn him not to eat this meat." If the believer eats, the unbeliever will think the believer is violating his conscience and that might actually disturb the unbeliever. In order to not give the unbeliever this false impression, Paul tells believers to abstain. He says it again in a surprisingly nonchalant manner with regard to the meat itself. Paul is not concerned about associating himself with false worship. He dismisses that concern in the next sentence, "For why should my freedom be limited by what someone else thinks?" He is concerned to love the pagan host. Love for another human being is a big deal (1 Cor 8:1; 13:1). Associating with false worship through consumption of meat is not as important.

SECOND, IT IS ABOUT LOVE AND WORSHIP

When I advocate that disciples can stay connected to their community, it may sound like I am ambivalent about evil and good, about orthodoxy and heresy, and about good practice and bad practice. I recognize the concern but I am not ambivalent about these crucial issues. Paul's words in this passage reinforce that commitment.

In 1 Corinthians, Paul draws hard lines between Christ-honoring behavior and Christ-denying behavior. He's dogmatic about it. Some behavior can destroy a believer for whom Christ died (1 Cor 8:11). Other behavior, Paul declares, is communion with demons that violates one's fellowship with Jesus (1 Cor 10:20–21). These are hard lines.

The boundary Paul draws concerns love. Concern for love dominates Paul's letter to the Corinthians, with his famous explanation of love's power in chapter 13. In chapters eight to ten, concern for love is the first issue that Paul discusses. Knowledge, Paul tells us, has limited value. He must be referring here to knowledge about the issue at hand: determining how believers should relate to meat consumed in pagan temples. Paul can describe theological principles such as monotheism and the non-existence of other gods. He can talk about who created the world and the materials from which idols are made. These are important issues. Then he adds, "not all believers know this" (8:7). The solution is not to *explain it all* to them so their knowledge increases. The solution is to act with regard to the weaknesses of these other believers. Paul calls believers to disregard their intellectual arguments for the sake of other believers. "So if what I eat causes another believer to sin, I will never eat meat again as long as I live" (1 Cor 8:13). Love is the principle that trumps all other priorities.

Paul's command to prioritize love has pushed me repeatedly to listen well to my friends and neighbors in Muslim Central Asia. To see the world through their eyes. Recently a close friend asked me an important question: "You seem to be doing a lot of work to help disciples stay in their context. Why not use a more straight-forward approach of proclaiming the Gospel and deal with the persecution and difficulties that come?" This question goes to the heart of what Paul is arguing for in his discussion of love and his abandonment of personal rights—learning to accommodate the vulnerable for the sake of the Gospel. Commentator Anthony Thiselton states the point of 1 Corinthians 9 succinctly: "In all cases [Paul's] strategy embodies sensitivity to where 'the other' stands."[14] Application of Paul's strategy involves paying attention to how those different from us experience the world.

In my opening parable, I described sitting in a Central Asian home observing Jesus talk to a Central Asian Muslim. The location of this story indicates what I've learned by working in Central Asia: the conversation takes place in the home of another. My own home is rather comfortable to me. I do not like traveling. I do not like being under another person's schedule for meals and sleep. I like to be in control of the house rules. When I enter someone's home, I am forced to adjust to the rules of their domain. I am out of my element—learning, listening, trying to discern how to do things the right way.

That is how it feels to present the Gospel in another culture. Some things I say in Central Asia make sense to people. Sometimes, no matter how well I speak their language, I do not make sense. Often, when I think that I have presented the Gospel in a "straight-forward" way, people get the wrong meaning. One of the clearest examples of this is what I have described in this book. Over and over people have heard my "straight-forward" invitation to the Gospel as an invitation to join my American cultural community. What is most comfortable to me may not be most effective in winning them to Jesus. At times, I have been shocked to find that little things I have done, which seemed completely unrelated to the Gospel, have communicated volumes about Jesus' authority and power in my life. Those things have often had to do with me being willing to be out of my element, not operating in what feels like a "straight-forward manner."

We need the ability to move into the comfort zone of others rather than stay in our own comfortable place. We do so compelled by our commitment to the Gospel and love for people. We believe that Jesus is supreme, that His word is powerful, that He reigns over this world for the good of those that trust Him, that He has reconciled us to God in the cross and that everything is now different. On this basis we move out of what feels comfortable to us and listen to how Muslims view the world. As Thiselton's commentary on 1 Corinthians explains—we do not live in fear of other spiritual powers in the world. Jesus reigns.[15] Even more, his powerful reign means we have freedom to love boldly at the cost of our emotional comforts. Regarding the decision to eat or not eat meat in 1 Corinthians 10:27-29, Thiselton notes, "the broad criterion for a decision about what to eat rests *not with 'my worries' or 'my overconfidence,' but with factors that relate entirely to the 'other person.'*"[16] I have learned to prioritize the voice and perceptions of flesh and blood Muslims over textbook representations of them. I can flex to listen well. Indeed, I can "become Muslim"—not in the sense of converting to become loyal to Mohammad or even by describing myself as "Muslim," but in the sense of seeing the world through their eyes—so as to win them to Jesus. This is the way we live within the boundaries of love, rather than knowledge.

In 1 Corinthians 8–10, Paul draws lines *beyond* love. He also draws lines concerning the worship of, and fellowship with, false deities. Though Paul isn't concerned about mere association between an act and false worship, he is concerned with direct participation in appeasing demonic powers through worship. This idolatry, identified by Paul, is out of bounds. The Corinthians should stop it.

Two points stand out in Paul's directions in chapter 10. First, as noted in Fee's description of the temple ceremony, there were multiple activities involved in the preparation, sacrifice, and consumption of the meat.[17] Paul shows a robust understanding of the differences involved and points out that aspects of the feast involve eating at "the table of demons" (1 Cor 10:21). Though the strong deny their connection to the physical idol at the center of the feast, Paul insists they are communing with spiritual power by what they do. Hays summarizes, "The God who demands exclusive allegiance will not tolerate cultic eating that establishes a bond with any other gods or powers."[18]

Secondly, and with crucial importance to the themes of this book, commentator Richard Hays points out that Paul's instructions contradict the "strong" believers' prioritization of social relationships. Hays summarizes the possible argument of the strong: "What possible difference can it make if they accept friendly invitations to other meals that just happen to be located in the shrine of some imaginary god?"[19]

Paul's answer, Hays explains, is that the Corinthian believers should prioritize love and be willing to abandon their own rights. Even more, Hays explains,

> [The] Corinthians who attend these temple meals are not only endangering the weak but also putting themselves in spiritual peril. By casually participating in idolatrous practices, they are putting Christ to the test (1 Cor 10:9) and provoking the Lord to jealousy (1 Cor 10:22).[20]

The "strong" believers have crossed a spiritual line that endangers their souls. This spiritual concern trumps the advantages social relationships might give them in advancing the Gospel.

Paul's admonitions call us to reject idolatry when we find it in our lives and in our community. It is important to draw lines in our communities and lives that keep us from communing with false spiritual powers. The cost of this may be the loss of social influence and connectedness. Even as I have argued for creative ways of maintaining social connectedness for the sake of the Gospel, maintaining social connections cannot supersede loyalty to Jesus. For Paul, communion with Jesus cannot be tainted by communion with false spiritual powers. Insofar as disciples in Muslim contexts engage in idolatry and communion with false spiritual powers, lead them away from that and teach them to "flee idolatry" (1 Cor 10:14). For disciples of Jesus in Muslim contexts, these same kinds of questions have to be asked.

Third, it is about making theological decisions in context

Each setting determines the dominant temptations to idolatry. Each setting must be dealt with in its own context. Paul makes this point by addressing the issue of meat sacrificed to idols without a single reference to the Jerusalem Council's decision on the issue. Paul certainly knew that decision. He was there when it was made and was responsible to pass on the letter explaining it to Gentile churches. He decides the issue differently when confronted with the context in Corinth. Despite the crucial importance to a cross-cultural worker like me of this seeming contradiction in practical theology, commentaries do not focus on this. I focus on geography, social relationships, theological development, and cultural differences when I read the New Testament. I see the relevance of Scripture's proclamations and its process for my work. This is a perfect example.

The instructions of Acts 15 were directed to the churches Paul had planted as recorded in Acts in Antioch of Pisidia, Iconomium, Lystra, and Derbe (Acts 13 and 14). These churches were in Asia, likely having larger Jewish communities that would be impacted by the behavior of Gentile believers. Jerusalem probably had some awareness of their context. But Corinth was in Europe. It was over 600 miles away from Antioch of Pisidia and over 1000 miles from Jerusalem. There were fewer Jews there, likely traveling rarely back and forth between Corinth and Jerusalem. So, while Acts 15:20 tells these disciples to "abstain from food polluted by idols," Paul tells the Corinthians, "You may eat any meat that is sold in the marketplace" (1 Cor 10:25). As Fee explains, "Paul takes a decidedly 'liberal' stance on this issue. [For him] it was . . . irrelevant whether [the meat] had been sacrificed or not."[21] This is decidedly contrary to the Jerusalem Council's request that Gentile believers "abstain from eating food offered to idols" (Acts 15:29). Corinth and Jerusalem were different contexts.

Some scholars solve this problem by suggesting that the historical sequence of events in Acts is different than the way Luke presents it. I have assumed that Luke is accurate and that his presentation is consistent with Paul's letters.[22] Paul feels free to act this way because the Jerusalem Council decision was limited by geography and possibly time.[23] It was a different context. Paul applies the eternal principles of redemptive history differently. This is local theologizing.[24] Again, Paul's apostolic position mattered, but that was not the only factor. His experience in the region trumped the apostolic directives of James and Peter back in Jerusalem. Paul seems to assume that the specific commands of the Jerusalem Council were not universal for all times and all places, even if the *principles* reached at the Jerusalem Council were. The degree of difference is significant enough for Paul that he does not even reference the decision in his discussion of meat in 1 Corinthians 8-10.[25] Instead, he deals directly with the Corinthians' questions and arguments. He forms a local answer to a local question. He does local theology.

Paul does local theology by engaging with rigorous detail in the Corinthians' lives. He provides nuance. He engages with arguments, refuting some and embracing others. As someone culturally near to the Gentile Corinthians, Paul does this knowledgeably and vigorously. Yet he does not shut down the process. Rather, he models a process seen throughout the New Testament, church history, and the movement of world missions. He gives the Corinthians space to process and engage Jesus' lordship over every aspect of their lives.

A quick reading of 1 Corinthians 8–10 will usually leave an American reader confused. Paul shifts back and forth between positive words about meat and all out denunciations. On one hand, he seems nonchalant about eating meat. "God made it. I can eat it," describes his conclusion in 10:25–26. Just a few verses earlier, however, he associates the sacrifices which prepare this meat as something offered to demons. In chapter 8, he includes the question of bothering a brother with this practice. Should this happen, he would never take a bite of meat for the rest of his life (1 Cor 8:13).

It is important to see how contradictory Paul can sound on the surface. He denies, then affirms, then releases. He goes back and forth and weaves in and out. It is hard to discern the precise line that he is drawing on the issues related to meat sacrificed to idols.

Paul is considering specific people, situations, forms and meanings as he gives these guidelines. He is not dealing in the abstract. Abstract law would be, "Idols are not real but demons are. Meat sacrificed to idols is meat given to a demon. If you eat that meat you are rejecting Christ and embracing a demon. Do not do it." But because of the particularity of the situation and Paul's deep understanding of the Greco-Roman context, he adds nuance. That nuance, from an outsider's perspective, can look like equivocation. It can look like Paul has abandoned right and wrong, truth and falsehood. It can look like Paul is speaking contradiction.[26] But he is not. He is doing local theology. He is imitating the incarnate Jesus for God's glory (1 Cor 11:1).

This challenges me. As an outsider, should I independently formulate solutions for how disciples in Muslim contexts discern false worship within their culture? From Paul's example, I believe the answer is "No." I must be willing to engage in the nitty gritty details of actual people, to frame their concerns under Jesus' lordship and to be motivated by love for others' good. I believe the New Testament is calling me to this.

The criticisms I receive of my views often relate to local theology. Local believers and cross-cultural workers must do together the hard work of examining local culture in light of God's universal Word. It is not possible to instinctively critique the decisions made in those contexts by simply translating those decisions into English or the culture of another context. Paul's nuance over what constitutes actual worship with demons is not intuitive to me. I cannot feel the distinction he makes. But I suspect the Corinthians understood it well.

I expect disciples in Muslim contexts to engage in a similar process of discerning biblically impermissible forms of false worship from within their own culture. The situation in Corinth was different from today. Neither Muslim contexts nor Western ones have physical idols to which people bow in reverence or make sacrifices. Idolatry is about more than prostrations and sacrifices. Kevin Higgins helpfully defines idolatry this way: "seeking . . . to commune with, placate, worship, and obey a spiritual being or entity other than God."[27] If we are honest, the temptation to commune with, placate, or worship a spiritual being or entity other than God confronts us every day. Disciples of Jesus in Muslim contexts, like all of us, have tough work to do. It will take time and the decisions may shock outsiders. The Corinthians were still participating in sacrificial meals in the presence of idols at least five years after Paul planted the church.[28] Jewish believers in Jerusalem would likely have been horrified to hear of such things.

Similarly, disciples in different Muslim contexts will differ in their conclusions. Some may find the sacrifice of a sheep in commemoration of Abraham's sacrifice of his son on their *Eid-i-Qurban* to be a mere remembrance of God's commands and provision. Others may sense an appeasement of evil spirits or an effort to atone for sin through animal sacrifice. Some may see the Muslim creed as invoking spiritual power for protection. Others may see it is recognition of their cultural-ethnic heritage, much as Americans do when they honor George Washington or say the pledge of allegiance.[29] I am not advocating mature believers continue any of these practices. I am observing these are some of the issues disciples in Muslim contexts grapple with as they grow and mature. There will be variations, but there will be lines to draw for each context—not universal rules, but universal principles. As believers from a non-Muslim background engaging with believers from Muslim backgrounds, I aim to focus on questions about idolatry itself, rather than mere association with idolatry.

My longing is for disciples in Muslim contexts to ask these questions about every sphere of their lives. Paul's model can be followed by asking, "How does love play into this consideration? What does our own local context imply for our approach? What does my communion with God through Jesus have to say about this issue? What lines do we need to draw so we are not engaged in false worship?" Disciplers need to ask tough questions about the issues facing disciples. Disciplers can and should weigh their own consciences in how they talk about these sensitive issues. The goal for the local disciple needs to be a conscience informed by the Holy Spirit and the Scriptures—not the assuaging of a foreigner's conscience. As missiologist Robert Priest notes in an insightful article on the development of a biblical conscience in cross-cultural settings, "Discipleship which bypass[es] native conscience may lead to superficial conformity or to a compartmentalized conformity."[30] I serve as a resource for answering these questions but not as the final arbiter. I long for disciples in Muslim contexts to engage the Scriptures as their final authority, consider their context, and do what is best, by the leading of the Spirit, in light of their consciences.[31]

All things must come to serve Jesus as Lord. He will have all. Mohammad, the Quran, the mosque, and even identity, only have place in the life of a true disciple of Jesus as servants of the world's true Lord. They either come as cultural prizes akin to the camels of Midian and the ships of Tarshish to bring splendor to God's temple glorious (Isa 60:4-7), or they do not come at all. The process for that subservient position may be gradual or drastic. But it is what the Good News of God's reign in Jesus demands.

When Michelle put on the burqa in 2006, she was one of few expatriates in our Central Asian country to do so. Others had done so at times, but rarely. Even today, some expatriate believers serving in the country would condemn the practice as an accommodation to culture and oppressive Islam.

None of us are fans of the burqa. It is hot and restricts vision. And no, we do not believe it is what God intends by modesty. Michelle's decision to step inside the burqa, to feel its weight, and to share the burden of Central Asian women continues to open doors for me. I cannot count the times I have seen people's faces brighten when they see or hear that she wears the burqa. The looks on their faces say, "You care about us. You want to be with us." Within the liberties of the Gospel, we can bear that burden out of love.

Can things like burqas and meat served on a religious holiday be forms of ungodly accommodation to culture? That is possible. The burqa itself is associated with a view of women that puts the burden of male temptation on women rather than male restraint. This is not God's ideal. Sacrificing animals can be a way of appeasing spirits. These interpretations of clothing and the slaughtering of animals are possible. Critics of disciples who retain connections to their identity of birth are right that they risk on-going association with false meanings.

Did Paul not do the same? He did not condemn eating meat that had been sacrificed to idols. He did not condemn stepping onto temple grounds. Would these actions not cause others to associate believers with idol worship? That is a risk, a risk that Paul took for the sake of love and for the sake of recognizing all of the world as God's true domain.

Disciples in Muslim contexts, like Paul, should reinterpret and reapply whenever possible in good conscience. When they cannot, they should discard the practices. They should take the tools of culture to serve God's greater purposes in the world with love—like reaching Muslim neighbors and friends.

Disciples in Muslim contexts are not much different than Western disciples. Some Westerners worship football teams. Some Western Christians enjoy football games (in American or international form!) as a gift from God. Some people idolize their smart phones. Some Christians use them as a tool for productivity and spiritual engagement. The simple use of culture and material goods for false worship does not taint them irrevocably. These seeming idolatrous practices are often reinterpreted within a culture. Association does not taint irretrievably. If it did, believers would have to leave this world entirely (1 Cor 5:10).

Part of being a disciple of Jesus is learning and re-learning how to distinguish elements that are communion with demonic powers from the parts God created for us to enjoy. Books are written on these topics. Sermons are preached. Table discussions tangle over them. Disagreements take place. This is part of the process of discipleship. It is part of the transformation for which Jesus came into the world. I grapple with Jesus' transformation of me in my context every day. I want my Muslim friends to engage in this transformation process in their context as well.

Listening well means listening to the Scriptures, to the context, to people, and to the work of the Spirit in the life of new believers and seekers. This pattern of listening empowers hearty discipleship, because it focuses on allegiance to Jesus, not cultural or religious identities or systems. Jesus commanded his followers to "teach all the commands" he had given his first disciples. He defines the foundation of those commands as loving God fully and loving one's neighbor as oneself. Allegiance to Jesus as the one who calls us to robust love is no light task. It requires thought, prayer, transformation, and humility. This life of love, embodied in communities and families, must happen in the Muslim world—in all the world—every day, for His glory to be revealed.

REFLECTION QUESTIONS

1. What elements of your culture involve idolatry or false worship?
2. In what ways do you associate with activities or things that could be used in false worship? In what ways do you do so for the sake of the Gospel and love for others?
3. What aspects of your culture present the greatest temptation to idolatry? What lines do you draw for yourself and your community to ensure that your loyalty to Jesus is not shared with false spiritual powers?
4. How can you show love to people outside of your community in ways that prioritize their understanding over your personal comforts?

---

1. Andrew F. Walls, "The Gospel as Prisoner and Liberator of Culture," in *Understanding Insider Movements* (Pasadena, CA: William Carey Library, 2015): 305–16.
2. Most Muslims believe it was Ishmael that Abraham laid on the altar, but the Quran never specifies the name of Abraham's son in the relevant passage.
3. Richard B. Hays, *First Corinthians* (Louisville, KY: Westminster John Knox Press, 2011), 172.
4. Hays, *First Corinthians*, 144.
5. Georges Houssney, "Jew to the Jew, Greek to the Greeks? Part 1," *Biblical Missiology*, http://biblicalmissiology.org/2010/07/08/jew-to-jews-greek-to-greeks-part-i/.
6. B. B. Blue, "Food Offered to Idols and Jewish Food Laws," in *Dictionary of Paul and His Letters*, ed. Gerald F. Hawthorne, Ralph P. Martin, and Daniel G. Reid (Downers Grove, IL: InterVarsity Press, 1993), 309.
7. Gordon D. Fee, *The First Epistle to the Corinthians* (Grand Rapids, MI: William B. Eerdmans, 2014), 397-398.
8. Hays, *First Corinthians*, 124.
9. Hays and Thiselton distinguish between the two issues as well, Hays, *First Corinthians*, 134; Anthony C. Thiselton, *1 Corinthians: A Shorter Exegetical and Pastoral Commentary* (Grand Rapids, MI: William B. Eerdmans Publishing Company, 2006), 2250, Kindle.
10. Jay Smith, "An Assessment of the Insider's Principle Paradigms," *St Francis Magazine* 5, no. 4 (August, 2009): 37-38.
11. Blue notes in his entry on the issue, "W. A. Meeks observes that by abandoning the standard Jewish regulations governing eating, the 'Pauline Christians gave up one of the most effective ways by which the Jewish community had maintained its separate identity in the pagan society'" Meeks, 97 as quoted in Blue, "Food Offered to Idols," 207.
12. Fee, *The First Epistle*, 426-427.
13. Fee, *The First Epistle*, 535.
14. Thiselton, *1 Corinthians*, 1994.
15. Thiselton, *1 Corinthians*, 2234.
16. Thiselton, *1 Corinthians*, 2273; emphasis original.
17. Fee, *1 Corinthians*, 397.
18. Hays, *1 Corinthians*, 167.
19. Hays, *1 Corinthians*, 159.

20. Hays, *1 Corinthians*, 159.
21. Fee, *1 Corinthians*, 530-531.
22. Douglas Moo provides a helpful outline of the problems related to this in the introduction to his commentary on Galatians. Douglas J. Moo, *Galatians*, Baker Exegetical Commentary on the New Testament (Grand Rapids, MI: Baker Publishing Group, 2013). For an argument for the Jerusalem Council coming after the letter to the Corinthians, see John Knox, *Chapters in a Life of Paul* (Macon, GA: Mercer University Press, 2000).
23. See also Moo, *Galatians*, 840
24. See Higgins' definition: "Theology becomes local when someone applies a previously revealed principle to a new context in such a way that the application of the principle differs from how it was originally applied. Although the principle is the same, the actions or behaviors that characterize how one is to obey the principle may be different in the specifics in another context." Kevin Higgins, "At Table in the Idol's Temple? Local Theology, Idolatry, and Identification in 1 Corinthians 8-10," *International Journal of Frontier Missiology* 31, no. 1 (Spring 2014): 30.
25. Bailey notes, "Paul could have simply issued a ruling such as, 'Barnabas and I agreed with the apostles in Jerusalem on this matter and I insist that our agreement be honored. No Christian is allowed to eat meat offered to idols, and that's final!" Kenneth Bailey, *Paul Through Mediterranean Eyes: Cultural Studies in 1 Corinthians* (Downers Grove, IL: IVP Academic, 2011), 233. See also Hays, *1 Corinthians*, 133.
26. Some biblical scholars take this equivocation to mean that the text itself is a composite of separate letters. In other words, the back and forth is so striking that they doubt the passage represents a coherent argument. None of the commentators cited in this chapter take that approach, but most of them note it. See Thiselton, *1 Corinthians*, 1673; Higgins, "At table," 29.
27. Higgins, "At Table," 33. Some readers may read this and think that worship of "Allah" fits this definition of idolatry because they presume that the God of the Old and New Testaments is different from the god "Allah" as described by the Quran. I have not addressed this issue in this book but have assumed throughout the book that those from monotheistic traditions may disagree about certain qualities of God but cannot ultimately be describing two different entities. In other words, I would say that Muslims I know have an inadequate, incomplete, often skewed understanding of God, but I would not assume that the God they worship is a completely different entity from the one described in the Old and New Testaments. In my own context, I use the existing word for God (which is not primarily "Allah"). I do not find it viable to talk about rival deities in my description of the Good News Jesus has brought into the world. Moreover, among those that have come to faith in Jesus, I have only heard them refer to their faith as confirming, fulfilling, or expanding on what they knew or suspected of God, but never as moving them to worship a different deity. For a description of the importance of using local terms to describe the God of the Bible, see Sanneh, *Translating the Message*. For a thorough discussion of the question about Allah being a different deity, see chapters four, five and six of Miroslav Volf, *Allah: A Christian Response* (New York, NY: HarperCollins ebook, 2011).
28. Hays, *1 Corinthians*, 5.
29. For a range of descriptions of how believers can or should relate to the Muslim creed see Brown, "Biblical Muslims," 65–74; Carlos Diaz, "Insider Approach to Muslim Ministry: A Latino Perspective," *Evangelical Missions Quarterly* 46, no. 3 (July 2010): 312–19; L. D. Waterman, "Do the Roots Affect the Fruits?," *International Journal of Frontier Missiology* 24, no. 2 (Summer 2007): 57–63. A significant part of the "back-story" so to speak for these questions is the influence of Christian traditions in the 6th and 7th century on the formation of Islamic practice. J. Dudley Woodberry addresses this in J. Dudley Woodbury, "Contextualization Among Muslims Reusing Common Pillars," *International Journal of Frontier Missiology* (1996):

171–86 and Rachel Pieh Jones explores her own journey engaging the pillars as a follower of Jesus with significant insight into their background. Rachel Pieh Jones, *Pillars: How Muslim Friends Led Me Closer to Jesus* (Walden, NY: Plough Publishing House, 2021).

30. Priest, "Missionary Elenctics," 305.
31. Priest notes concerning the time and process necessary to develop a healthy conscience: "With conversion individuals have a new allegiance (to Christ), a new motivation to live up to their own conscience (love for Christ and gratefulness to him), a new power for living up to their conscience (the indwelling Holy Spirit), and a new source of authority—the Scriptures—which exercises authority over their conscience and gradually corrects and deepens the moral insights and sensitivity of conscience. But the moment of conversion does not miraculously give an Aguaruna the same conscience as that of the missionary or that of an Utku, Apache, or Japanese Christian, or even the same conscience as that of a more mature Aguaruna believer. Sanctification is a process which affects the content of conscience. And it is a process. Central to that process is instruction in, meditation on, and submission to the Word of God." Priest, "Missionary Elenctics," 311.

CONCLUSION

A Breakthrough Envisioned

I'm at the green metal gate again. My burqa-clad wife stands next to me. I knock and wait.

A young boy comes to the gate. This time, he sees me and grins. We step into the yard. A woman, wearing a head scarf emerges from a door at the side of the house. She calls out, "Welcome." Michelle has lifted up her burqa. The woman steps forward and hugs her. Then she puts her hand on Michelle's head and pulls the burqa off her head entirely. My wife has a head scarf underneath and the two women hug again and exchange kisses on each cheek.

My friend, Aziz, emerges. He cheers, "Welcome, welcome." And then husband and wife lead us from the gate to the house entrance together. We enter a long room. In the corner, an old lady is reclining. We go over and hold her hand. She does not stand but smiles and bends forward to kiss Michelle when she comes near. The family scrambles. They chatter discreetly about setting out tea and cups and fruit. Aziz and his wife sit down together. We raise our hands, open palmed, to the air. I thank God that we can sit together. I express praise for the work of Isa al Masih. We lift our hands to our foreheads and then wipe them across our faces like we are washing them.

Aziz and Farishta have been following Jesus for a year now. Farishta met Michelle when she was visiting neighbors. Michelle learned about a poorly done C-Section that had left Farishta with a massive infection. She was in great pain and unable to care for the baby who had just been born. Michelle prayed for her in Jesus' name. She improved dramatically in a few days. Farishta credits Jesus with her healing.

After this, Aziz invited me to talk. I asked him if he would be willing to hear the "whole story." I started visiting every week or so to talk about a story from the Old Testament. Aziz was full of questions. He kept affirming that the stories we were reading were his stories too. He believed in the *Tawrat* and the *Zabur* and the *Injil* as well.[1]

We found a copy of the Quran in Aziz's language. We read the verses that said these other books—the Old and New Testaments—were from God. We even read a verse that said if Muslims had questions about them they should ask Christians about them. I told him that I was there to answer his questions.

Aziz began talking to his brother about what he was reading. His brother talked to a cousin in a nearby village. That cousin told his family. About the time Aziz and I began talking about the life of Jesus, that distant cousin told the others one of his sons was having seizures. He had taken the boy to a mullah to have Quranic verses recited over him. They had sacrificed a sheep and given the meat to the poor and to the mullah. The boy improved temporarily but then the seizures continued. Aziz asked me what he should do. I asked him what he thought he should do. We read some verses from John 14 that said Jesus would give even greater works to his followers. Aziz said, "I'm following Jesus. Maybe Jesus will give me these works too."

One night, he, his brother, Farishta, and a few other members of the family all went to this cousin's house and prayed. They prayed all night in Jesus' name for the boy's healing. The next day, the boy was better. The family says they want to follow this Jesus too. Aziz has started going to their village regularly to tell stories we studied together.

The experience has challenged some of their practices. As they prayed over the boy, Aziz felt prompted to take off the fetishes that had been given to the boy by the mullah. It was only after they removed these that the boy improved. They have understood this as a sign from the Lord that the fetishes have evil powers associated with them that Jesus alone can overcome. But the fetishes have Quranic verses written on them. They are finding their devotion to Jesus to be in conflict with this communal practice of making fetishes. Right now, they are praying, studying, and talking about what to do with these things. At the same time, they are committing themselves all the more to seeing Jesus' authority over sickness and evil spiritual forces by removing the fetishes from their children.

Farishta has always been a seeker. Even before she met Michelle she would correspond with religious teachers in other countries through Facebook. She asked one of them where in the Quran it said she had to say the Muslim creed. He was stumped. He admitted the creed is not actually stated in the Quran itself but it was important. Farishta processed this and began exploring how she could express her allegiance to Jesus more clearly. She now confesses, "There is only one God, and Jesus is the Word of God." She has started incorporating this creed into her daily prayers.

A few months later, a relative of Aziz criticized him because I had been at their house. The relatives said to Aziz, "You've become one of those *Kafirs*. You're going to ruin our family name in the community." Aziz asked me to stop visiting for a while. That was hard for both of us. But during that time, Aziz had a dream. A house was burning down all around him. In the dream, he saw the two of us standing together and holding a copy of the *Injil*. He told me, "God is going to protect us. I know that I have found hope in the words of Jesus."

After this dream, Aziz invited me to his house again. But he told me that we should not come too often. He has started to notice a pattern. When his neighbors notice me visiting his house frequently, they tend to respond to his mentioning of Jesus' name with suspicion in their eyes. But when I am absent for a while and he mentions the name of Jesus, people listen. We are trying to figure out what this means for our ongoing relationship and the things God is doing.

Asking Questions

This story is not the story of a single person or family. The Aziz and Farishta of this story are a conglomeration of many relationships and conversations I've had with Central Asians over the past decade and stories I've heard about the Gospel breaking through in Muslim communities. It is an imagined vision, highly informed by real events, as to how that breakthrough might happen in my community. Perhaps this story leaves you with a list of questions. Would such disciples attend the mosque? How will they relate long-term to the existing religious community? As they follow Jesus, will they continue to reference the Quran? I have these questions too. These are the kinds of question that come in pursuit of Jesus' supremacy among Muslims at the edges of the kingdom. Not everything is so clear on the periphery.

But on my journey, I have learned Jesus is supreme. He is able to step into any space of earth and call to himself his people, his flock. In Acts 10, Peter got a glimpse of the work that Jesus was doing. Many have pointed out that while we call the book of Acts "the Acts of the Apostles," Luke introduces the book as a continuation of what "Jesus began to do" (Acts 1:1). Luke affirms the stories of Acts are the works Jesus continues to do.

Peter was doing his noon prayers when he saw a disturbing vision (Acts 10:3). Peter had reasons to resist an invitation to a pagan home. The act—as he understood it—was equivalent to eating a dog or a pig—unclean meat that had never passed his lips. But God was at work. One day earlier God had given a vision to a pagan centurion. God told the centurion his prayers had been accepted and he should find Peter who had a message for him. Cornelius sent men to find Peter. They were standing at the door when Peter's vision ended.

Peter could have asked a lot of questions of God. What about this pagan centurion's temple worship? What about his allegiance to a Roman state which claimed to have a deity at its head? What about circumcision? What will Peter's Jewish friends think? What . . . what . . . what? But instead Peter obeys God and goes with Cornelius' emissaries.

Peter steps into a Gentile home for the first time and sees the family gathered. Cornelius has invited quite a crowd—"his relatives and close friends" (Acts 10:24). Cornelius relates his vision. Peter talks about Jesus. As he does so, Cornelius and his family begin speaking in tongues, just as Peter had done on Pentecost after Jesus' death and resurrection. Peter and his Jewish companions recognize the work of the Holy Spirit. They are all shocked to find the Spirit in a pagan home. Those questions—temple, circumcision, associations, rival systems of authority—surely, they were all there as well. In spite of certain questions, Peter is faithful and baptizes them.

I find myself in good company. I am trying to learn what it means that God "shows no favoritism," as Peter explains (Acts 10:34). Jesus is willing to meet people where they are. I am trying to understand how Jesus goes before us calling us to go there too. I am trying to embrace Jesus' supremacy at the edges of the kingdom.

Partnering Globally in Preparation for Caravans of Splendor

One of the Central Asians that visits our home on a weekly basis is a 70-year-old woman whom we affectionately call the "Milk Lady." Every day, this woman collects milk from different homes in her village. The homes have excess milk from one or two cows. She then carries that milk into our town to sell the milk door-to-door. She makes a two-cent profit on each cup of milk sold, with a total profit of two to four dollars per day. We have a standing order for two gallons of milk and as many eggs as she can gather and carry for each week.

The Milk Lady speaks only one language. She has never gone more than ten miles from her village. She was married to a 60-year-old man when she was thirteen and widowed by the time she was twenty. She has one son still living. We do not know how many children she has total, because her daughters never return home to visit her and she never mentions them. She has a few grandchildren, one of whom has lived with her since the girl's father passed away. She cannot read. She has no cell phone. She lives on a dirt floor with no electricity and heats her house in the winter with the goat dung we donate to her each year. Her experience of the world is so different than mine. She has been told that the world contains only two kinds of people: Muslims and *Kafirs*. We and a few other foreigners in our town are likely the only *Kafirs* that she has met. We are not sure if she thinks of us as *Kafirs* or as strange, generous Muslims from some other part of the world.

When I think about the Gospel spreading in our town, I think about the Milk Lady. I wonder what it will take for the words about Jesus to come to her as good news, in terms that she can understand. One of the hardest things to explain to our American friends is how hard that process can be. Yes, we have told the Milk Lady about Jesus. Yes, we have told her this is Good News. But the look in her eyes and the way she responds, we know it makes little sense. Yes, the Holy Spirit's intervention is essential. But most cross-cultural workers describe a moment when something similarly miraculous happens—people hear the words about Jesus as applying to their people. They see Jesus as of them and for them. How can that happen?

What will it take for a person with an isolated worldview like the Milk Lady to hear that Jesus is for her? That question is why discipleship within context matters to me. That is the question that drives my questions, longings and searching, for my host community.

I have sought to give you my voice—to give context, smell, taste, and place—to the decisions I have made as I have engaged Central Asians with the Gospel. Maybe you are still uncomfortable. Maybe you still have reservations. I long for that discomfort and even those reservations to strengthen our devotion to Jesus and his cause in the world, not undermine it.

In celebrating the diversity of Christ's body, I do not want those with reservations about the approaches laid out in this book to be held back. I do not want readers to ignore these issues or quietly simmer with frustration. I want all of us, as brothers and sisters in Christ, to talk, to share our concerns and experiences, and to wrestle with the Scriptures together. Part of the glorious diversity Christ gives us is the privilege to engage one another with our different perspectives as reconciled sinners. This happens repeatedly in Paul's letters. I think it is why Paul closes out Romans, with a call to unified engagement: "Each of us will give a personal account to God. So, let's stop condemning each other" (Rom 14:12-13). Those that have concerns serve me with their questions. I have experienced this many times while writing my thoughts. Those questions and concerns drive me deeper into Scripture. Similarly, I hope to serve the body of Christ in my sending country by reporting on insights gained from the frontlines. I hope I make some people uncomfortable. I want that discomfort to lead to greater devotion to Jesus and disregard for all rivals. I long for a glorious partnership to see God's kingdom break through where Satan has held sway for centuries. That kind of partnership requires patience, respect, listening, and a lot of prayer. May God help us all to abound in these things.

I long for the global church to see without blinders. I believe Muslims have treasures to bring into the heavenly Jerusalem—caravans of splendor. I believe they will help us see more of God's beauty and glory than we currently see. I could keep these treasures to myself. The paradigm I have presented, and even the sympathy I have tried to communicate for Muslims, is controversial. I could hide this information, receive support from Americans that may find them hard to embrace, and continue serving in Central Asia. But this approach cheats the American church out of the treasures and insights of another cultural interpretation of the Gospel. It is true discipling within Muslim contexts is counter-intuitive and even offensive to some. The challenge that this discomfort and seeming offense provide can raise our eyes above the boundaries of our own culture and Christian experience to the boundless splendor God intends for us to see in his redemption of the nations. As disciples of Jesus in Muslim contexts integrate their past with the lordship of Jesus, their past will be purified. It will become the shining gold that God placed in their cultural background with a view to its redemption. If we in any way marginalize these disciples because they make us uncomfortable, we risk missing out on the glory that God wants us to see displayed through them.

We grow in our understanding of this glory as we each share with one another aspects of God's glory that we see. I aim to contribute to that global act of worship through these stories and reflections. Embracing these disciples is not first and foremost about strategy. It is not about bypassing resistance to hoodwink Muslims into the kingdom. It is not about numbers or even multi-culturalism. It is about expanding our vision to anticipate with joy the splendor God intends to reveal. It is about seeing how big God is, how active he is in the world, and how immeasurable he is in his love. It is about seeing him and celebrating who he is for the ages to come.

Looking for that Expanded Vision

While writing this book, I sent draft copies to different friends and colleagues across the globe. In response, one friend told me about a story from William Miller written in the nineteenth century.[2] The story so encapsulated my hope in doing cross-cultural Gospel ministry among Muslims that it brought tears to my eyes.

Miller envisioned a room with a treasure box in the center. He went to that treasure box and found many beautiful items, gold pendants, diamond rings, rubies, and all manner of splendor. As he was admiring the treasures, some other people came into the room. They bumped him out of the way and began looking at the treasures as well. Indeed, they started spreading them throughout the room. Miller was deeply troubled. He started to shout at the visitors to leave the treasures alone. They were not only spreading them around they were tarnishing them in the process—muddying them and staining them with their grubby hands. But then someone with authority entered the room. The authority figure looked at Miller and told him to leave the people alone. After a while, the people all left the room and Miller was left alone with the person in authority.

This person started walking around collecting the treasures. Shockingly, the visitors had not only tarnished the jewels, they also brought trash in with them which they left behind. But the authority collected trash and jewels alike. He sorted them and cleaned them. As Miller watched, he was amazed. As the person polished the jewels they shined brighter than before the visitors came. As the person placed the jewels back into the box the most shocking thing of all happened—they no longer fit in the box.

The person then left the room to bring back another treasure box. This one was much larger than the first. It overflowed with the jewels as they were placed inside. Miller was amazed. The visitors, with all of their grub and trash, had somehow increased the beauty and amount of the treasure.

Miller's vision is nothing but a rearticulation of Jesus' parables and the heavenly vision in Revelation. Jesus told us not to pull out the weeds. On that day, He will sort the weeds out from the wheat (Matt 13:24-43). The expansive treasure the visitors bring resonates with the vision in Revelation (Rev 21:24–27). The nations bring their treasures into the heavenly Jerusalem and make God's house beautiful. This process is one we could hardly expect. It looks like unreasonable risk. Yet, somehow, splendidly, God makes it more than we could have ever imagined.

This is what it means to embrace Jesus' supremacy among disciples of Jesus in Muslim contexts. It is a journey to exult in God's power to save, not only from the evil and corruption of this world, but in the setting in which he placed us. It is a journey to embrace the transformation of everything—nothing stays the same—as Jesus reigns. It is a journey to admit that the treasure is not ours to protect and that the final work of cleansing and purification is God's to complete. I hope you will join me in that journey. I cannot wait to see how it ends.

---

1. Recall that these books, *Tawrat*, *Zabur* and *Injil* are what the Quran uses to refer to the Torah (first five books of the Old Testament), the Psalms, and the Gospel.
2. Ellen G. White, "William Miller's Dream," http://everythingimportant.org/WilliamMiller/.

APPENDIX A

A Discussion of Religion, Culture, Ethnicity, Gentiles, Muslims, and Jews

One of the most difficult issues to sort out in my journey in the Muslim world has been how religion and culture intersect. Indeed, if you have read through this book and particularly chapters 3 and 8, you likely have lingering questions about the way I distinguish between what some might call "cultural Muslims," "ethnic Muslims," and "religious Muslims." If you do, you are in good company.

I am still grappling with these key issues. One of the comforts I have found in that journey and a point that I believe reinforces the arguments in this book is that this issue is historically a thorny one. A book like this is cross-disciplinary. It touches on issues of history, anthropology, sociology, theology, and biblical exegesis. In researching the book, I have had to bounce between these disciplines with limited ability to dig into the depths of each topic. I hope that others will continue to explore the untapped terrain.

The three most prominent fields that need exploring on the issue of religious identity in missions are history, anthropology, and New Testament studies. Each of these fields today indicate how complex it is to define and distinguish religion and religious identity from other spheres of life.

Appendix A

For instance, historian of religion, Brent Nongbri, in his book on the complications of this issue, writes:

During the past thirty years, this picture [of religion as easily distinguished from other elements of a society] has been increasingly criticized by experts in various academic fields. They have observed that no ancient language has a term that really corresponds to what modern people mean when they say "religion." They have noted that terms and concepts corresponding to religion do not appear in the literature of non-Western cultures until after those cultures first encountered European Christians. They have pointed out that the names of supposedly venerable old religions can often be traced back only to the relatively recent past ("Hinduism," for example, to 1787 and "Buddhism" to 1801). And when the names do derive from ancient words, we find that the early occurrences of those words are best understood as verbal activities rather than conceptual entities; thus the ancient Greek term *ioudaismos* was not "the religion of Judaism" but the activity of Judaizing, that is, following the practices associated with the Judean ethnicity; the Arabic *islām* was not "the religion of Islam" but "submitting to authority." More generally, it has become clear that the isolation of something called "religion" as a sphere of life ideally separated from politics, economics, and science is not a universal feature of human history.[1]

Nongbri's book, *Before Religion*, is a catalog of how our framework for understanding "religion" as something readily distinguished from other elements of human experience, society, and culture is something that came about primarily in the modern era, over the last three hundred years.

Significantly, Nongbri also notes, with many others, that "religion" in the West is presumed to be private belief, first and foremost. As he describes the popular American understanding of religion he notes, "Religion is not political, not concerned with current events; it is about 'the heart.' It is 'unobtrusive.'"[2] I suspect that most evangelicals will feel conflicted about this kind of statement. Within America, we tend to dislike the way the broader culture wants to isolate Christian belief to a private arena. But I also suspect that the influences of our culture impact how we understand the word "religious" to be used.[3]

Most definitions of religion focus on this inner dynamic. The definition, for instance, of anthropologist Clifford Geertz is often cited in these discussions.

His definition demonstrates how complicated it is to define religion as well as how most Western scholars focus on interior belief. According to Geertz, "Religion" is

> (1) A system of symbols which acts to (2) establish powerful, pervasive, and long-lasting moods and motivations in men by (3) formulating conceptions of a general order of existence and (4) clothing these conceptions with such an aura of factuality that (5) the moods and motivations seem uniquely realistic.[4]

Geertz' definition is interesting in that he tries to connect external forms (a system of symbols) with the feelings that are going on inside people (moods and motivations). But ironically, Geertz so emphasizes these interior aspects of this phenomenon that some, as Nongbri notes, suggest he actually rules out more externally oriented religions like Islam and Catholicism.[5]

More to the point, as Geertz indicates in his book in which he attempts to describe to Islamic communities, *Islam Observed*, it is strikingly difficult to separate the cultural and ethnic aspects of a culture from its religious aspects. After describing how difficult it is to define religion, Geertz can only say the phenomenon he is describing is something almost everyone will regard as having "vaguely to do with 'religion'".[6] Nongbri calls this the "I know it when I see it" approach to defining religion.[7] Unfortunately, this is highly subjective and all the more prone to privilege outsiders in defining "religion" for a community. Indeed, most of the criticism of this concept of religion has to do with Westerners imposing their cultural patterns on the rest of the world.[8]

Throughout this book, I have tried to demonstrate how some of those presumed patterns break down when interaction takes place with actual human beings. Recent anthropologists emphasize this point over and over again. Taking one example, anthropologist Robert Canfield, in his study of a largely Shi'a Muslim community in Central Asia reports how the people in that community described those who converted from one of their Shi'a sects to a Sunni sect as those who had changed their ethnicity. They were "Hazara" (an ethnic name) but became "Tajik" (another ethnic name). This, again, indicates the difficulty of assuming a black and white distinction between ethnic, social, cultural, and religious identities.[9]

In pointing out the difficulty in separating out religion from culture, I am not saying that the things modern religious adherents associate with religion (worship, holy books, rituals) do not exist. They certainly do. The problem is that they are not always easily distinguishable from a community's sense of itself as an ethnicity and as a culture.

We face this same problem when we come to the question of "Gentiles" and "Jews" and their own identity, culture, and ethnicity. Was "Gentile-ness" for instance always tied to religious activity as distinct from culture? How did it relate to ethnicity? In chapter three, I argued that Gentile-ness had some associations with pagan religion within the New Testament context and that Gentiles did not have to become Jews in order to follow Jesus. The Greek term for "Gentiles" is *ethnos*. Though "Gentiles" is the most common way it is translated, it is also translated as "nations," "heathens," and "people."[10]

The New Testament writers move between positive descriptions of Gentiles coming to faith in Jesus and their worship of the God of Israel and implicitly negative uses of the word in their calls to separate from the false worship of Gentile communities. So, for instance, "Gentiles are fellow heirs, members of the same body, and partakers of the promise in Christ Jesus through the gospel" (Eph 3:6) and these same Gentile believers in Ephesus are told to "no longer walk as the Gentiles do" (Eph 4:17). This way of talking is ironic, of course, because Paul rebukes Peter for hypocrisy in that he lives "like a Gentile and not like a Jew" while forcing Gentiles to live like Jews (Gal 2:14). Is living like a Gentile a good thing or a bad thing? For Paul, it can be both.

These contexts are different, and my point is not to suggest that Paul is contradicting himself. Not at all. I simply point out that there is a variety of ways of talking about Gentiles using the exact same Greek word to describe them. This reinforces Nongbri's point that the New Testament does not have an easily distinguishable term for "religious identity," let alone "religion." Sometimes the New Testament talks about Gentiles as an ethnic-cultural group. Sometimes it talks about Gentiles as connected to pagan behavior.

The degree to which first century Jews associated Gentiles with pagan behavior suggests to me that it would have been hard for them to completely distinguish ethnicity from what we tend to call religious behavior. New Testament scholar John Barclay, for instance, analyzes Paul's descriptions of "Gentiles" in his writings this way:

> Paul most commonly categorizes humanity in terms of the simply biblical division between 'Jews' and 'Gentiles/the nations'... The biblical disdain for 'uncircumcised Gentiles' is evident in the associations Paul builds around these terms. He contrasts Jews with 'Gentile sinners' (Gal 2.15), and assumes that the latter have minimal moral standards (a certain sexual sin is found 'not even among the Gentiles', 1 Cor 5.1); indeed, he summarily dismisses them as 'Gentiles who do not know God' (1 Thess 4.5). Although he understands himself to be 'an apostle to the Gentiles', he considers his converts as somehow lifted out of this negative category: the Corinthian Christians were, he says, '*formerly* Gentiles' (1 Cor 12.2). Although his life's work consists of establishing communities made up of Jewish and non-Jewish believers, each of equal dignity, Paul retains the assumption that the non-Jewish world is a cess-pit of godlessness and vice (Rom 1.18-31; Phil 2.15).[11]

I point out all of this to show that the New Testament can talk in multiple ways about Gentiles and "Gentile-ness." It can describe Gentiles as *staying* Gentiles because the Gospel is for them and God is the God of the Gentiles too (Rom 3:29). And it can talk about the Gentiles being "former Gentiles" (1 Cor 12:2) who separate from the wicked behaviors of their community. Again, Paul uses the same term for both issues.

Fundamentally, after wrestling with the issues surrounding identity in Central Asia, I came to realize that my tendency to limit "Gentile" to a solely ethnic category in the New Testament was unwarranted. In reading the New Testament this way I was blocking out the tensions within redemptive history over the inclusion of Gentiles and their "religious" associations. To see how prominent this is, try reading the New Testament and substituting the word "pagan" for every reference to "nations" (*ethnos*) or "Gentiles" that you find. The New Testament does not use the word *ethnos* in this way every time, but neither does it simply mean "non-ethnically Jewish" when it uses the word. I can no longer deny a religious tinge to the term *ethnos* and my reading of the New Testament is dramatically affected by having this blinder removed.

This brings us to the issue of Muslims. In this book, even though I argue that genuine disciples of Jesus can legitimately identify themselves as Muslims and retain a connection to the community, I have been careful to distinguish between "Muslims in general" and those that give allegiance to Jesus within their Muslim communities. In doing so, I am trying to do the same thing that the New Testament does with the term Gentile. In some cases, I am emphasizing the radical generosity of the Gospel for all peoples. In other cases, I am trying to distinguish between those that are loyal to Jesus and those that are loyal to Mohammad even though they might be within the same socio-ethnic category. Some have suggested that I use the term "cultural Muslim" and "religious Muslim." If this kind of categorization helps you to understand how believers could still call themselves "Muslim" while giving ultimate allegiance to Jesus, then you should think in those terms. I have not always used that distinction because it is a distinction that we are imposing from the outside. As a student of culture, I am intent on listening to how people describe themselves first so that I do not impose my paradigms upon them.

As I described in chapter five, many of my friends use the term "Muslim" in positive terms that emphasize integrity and devotion to God. When they use the term this way, do they mean it culturally, ethnically, religiously? When someone calls me a "good Muslim" because of my unwavering devotion to Jesus, is this a cultural or religious use of the term? When Hajji Odam says that I can no more separate him from his Muslim identity than I can separate his body from his skin, is he using the term culturally, ethnically, or religiously? Some individuals may have clear answers for each of those questions. I do not. The first two were probably a mix of what we tend to call "culture" and "religion." The third was probably used ethnically. But in all cases, my friends are using the exact same term to describe different phenomenon. That ambivalence and confusion, then, shines through in my own descriptions and readings of the situation. As I look at the massive amount of ink spilled over this issue, I find myself in good company.

Related, however, to this issue of "religious Muslim" and "cultural Muslim" is the fundamental assumption I frequently hear from critics of the ideas in this book that we all understand exactly what a "Muslim" is. In Chapter five, I sought to challenge that fundamental assumption. Muslims are diverse. Islam is diverse. Anthropologist of Islam, Gabrielle Marrinci notes it this way:

During my years of study, books and teachers explained that Islam is a religion based on theological precepts and a particular history. During my research, I learned that the Islam of books, theology and history is nothing other than a ghost hunted for by both the believers as well as the academics.[12]

Most of the objections I receive about my use of the term Muslim center around academic definitions of Islam or verse citations from the Quran that show a fundamental conflict between the Bible's teachings and the Quran. The warning I offer to such an approach is that all Muslims are different, and all Muslim communities are different. It is true that there is a fundamental conflict between formal, Sunni Muslim theology and Christian theology. I accept that.[13] But this formal conflict may or may not have relevance to the average Central Asian Muslim who has likely never read the Quran nor the Hadith.[14] We have to engage Muslims as people, not as textbooks. And people, myself included, are strikingly messy, confused, contradictory and inconsistent. We have a mix of motivations, theologies, philosophies, and relationships that influence the way that we interact with ourselves, our community, and God.

Because of that mixture and confusion, I have come to see my best hope in parsing out the differences in culture, religion, allegiance, community, and associations is to be highly simplistic in my approach to discipleship. I talk about Jesus and his supremacy. I study the Scriptures chronologically with disciples. I ask them to obey what they read and teach them that the Holy Spirit is present and active to help us obey what the the Scriptures say. Then I watch, often with surprise, as I see the Holy Spirit help disciples prioritize their next step in following Jesus. In every case of discipleship with which I have been involved, that first step has not been to denounce Islam. Rather, it has often been to love a father (like God loves us), forgive an offense (as God forgives us in Christ), confess an offense (because God's forgiveness is ready at hand), work with integrity, speak honestly, and share about God's love with a friend or cousin. Watching that process as well as seeing the way God sorted through messy issues in the New Testament and church history encourages me to trust God's timing and wisdom to sort out these issues of culture, religion, allegiance, community and association as Muslims in Central Asia commit themselves to Jesus. I am confident that the living Christ through the Holy Spirit and the revealed Scriptures will do this effectively. I aim to be a partner in that process, a co-worker with God as Paul boldly puts it, who builds on the sole foundation that can exist in this world, the Lord Jesus Christ (1 Cor 3).

---

1. Brent Nongbri, *Before Religion*, 2.

2. Nongbri, *Before Religion*, 19.
3. Joel Green, in his analysis of conversion on Luke-Acts, suggests that "an individual-oriented, feeling-based interior religion" is "axiomatic for many," even New Testament scholars. Joel B. Green, *Conversion in Luke-Acts: Divine Action, Human Cognition, and the People of God* (Grand Rapids, MI: Baker Academic, 2015), 409, Kindle.
4. Clifford Geertz, "Religion as a Cultural System," in *Anthropological Approaches to the Study of Religion* (New York, NY: Frederick A. Praeger Press, 1966), 4.
5. Nongbri, *Before Religion*, 7.
6. Clifford Geertz, *Islam Observed: Religious Development in Morocco and Indonesia* (Chicago, IL: University Of Chicago Press, 1971), 96.
7. Nongbri, *Before Religion*, 15.
8. The most well-known example of this critique comes from Edward Said, who defined this phenomenon as "Orientalism." He was particularly concerned that definitions of Islam tend to shore up a sense of Western superiority rather than actually understand the people they describe. Edward W. Said, *Orientalism* (New York, NY: Vintage, 1979). Richard King addresses the issue with regard to the definition of religion in *Orientalism and Religion: Postcolonial Theory, India and 'The Mystic East'* (New York: Routledge, 1999), 46-72. H. L. Richard provides a summary of the issues involved in "Religious Syncretism as a Syncretistic Concept," in *Understanding Insider Movements*, ed. Harley Talman, and John Jay Travis (Pasadena, CA: William Carey Library, 2015), 363–74.
9. R L Canfield, *Faction and Conversion in a Plural Society: Religious Alignments in the Hindu Kush* (Ann Arbor, MI: University of Michigan, 1973), 117.
10. J. A. Manickam, "Race, Racism, and Ethnicity," in *Global Dictionary of Theology*, ed. William A. Dyrness, and Veli-Matti Kärkkäinen (Downers Grove, IL: IVP Academic, 2008), 723.
11. Barclay, *Jews in the Mediterranean Diaspora*, 388.
12. Marranci, *The Anthropology of Islam*, 472.
13. Even as I accept this caveat, it is still amazing to see the historic diversity of formal theology among Islamic scholars. See especially Joseph Cumming, "God, Word and Spirit: The Doctrine of the Trinity in the Qur'ān and Islamic Interpretation" (PhD dissertation, Yale University, 2020) and Corrie Block, *The Qur'an in Christian-Muslim Dialogue: Historical and Modern Interpretations*, Culture and Civilization in the Middle East (New York: Routledge, 2013).
14. The Hadith are the traditionally collected sayings by and of the prophet Mohammad within Islam. The collections of Hadith are considered second only to the Quran in importance for faith and practice for Muslims.

APPENDIX B

Reflections on the C1-C6 Spectrum[1]

In 1997, I made my first foray into missions as a recent college graduate. I went to a post-Soviet, Muslim-majority country in Central Asia with the intent of exploring my calling to the Muslim world. During my two years there, unbeknownst to me two articles were published in *Evangelical Missions Quarterly* that would both trouble and inform my years of service in Muslim Central Asia. When I returned to the US in 1999 and was pursuing a seminary degree, I read those two articles as part of my training. One was John Travis' "C1 to C6 Spectrum."[2] The other was Phil Parshall's provocatively titled response: "Danger! New Directions in Contextualization."[3] For those at my seminary and church who were interested in missions, the "C" issue was front and center. We were all ready to define ourselves by the letter "C," along with an appropriate number from 1 to 6.

I write now after more than fifteen years of living and working among Muslims in two countries in Central Asia. I no longer wish to define myself by the letter "C" and a number. I do, however, find the foundational questions of a debate made public by those initial articles to be of ongoing concern to the task of missions among Muslims. In this chapter, in honor of Phil Parshall's tremendous contributions to the issues of contextualization and mission among Muslims, I will lay out my own series of "Cs" both in summary of the debate raised by those two seminal articles and in anticipation of their ongoing impact. The five C's I will address are Controversies, Clarifications, Challenges, Continuation, and Cautions.

Controversies

In this section, I will first outline the basic elements of the spectrum and summarize Parshall's response to the model. Then I will mention important clarifications that have emerged since Parshall and Travis' 1998 articles. Travis listed six ways that groups of believers in Jesus from Muslim backgrounds, at the time, were expressing their faith in Christ in terms of language, culture, and religious identity. Travis called this the spectrum of "Christ-centered communities," hence the "C-Spectrum."[4] The spectrum has often been read as a "contextualization" scale, and that is how I read it in 2000. C1 meant far from local culture and C5 or C6 meant the gospel could be indistinguishable from local culture.

Note that the intended "C" of the spectrum is closer in meaning to "church" than "contextualization."[5] Travis' "C-Spectrum" was about existing "churches" within a Muslim context. These "Christ-centered communities" all work out how to "retain," "reinterpret," and "reject" elements of their own culture in relationship to foreign cultures as they live out devotion to Jesus as Savior.[6] These communities are highly varied, just as they vary in their location around the globe.

The spectrum itself presented three main areas of distinction between the different ways *gathered* believers from Muslim backgrounds "worship Jesus as Lord":[7] language, culture, and religious identity. Each number on the scale indicates a different aspect of these three dimensions that is different from the one to the left. To show these different aspects, below I have indicated the key difference from one number to the next. For instance, the difference between C1 and C2 hinges on which language is used in the gathered community of believers. The chart on the following page is how I have visualized the spectrum.

Parshall's focus, however, was on "contextualization," as his own article's title indicated.[8] Contextualization has tended to mean the work that a "foreign missionary" does to explain the gospel and its implications in context.[9] Parshall's own work[10] describes potentially controversial ideas that moved missionaries deeper into the practice, thought, and community of Muslims to

Appendix B | 155

The "C-Spectrum"
Christ-centered communities among Muslims and how they relate to language, culture, and identity

Category	C1	C2	C3	C4	C5	C6
Language	Non-native	Native	Native	Native	Native	C1-C5
Culture	Non-native	Non-native	Religiously "neutral."* Local culture retained.	Retain many religious forms but give them fresh biblical meaning.	Retain many religious forms but give them fresh biblical meaning.	C1-C5
Religious Identity	"Christian"	"Christian"	"Christian"	"Jesus Follower." "Usually not seen as Muslims by the Muslim community."***	"Legally and socially within the community of Islam."**	C1-C5

* Travis, "The C1 to C6 Spectrum: A Practical Tool."
** Ibid.
*** Ibid. Additionally, Travis argues that C5 believers "Meet regularly with other C5 believers" and "Unsaved Muslims may see C5 believers as theologically deviant and may eventually expel them from the community of Islam."

whom they sought to explain the gospel. In *Muslim Evangelism*, <u>for instance</u>, Parshall opens up questions about baptism, prostrations, liturgy, holidays, etc. The framework for these questions is often the missionary's position on these issues and the missionary's promotion of them. Parshall's response to the C Spectrum in 1998 focused particularly on the role of the missionary. His primary critique in "Danger! New Directions in Contextualization" was the possibility of foreign missionaries identifying as Muslims—a point that never comes up in Travis' C-Spectrum. But Parshall was also concerned that the pursuit of C5 models would lead to sub-biblical theological communities. He cites a study on a community of believers who identified as Muslims, confessed Jesus as their only Savior, but had mixed views on the Trinity and the role of the Qur'an.

In a sense, then, the debate of the past two decades has essentially been two debates, sometimes overlapping and sometimes occupying separate domains of concern. On the one hand, the question is how missiologists view, describe, and engage existing and burgeoning movements to Christ with a variety of expressions and ways of relating to MBBs' birth cultures. On the other hand, the question is how foreign missionaries themselves should engage Muslims with the gospel and the role they should play in discipling believers within the context of the missionaries' host cultures.

The tension between these two questions has much to do with whether the spectrum is prescriptive or descriptive. The heat of the debate, in one sense, has been over the degree to which any of the spots is the target for discipleship. Though there are critics of C4,[11] the primary conflict has been between the C4 and C5 regions of the spectrum. The distinction between the two, in Travis' original C-Spectrum, was that the C4 communities defined themselves as outside the "religious"[12] identity of their birth community, whereas the C5 communities tended toward retaining their formal or "legal"[13] religious identity within their birth community.

Travis did not explain how Muslim background believers might continue to relate to the mosque, the *Shahada* (Islamic creed) and the Qur'an. Rather, he simply noted that they retain a "Muslim" identity in their community, even as they deviate theologically from their birth community, particularly regarding Jesus' death, resurrection, and personhood, and the reliability and importance of the Old and New Testaments. The unaddressed questions in Travis' brief article, as evidenced in Parshall's response, became a prime concern for those debating and applying the spectrum regarding its application to Muslim evangelism.[14] As I have engaged the C Spectrum over the past two decades and considered its future use, I have sought to parse out the different descriptive elements and prescriptive interpretations of it. Next, I will address both descriptive and prescriptive approaches, particularly as they relate to my engagement with the spectrum on the field.

Clarifications

In my own pre-field reckoning with the C Spectrum, I had misconceptions about the C5 category that had to be clarified both through a better understanding of the terms being used and through face-to-face interactions with believers who could be considered C5. I have found that many missiologists and practitioners shared these misconceptions. This lack of clarity often distracted from meaningful discussion about missionary strategies. In this section, I seek to remove those obstacles and get to the core issues involved for both the descriptive and prescriptive tasks on the field. In particular, I have identified three key clarifications missiologists need to make regarding the C5 category.

First, many have posited that C5 communities simply seek to avoid persecution.[15] This has been consistently denied by observers of C5 communities. As Higgins, Jameson, and Travis note in their article, "Misunderstandings about Insider Movements," C5 believers are persecuted. C5 believers have been killed, imprisoned, tortured, and harassed for their allegiance to Jesus.[16] Some of the C5 believers I have met on the field have experienced death threats and exile. A proper understanding of the scale recognizes that C6 believers (by definition) are in the difficult position of hiding their faith for fear of persecution. The C6 category could be understood as a secret expression of any of the C1-C5 categories.[17]

Relatedly, the second clarification is in regard to the misconception that the retention of one's religious identity from birth, particularly the term "Muslim," involves no change in allegiance or theological formulation. In particular, we tend to rigidly associate the identity term "Muslim" with traditional Islamic positions that oppose central biblical teachings, like Jesus' divinity and crucifixion.[18] This assumption misunderstands the spectrum and the terms of description. C5 believers, though retaining a nominal affiliation with their birth community and social connectedness, have reoriented their theology and lives toward Jesus as Lord and Savior. This is a radical departure in conviction from the faith of their birth communities. Some have proposed that this dynamic is best explained as "cultural insider/theological outsider." Over the past fifteen years, I have met C3, C4, and C5 believers on the field. Each kind of believer has a dramatic account of conversion tied to Jesus' transformative power.

This leads to a final clarification from the spectrum's original definition, namely, that C5 believers have no expression of "church" as a distinguishing community of believers. Tennent infers, for instance, that the C5 approach is primarily individualistic without any corporate gatherings.[19] And Nikides argues that C5 believers do not baptize or practice the Lord's Supper.[20] Yet the statements at the beginning of this chapter showed that the *gathering of believers* was crucial to defining all the Cs of the spectrum. Moreover, Higgins and Naja both describe sacraments as being part of the C5 movements they studied.[21] Insofar as "doing church" refers to multiple believers gathering for prayer, worship, and reading of the Christian Scriptures, the C5 part of the spectrum fits this description.

Challenges

Recognizing the key clarifications regarding elements of the C Spectrum, I have observed ongoing challenges that the C1-C6 Spectrum, and the debate surrounding it, exposes for practitioners like myself: the tension between prescriptive and descriptive approach; the difficulty of distinguishing between religion, culture, and identity; and the evolving definitions of syncretism. I turn to those challenges now.

Prescriptive or Descriptive?

I have already noted the tension within debate surrounding the C Spectrum between prescriptive and descriptive approaches. For myself, I found that I was inclined to take the descriptive elements of the C1-6 spectrum and turn them into "ministry targets." As others have done, I idealized the C4 category when I entered the field, believing that space entailed gospel integrity: these groups were not co-opted by foreign identity, but stayed pure in light of the corrupting influences of Islam. I sympathized with Parshall's desire to avoid the risks of syncretism assumed to be part of the C5 space.

Yet I have found that simply using the C1-C6 spectrum to prescribe a certain plot on the continuum oversimplifies the task of missions in the Muslim context in two significant ways. First, the spectrum, as all heuristic tools must do, assumes distinctions that can be extremely difficult to tease out in real life — namely the distinction between religion and culture. Second, and relatedly, the problem of "syncretism" and its place on the spectrum continually tempts us to engage in "arm-chair missiology." In other words, we can too easily be drawn to evaluate and second-guess decisions others make (local believers and missionaries) outside of our own ministry context. These two issues are problematic for our use of the spectrum and application of it and, hence, bring us into the two additional challenges the C1-C6 Spectrum faces.

The Difficulty of Distinguishing between Religion, Culture, and Identity

I first confronted the tension between religion, culture, and identity when I moved to a small conservative town in Central Asia. My wife and I preferred the local clothing to Western garb and spoke the minority dialect, rather than the trade language or English. We were primarily identified as Muslims for these acts, despite not participating in any religious ceremonies associated with the mosque. Our training had taught us that "clothing" and "language" were cultural issues, not religious. It's been evident to us over the years that this simple division of categories is far from the reality.

The distinction between the C3, C4, and C5 categories hinges on the term "religious." C3 believers use "religiously neutral" forms.[22] C4 and C5 believers use "religious forms," but invest them with biblical meaning.[23] C5 believers retain their birth "religious identity." So much of one's reading of the spectrum depends on one's assumption about what is "religious" and what is "cultural." The social sciences have often demonstrated how "religion" can be a political and social marker as much or more than a theological one.[24]

Additionally, it can be difficult to determine what is a "neutral" religious act. For instance, wearing the traditional *shalwar kamees* style of dress for men in which the shirt extends to the man's knees can be understood to be an imitation of the Prophet Mohammad's dress, thus a keeping of the *sunna* (tradition). Was this, then, a statement of loyalty to the Prophet, or merely a cultural decision? In keeping with my experience, anthropologists have long struggled with explaining and defining "religion" as a distinct element of culture.

This particular discussion has a couple of crucial components. On the one hand, there is the question about "essentialism," or definitions of world religion, particularly Islam, that reduce them to their "essential doctrines and practices."[25] Social scientists have increasingly questioned this perspective, suggesting that each community and even each individual engage a variety of practices and beliefs that can hardly be encapsulated under a single umbrella of "Islam."[26]

But communities themselves are often "essentialist" in their definitions of "Muslim." This plays into the repeated concern that C5 believers are deceptive about their core convictions. For instance, if the local community defines "Islam" in one way and C5 believers vary from that depiction theologically, have they not fundamentally left that community? This is a legitimate question. In practice, I have been genuinely surprised at the way different groups and individuals negotiate their identity and practice in order to meet the requirements of Muslim identity in varying circumstances. One friend, for instance, told me about his atheistic convictions while thumbing his prayer beads. I am not commending his convictions. Rather, seeing lines of religious barriers crossed and re-crossed in practice has suggested to me that using "religion" as a primary category within the spectrum has its limitations.

A second component of how difficult it is to distinguish religion, culture, and identity involves ongoing debates about the definition of "religion" and to what degree our current conception of religions and their boundary lines are tied to modernity and the Enlightenment. Brent Nongrbi, in *Before Religion*, argues that common definitions of religion which distinguish it from other elements of society have been "increasingly criticized by experts in various academic fields" over the past thirty years. Historians have "observed that no ancient language has a term that really corresponds to what modern people mean when they say 'religion.'"[27] Moreover, they have discerned that many of the names associated with major religions first emerged after encounters with European Christians.[28] Others note, in this same vein, that the creation and enforcement of religious categories were often associated with Western colonial rule.[29] Increasingly, biblical scholars are alluding to these same issues. N. T. Wright, in his description of the apostle Paul, resists "Post-enlightenment" categories that parse out "religion" as a distinct element of life and culture, seeking in his own work to "put back together the worlds that the Enlightenment split apart."[30]

This is not to say that this perspective on religion and particularly distinct categories of "world religion" is settled. Postcolonial writer Pnina Werbner, for one, maintains there are pre-Enlightenment terms for world religions and the concepts of religion.[31] But the lack of clarity on this issue exposes the tension within the C Spectrum that contributes to the debates surrounding it, let alone its field application.

Evolving Definitions of Syncretism

Another challenge raised by employing the spectrum as a prescriptive model is the nature of syncretism. Parshall's expressed cautions in 1998 concerning the C5 fellowships were that they ran the risk of becoming syncretistic in their ongoing association with the local mosque. Within the C1-6 Spectrum itself, though, where does "syncretism" fit? The short answer is that it doesn't. The spectrum as a descriptive scale simply presents the different ways believers in Muslim contexts are following Jesus. It doesn't detail how successfully they do so.

In practice, I used the spectrum pre-field as a tool to decide what was syncretistic and what was not. As I noted above, I liked the C4 groups instinctively. They seemed to parse out what was good and bad and maintain the purity I idealized. In reality, though, I've found that most groups have syncretistic elements regardless of their approach to culture, language, or identity.

This observation fits with the developing reflections on syncretism over the past forty years. Imbach, for instance, defined syncretism in 1984 in a way that depended on the earlier concept of "essentialist" religion that we noted above. In the Evangelical Dictionary of Theology, he defines it as the "process by which elements of one religion are assimilated into another religion resulting in a change in the fundamental tenets or nature of those religions."[32] Imbach's definition raises some of the key questions being asked over the past few decades through this very debate and within the field of anthropology: What is religion? What are the fundamental tenets of a "religion," and to what degree is change bad or unexpected?

This tension is recognized by Moreau in his definition of the term sixteen years later:

> Syncretism. Blending of one idea, practice, or attitude with another.

> Traditionally among Christians it has been used of the replacement or dilution of the essential truths of the gospel through the incorporation of non- Christian elements.... Syncretism of some form has been seen everywhere the church has existed. We are naïve to think that eliminating the negatives of syncretism is easily accomplished.[33]

Moreau removes the term "religion" from his definition and focuses on the "dilution of essential truths." This moves the discussion toward the issue of convictions; however, they are lived out in the forms of the community, and away from the potential focus on rituals and forms that could dominate Imbach's definition.

Most recently, Shaw[34] and Burrows[35] outline how what may be perceived as "syncretism" can often be part of the necessary process of "hybridity" as the gospel penetrates the core of a community. Shaw, appropriating Hiebert's model of "Critical Contextualization,"[36] describes how even Shamanistic practices among the Samo became redefined in a biblical manner as the tribe redirected "their religious experience toward the creator's intention" in Christ.[37] In the subsequent chapter from the same volume, Burrows describes how our own understanding of this process is in ongoing flux. As he says, "[We] are only beginning to acknowledge the way in which the culture of the evangelizers and the culture of the hearers of the Word interact with one another."[38] He goes on to detail how he understands this process as necessary "hybridity"—not a process that dilutes the central message of "God and God's relationship to all of humanity ... in Jesus' ignominious death and logic-defying resurrection," but one that is indeed necessary "when Christian faith begins to mature among a people."[39] From this vantage point, "syncretism" as "hybridity" is "inevitable."[40] My own encounter with the issue of syncretism led to another crucial development in missiological thinking—namely, that externalism can be as much or more of a cause of syncretism than the mere mixing of ideas. In my early work with believers on the field, I found that external conformity on an issue, including the exclusion of former "religious" activities, did not necessarily mean heart-level engagement with the gospel.

Sometimes in an effort to avoid the mixing of religious categories, missionaries have unintentionally failed to introduce the gospel to the core concerns of a community. This can be quite evident within translation efforts. Harriet Hill describes how the avoidance of theologically loaded local terms actually distorted biblical truth rather than reinforcing it[41]—a point made at length, as well, in Lamen Sanneh's *Translating the Message*.[42]

In short, missiologists have had to reckon with the possibility that hidden presuppositions pose a risk of unbiblical syncretism. Neglecting to dig into the roots of cultural and religious presuppositions leaves them untouched and therefore persistent. This fundamental point has increasingly cautioned me against using the C Spectrum as a "syncretism" diagnostic tool. Each point on the spectrum runs the danger of syncretism, and no point provides an antidote against its dangers.

Continuation

The controversies raised by the C Spectrum are likely to continue, but in the midst of that we do well to learn as much as we can to move forward this discussion in productive and healthy ways. The value of the C Spectrum's continuation, then, depends on our ongoing learning and reflection. For those working in the field—particularly in pioneer settings—what can we make of the issues surrounding the C Spectrum and the challenge it presents on the descriptive and prescriptive fronts?

Regarding the latter, we have tremendous opportunity to keep learning from field developments. In 1998, there were a few movements to Christ among Muslims, the Islampur movement included. As of 2014, Garrison reported seventy movements to Christ in twenty-nine countries. He defined a movement as "100 new churches or 1000 baptisms that emerge/happen within a two-decade period." All of these seventy movements that he cited had begun in the last twenty years.[43] Anecdotally, these movements fall across the spectrum in terms of identity and association. This increase in movements represents a tremendous opportunity to evaluate and learn from God's work among Muslims, particularly in light of the questions this chapter has raised.[44] As a field worker, I seek to learn from the ongoing research and insights.

Yet I also have to sort out how I, as a foreign missionary, can faithfully announce Jesus' good news and relate to fellowships formed around that message. In my efforts to envision the goals for my own ministry of evangelism and discipleship and the prescriptive takeaways from the C Spectrum debate, I have come to resonate with the heart of Parshall's concern. In particular, both the C Spectrum and Parshall's writings pose the question: *How can believers be culturally and socially connected with their existing communities even as they embrace biblical norms that differ from that community?* This is a fundamental missiological question, raised in multiple books and articles over centuries.[45]

I have tended, then, to see two primary "ditches" that believers and cross-cultural missionaries are trying to avoid. The first is the ditch of isolation. Too great a distance culturally from a community labels the gospel as colonial or foreign or outsider. We believe, however, that God has come near to every human community in the gospel. As Andrew Walls puts it, "God accepts us as we are," including who we are in our group relations.[46] On the other hand, we seek to avoid the ditch of ungodly compromise—a condition in which the distinctives of Jesus' lordship and exclusive saving work are minimized or lost. In pursuit of effective discipleship and biblically grounded churches, I propose that we all aim for a target space between these two ditches.

At the end of the day, there is a distinction between the ways a group of believers see their associations and disassociations: Do they align primarily with foreigners or an existing historic church? Do they still see themselves as Muslims, or something in between as Kim discussed in chapter 4.[47] But though these are important questions, they are ultimately symptomatic of the core issues of engagement, cultural isolation, and syncretistic accommodation, which are our primary concerns. Moreover, these two ditches can be manifested at any point on the C Spectrum. Those inclined to foreign culture also run the danger of subsuming Jesus' lordship under other authorities (including foreign culture itself). Those inclined toward local cultural norms can isolate themselves and become insular or ethnocentric, failing to obey Jesus' command to make disciples of all nations. One can envision a prescriptive scale that exposes the ditches of isolation and compromise on each side, but two-dimensional models like the C1-6 scale have their limitations. They further a binary perspective that has so frequently plagued these discussions. No particular pattern of discipleship or evangelism protects us from the dangers of syncretism, accommodation, or isolation.

Acknowledging these ditches helps us process the debate surrounding the C Spectrum. We recognize that there can be compromised groups which have not given full allegiance to Jesus' lordship. We also recognize the danger of a colonial or ethnocentric paradigm which co-opts local groups into foreign or majority languages and cultures. Therefore Parshall's advocacy for C4 communities seems to be an appropriate ideal of "church" in a Muslim community: Believers distinguish themselves for their faith commitments but <u>aim to remain</u> part of their community in some meaningful way. However, as I discussed above, we come to acknowledge that this ideal may be pursued at any position on Travis' C Spectrum, even as the dangerous ditches threaten each group on the spectrum. This allows us to retain the C Spectrum as a descriptive tool while still encouraging reflective inquiry into what marks "Christ-centered communities" and how missionaries contribute to their development.

This still leaves us with the hard work of ministry in context under Jesus' lordship. I live in a pioneer setting with few believers and no historic church. In this context, my role is to observe what God is doing across the Muslim world in the various expressions of faith emerging over the past twenty years, to discern my own context by listening respectfully and well to my community, and then to proclaim Jesus' love and authority in that context. For believers and seekers inclined toward foreign identification and foreign paradigms, we exalt Jesus as Lord of every community and Savior of all who believe, no matter what community they were born into. For those inclined to uncritical adaptation of birth culture to their new faith, we exalt Jesus' authority over all authorities, including the traditions they have received from the past. We evangelize and disciple based on context and the needs and tendencies of the seekers and believers we meet.

Based on conscience and calling, missionaries are drawn to different approaches regarding continuity of identity, culture, and language. This diversity is appropriate and necessary. It is part of the distinctive gifts that the Spirit has given Christ's body, including those involved in the missionary task. Though we study the Scriptures intently, live according to our consciences, and argue for our paradigms, the Holy Spirit leads in surprising ways. We are ultimately servants of the Lord—not of our paradigms and models. I have repeatedly met missionaries who aimed for a C3, C4, or C5 church, only to see a different kind of church emerge through the Spirit's leading within the contextual demands. God calls each community and each believer within his or her own context; and we need to respect that calling and the beautiful power of the Spirit to fulfill God's purposes for each community and the individuals within them. We must also be wary of hindering the gospel from reaching into new, unengaged communities because of biases developed outside (or inside) of the community context.

Cautions and Conclusion

In my current host country in Central Asia, I have observed an intense conflict between a modernist agenda and traditional values. Modernists are drawn to the West, including its impulses to secularism. Traditionalists seek to uphold traditional culture, often using Islamic terminology to do so, but not necessarily based on so-called Islamic orthodoxy. In many ways, this competition between modern and traditional runs through the very heart of families. City-dwelling families often lean one way, even as they have relatives in distant villages committed to another way. How do we speak the truth of the good news of Jesus' death and resurrection and glorious salvation for all (traditionalists and modernists included) who put their faith in him? Is Jesus only for traditionalists? Is Jesus only for modernists? Of course not. He is for all of the people of all nations and all peoples in all contexts (Rom 3:29–30). Our contextualization of that foundational message must not yoke the gospel message to one particular side in the ongoing conflict.

The huge temptation in each context is to universalize the experience of an individual believer or group of believers to all Muslims in that context or to all Muslim contexts. The reality is that even within the same country or people group, those who find Jesus come from a variety of perspectives. Some are traditionalists; some are inclined toward foreignness; and some lie somewhere in between. In my ministry, I engage some who have been drawn into the gospel message *because* of the positive words about Jesus in the Qur'an and the Hadiths. And I engage with others who are drawn to the gospel message because they were repulsed by the violence they saw as inherent to Islam. To universalize either of these experiences is to predecide where all Muslims will fall on the C Spectrum. I believe this is a mistake that has dominated the C Spectrum debate. Advocates of each point on the scale can point to some believer somewhere who shows the dangers of other points. As those engaging cross-culturally with the gospel, we must be careful lest we unintentionally hinder the Spirit's work in different contexts from our own.

It is my hope that in the next two decades of discussion on the C Spectrum, other models of analysis will continue to emerge. But most of all, I pray that non-Muslim background contributors to the discussion will prove to be peacemakers (blessed are they) as they help Muslim background believers to rightly debate and process their diverse experiences under the lordship of Christ. If we sow division and exasperate the historic tensions between peoples, we will not be living in accord with the gospel that we preach (Gal 5:13–15).

Phil Parshall modelled this reflective engagement. He did so by calling for a greater move toward Muslim contexts in terms of cultural behavior and even spiritual language. He did so by his polite engagement with those with whom he disagreed. He did so, most strikingly, by his "removal of the Fatwa"[48] against any suspicion of motives or faith among fellow missiologists and practitioners. We do well to follow Parshall's lead on this as the gospel penetrates new people groups among Muslims in deeper and wider ways over the next decades.

References

Ayub, E. 2009. "Observations and Reactions to Christians Involved in a New Approach to Mission." *St. Francis Magazine* 5 (5): 21–40.

Barth, F. 1969. "Introduction." In *Ethnic Groups and Boundaries: The Social Organization of Culture Difference*, edited by Fredrik Barth, 9–38. Oslo, Norway: Universites for laget.

———. 1994. "Enduring and Emerging Issues in the Analysis of Ethnicity." In *The Anthropology of Ethnicity: Beyond 'Ethnic Groups and Boundaries*, edited by Hans Vermeulen and Cora Govers, 11–32. Amsterdam, NL: Het Spinhuis.

Burrows, W. 2018. "Theological Ideals, Cross-Cultural Realities: Syncretism and Hybridity in Christian Culture Crossings." In *Traditional Rituals as Christian Worship: Dangerous Syncretism or Necessary Hybridity?* edited by R. Daniel Shaw and William R. Burrow, 20–36. Maryknoll, NY: Orbis.

Canfield, R. L. 1973. *Faction and Conversion in a Plural Society: Religious Alignments in the Hindu Kush*. Ann Arbor, MI: University of Michigan.

Corwin, G. 2007. "A Humble Appeal to C5/Insider Movement Muslim Ministry Advocates to Consider Ten Questions." *International Journal of Frontier Missiology* 24 (1): 5–20.

Daniels, G. 2018. "Conclusion: Learning from the Margins," In *Margins of Islam: Ministry in Diverse Muslim Contexts*. Pasadena, CA: William Carey Library.

Daniels, Gene and Warrick Farah, eds. 2018. *Margins of Islam: Ministry of Diverse Muslim Contexts*. Pasadena, CA: William Carey Library.

Dixon, R. 2009. "Moving on From the C1-C6 Spectrum." *St. Francis Magazine* 5 (4): 3–19.

———. 2016. "When C4 Is Not Biblical in Many Respects." https://biblicalmissiology.org/2020/10/07/when-c4-is-not-biblical-in-many-respects/

Duerksen, Darren T., and William A. Dyrness. 2019. *Seeking Church*. Carol Stream, IL: InterVarsity.

Farah, W. 2018. "How Muslims Shape and Use Islam: Towards a Missiological Understanding." In *Margins of Islam: Ministry of Diverse Muslim Contexts*, edited by Gene Daniels and Warrick Farah. Pasadena, CA: William Carey Library.

Garrison, D. 2014. *A Wind in the House of Islam: How God Is Drawing Muslims Around the World to Faith in Jesus Christ*. Monument, CO: Wigtake Resources LLC.

Geertz, C. 1971. *Islam Observed: Religious Development in Morocco and Indonesia*. Chicago: University of Chicago Press.

Greenlee, D., ed. 2005. *From the Straight Path to the Narrow Way: Journeys of Faith*. Waynesboro, GA: Authentic.

———, ed. 2013. *Longing for Community*. Pasadena, CA: William Carey Library. Hiebert, P. G. 1987. "Critical Contextualization." *International Bulletin of Missionary Research* 11 (3), 104–12.

Higgins, K. 2009. "Speaking the Truth About Insider Movements: Addressing the Criticisms of Bill Nikides and 'Phil' Relative to the Article 'Inside What?'" *St. Francis Magazine* 5 (6): 61–86.

Higgins, K., R. Jameson, and H. Talman, 2015. "Myths and Misunderstandings About Insider Movements." In *Understanding Insider Movements: Disciples of*

Jesus Within Diverse Religious Communities, edited by Harley Talman and John Jay Travis. Pasadena, CA: William Carey Library.

Hill, H. 2007. "The Effects of Using Local and Non-Local Terms in Mother-Tongue Scripture." *Missiology: An International Review* 24: 383–96.

Imbach, S. R. 1984. "Syncretism." In *Evangelical Dictionary of Theology*, edited by Walter A. Elwell, 1062. Grand Rapids: Baker.

Jenkins, P. 2011. *The Next Christendom: The Coming of Global Christianity*. New York: Oxford University Press.

Kraft, K. A. 2012. *Searching for Heaven in the Real World: A Sociological Discussion of Conversion in the Arab World*. Oxford: Regnum Books International.

Lingel, M., J. Morton, and B. Nikkedes, eds. 2012. *Chrislam: How Missionaries Are Promoting an Islamized Gospel*. i2 ministries.

Marranci, G. 2008. *The Anthropology of Islam* [Kindle Edition]. New York: Berg Publishers.

Moreau, A. S. 2000. "Syncretism." In *Evangelical Dictionary of World Missions*, edited by A. Scott Moreau, 924. Grand Rapids: Baker.

Morse, G. 2017. "Why Are So Many So Silent? The Insider Movement in America." https://www.desiringgod.org/articles/why-are-so-many-so-silent.

Morton, J. 2011. "Insider Movements and the Historical Approach." *Journal of Biblical Missiology*, February 8, 2011. http://biblicalmissiology.org/2011/02/08/insider- movements-and-the-historical-approach.

Naja, B. 2013. "A Jesus Movement Among Muslims: Research from Eastern Africa."

International Journal of Frontier Missiology 30 (1): 27–29.

———. 2013. "Sixteen Features of Belief and Practice in Two Movements Among Muslims in Eastern Africa: What Does the Data Say?" *International Journal of Frontier Missiology* 30 (4): 155–60.

Nikides, B. 2009. "A Response to Kevin Higgins' 'Inside What? Church, Religion and Insider Movements in Biblical Perspective." *St. Francis Magazine* 5 (4): 92–113.

Nongbri, B. 2013. *Before Religion.* New Haven, CT: Yale University Press.

Parshall, P. 1980. *New Paths in Muslim Evangelism: Evangelical Approaches to Contextualization.* Grand Rapids: Baker.

———. 1998. "Danger! New Directions in Contextualization." *Evangelical Missions Quarterly* 34 (4): 404–6, 409–10.

———. 2004. "Lifting the Fatwa." *Evangelical Missions Quarterly* 40 (3): 288–93.

———. 2007. *Muslim Evangelism: Contemporary Approaches to Contextualization.* Colorado Springs, CO: Biblica.

Prenger, H. 2017. *Muslim Insider Christ Followers: Their Theological and Missiological Frames.* Pasadena, CA: William Carey Library.

Richard, H. L. 2014. "Religious Syncretism as a Syncretistic Concept: The Inadequacy of the 'World Religions' Paradigm in Cross-Cultural Encounter." *International Journal of Frontier Missiology* 31 (4): 209–14.

Ripken, N., and G. Lewis. 2013. *The Insanity of God: A True Story of Faith Resurrected.* Nashville: B&H Publishing.

Sanneh, L. 1996. *Translating the Message: The Missionary Impact on Culture.* Mary Knoll, NY: Orbis.

Sciortino, G. "Ethnicity, Race, Nationhood, Foreignness, and Many Other Things: Prolegomena to a Cultural Sociology of Difference-Based Interactions," In *The Oxford Handbook of Cultural Sociology,* edited by Ronald N. Jacobs, Jeffrey C. Alexander, and Philip Smith, 365–89. Oxford: Oxford University Press.

Shaw, R. D. 2010. "Beyond Contextualization: Toward a Twenty-First-Century Model for Enabling Mission." *International Bulletin of Missionary Research* 34 (4): 208–15.

———. 2018. "The Dynamics of Ritual and Ceremony: Transforming Traditional Rites to Their Intended Purpose." In Traditional Rituals as Christian

Worship: Dangerous Syncretism or Necessary Hybridity? edited by R. D. Shaw and William R. Burrow, 1–19. Maryknoll, NY: Orbis.

Smith, J. 2009. "An Assessment of the Insider's Principle Paradigms." *St. Francis Magazine* 5 (4): 20–51.

Talman, H., and J. Travis, eds. 2015. *Understanding Insider Movements: Disciples of Jesus Within Diverse Religious Communities*. Pasadena, CA: William Carey Library.

Tennent, T. C. 2006. "Followers of Jesus (Isa) in Islamic Mosques: A Closer Examination of C-5 'High Spectrum' Contextualization." *International Journal of Frontier Missions* 23 (3): 101–15.

Travis, J. 1998. "The C1 to C6 Spectrum: A Practical Tool for Defining Six Types of 'Christ-centered Communities' ('C') Found in the Muslim Context." *Evangelical Missions Quarterly* 34 (4): 411–15.

———. 2015. "The C1-C6 Spectrum After Fifteen Years: Misunderstandings, Limitations, and Recommendations." In *Understanding Insider Movements: Disciples of Jesus Within Diverse Religious Communities*, edited by Harley Talman and John Jay Travis, 489–96. Pasadena, CA: William Carey Library.

Travis, J., and A. Travis. 2013. "Roles of 'Alongsiders' in Insider Movements." *International Journal of Frontier Missiology* 30 (4): 161–69.

Trousdale, J. 2012. *Miraculous Movements: How Hundreds of Thousands of Muslims Are Falling in Love with Jesus*. Nashville: Thomas Nelson.

Walls, A. F. 1996. "The Gospel as Prisoner and Liberator of Culture." In *The Missionary Movement in Christian History: Studies in the Transmission of Faith*. Maryknoll, NY: Orbis.

Watson, D., and P. Watson. 2014. *Contagious Disciple Making: Leading Others on a Journey of Discovery*. Nashville: Thomas Nelson.

Werbner, P. 2010. "Religious Identity," In *The Sage Handbook of Identities*, edited by Margaret Wetherell and Chandra Talpade Mohanty. Thousand Oaks, CA: SAGE Publications.

Woodberry, J. D, ed. 2011. *From Seed to Fruit: Global Trends, Fruitful Practices, and Emerging Issues Among Muslims*. Pasadena, CA: William Carey Library.

Appendix B

Wright, N. T. 2013. *Paul and the Faithfulness of God*. Minneapolis: Fortress.

---

1. This article was originally published as Williams, Joseph S, "Two Decades of the Letter 'C'," in *The Life and Impact of Phil Parshall: Connecting With Muslims*, ed. Kenneth Nehrbass and Mark Williams (Littleton, CO: William Carey Publishing, 2021), 71–90 and is republished by permission.
2. Travis, "The C1 to C6 Spectrum."
3. Parshall, "Danger! New Directions in Contextualization."
4. The original article was defined as a "spectrum," but it is often called a "scale." I have retained the original term in this article.
5. I have confirmed this in personal correspondence with Travis.
6. See Travis and Travis, Travis and Travis, "Roles of 'Alongsiders' in Insider Movements," 162. In the original article (1998), Travis only mentions "reject" and "reinterpret."
7. Travis, "The C1–C6 Spectrum After Fifteen Years: Misunderstandings, Limitations, and Recommendations," 492.
8. Parshall, "Danger! New Directions in Contextualization."
9. Contextualization may not be explicitly defined this way, but in Parshall's own writings it clearly comes out as the framework for discussion.
10. See Parshall, *Muslim Evangelism: Contemporary Approaches to Contextualization*. The original edition was Parshall, *New Paths in Muslim Evangelism: Evangelical Approaches to Contextualization*.
11. Dixon, "When C4 Is Not Biblical in Many Respects."
12. I use quotation marks in the first use of this term "religious," for reasons that I will explain in a later section, but I will refrain from doing so in future instances. Yet it should be clear that this is one of the disputed terms in this discussion.
13. Travis, "The C1 to C6 Spectrum."
14. Many of the articles have been collated into a couple volumes. Additionally, Corwin's exchange with C5 observers in 2007 provided a substantive description for the discussion. See Corwin, "A Humble Appeal to C5/Insider Movement Muslim Ministry Advocates to Consider Ten Questions." See also Talman and Travis, eds., *Understanding Insider Movements: Disciples of Jesus Within Diverse Religious Communities*; and Lingel, Morton, and Nikkedes, eds., *Chrislam: How Missionaries Are Promoting an Islamized Gospel*.
15. See Ayub, "Observations and Reactions to Christians Involved in a New Approach to Mission"; and Morse, "Why Are So Many So Silent? The Insider Movement in America."
16. Higgins cites a specific C5 leader who was "repeatedly beaten, given electric shocks, hung upside down by his feet ... and forced to watch several men have their throats cut." Higgins, Jameson, and Talman, "Myths and Misunderstandings About Insider Movements," Location 1680.
17. According to my correspondence with John and Ann Travis, this was not their intention. Because C1-C5 are defined as groups, an individual hidden believer does not fit into any of those categories. I work in a setting with few gathered groups and have tended to see the spectrum in light of identity, language, and culture for both individuals and groups. In this sense, I am speaking of the secret believer's disposition toward those five categories.
18. See Dixon, "Moving on From the C1-C6 Spectrum"; Nikides, "A Response to Kevin Higgins' 'Inside What? Church, Religion and Insider Movements in Biblical Perspective'"; and Smith, "An Assessment of the Insider's Principle Paradigms."
19. Tennent, "Followers of Jesus (Isa) in Islamic Mosques."
20. Nikides, "A Response," 97–98.

21. Higgins, "Speaking," 67; Naja, "Sixteen Features," 156.
22. Travis, "The C1 to C6 Spectrum."
23. Ibid.
24. See Barth, "Introduction"; Barth, "Enduring and Emerging Issues in the Analysis of Ethnicity." Canfield shows how Barth's paradigm applies to the use of religion as a political marker. See Canfield, *Faction and Conversion in a Plural Society: Religious Alignments in the Hindu Kush*. See also Giuseppe Sciortino, "Ethnicity, Race, Nationhood, Foreignness, and Many Other Things: Prolegomena to a Cultural Sociology of Difference-Based Interactions."
25. Daniels, "Conclusion: Learning from the Margins," location 5144.
26. As Marrinci puts it in his *Anthropology of Islam*, "During my years of study, books and teachers explained that Islam is a religion based on theological precepts and a particular history. During my research, I learned that the Islam of books, theology and history is nothing other than a ghost hunted for by both the believers as well as the academics," 472. Yet recognizing the diversity of beliefs and practices still leaves us grappling for words to describe the common elements between these so-called "Islams." As Farah notes on this question, citing Ahmad's *What Is Islam?* there are two errors we can fall into in this discussion: The first error is to place Islam in a rigid framework that is unable to account for the diversity of Muslims around the world who often contradict one another. The second error is to claim that there is no such thing as Islam, but instead only islams imagined by each Muslim. "How Muslims Shape and Use Islam: Towards a Missiological Understanding," location 664.
27. Nongbri, *Before Religion*, 7.
28. Ibid.
29. Duerksen and Dyrness, *Seeking Church*; Richard, "Religious Syncretism as a Syncretistic Concept."
30. Wright, *Paul and the Faithfulness of God*, 35.
31. Werbner, "Religious Identity," 238.
32. Imbach, "Syncretism," 1062.
33. Moreau, "Syncretism," 623.
34. Shaw, "The Dynamics of Ritual and Ceremony: Transforming Traditional Rites to Their Intended Purpose."
35. Burrows, "Theological Ideals, Cross-Cultural Realities: Syncretism and Hybridity in Christian Culture Crossings."
36. Hiebert, "Critical Contextualization."
37. In this particular case, Shaw had observed in 1972 the Samo community use glossalalia (tongues) to summon a dead shaman's spirit. Fifteen years later, Shaw discovered (to his great surprise) that after many in the community had come to faith they were speaking in tongues, with interpretation, in their church services, using some of the same musical patterns as the 1972 ritual. This had emerged without the involvement of "Pentecostal" missionaries. Shaw, "Dynamics of Ritual," 14–15.
38. Burrows, "Theological Ideals," 26.
39. Ibid., 27.
40. Ibid.
41. In an effort to avoid using a local term for "demons" that came from the local spiritual language, the translators created a new term for the idea of "demons." As a result, it appears that the local term (and beings) they decided against remained within the believing community's worldview and were largely untouched by the teaching of the Scriptures. Jesus has power to cast out demons (using the new term), but not the supernatural malevolent beings never mentioned in the Scriptures but existing within their previous worldview. This contrasts with what happened when local, non-ideal terms were used. The term for "Satan," though originally

implying a sometimes malevolent, sometimes benevolent, being, changed over its eighty years of use in the translated Scriptures. Believers reassigned the meaning of the term to refer to a malevolent being that was opposed to God's will. Hill, "The Effects of Using Local and Non-Local Terms in Mother-Tongue Scripture."

42. The late Catholic missiologist, who came from a Muslim background himself, argued that the use of local terms, even ones linked deeply with existing religions, created a connection with the past necessary for the gospel to engage all elements of the culture. Describing this process in another African language, he writes, "[When] new converts prayed to the God of Jesus Christ as *ndina*, for example, they created an overlap to preserve and perpetuate the earlier notions in the environment of the new dispensation. [This] ... helps to legitimize change and resolve, without bypassing, potential difficulties. The point of convergence remains the familiar medium of the vernacular and its often-hidden presuppositions." Sanneh, *Translating the Message: The Missionary Impact on Culture*, 177.

43. Garrison, *A Wind in the House of Islam: How God Is Drawing Muslims Around the World to Faith in Jesus Christ*, Location 135.

44. A short listing of some of the volumes to emerge recently shows the salient insights. Prenger has supplied insights into the thinking and practice of C5 leaders—thinking and practice which reflects great diversity on some of the key issues like the role of the mosque and the Quran. Prenger, *Muslim Insider Christ Followers: Their Theological and Missiological Frames*. Naja provides a detailed study of two movements in East Africa ("Sixteen Features"). Kraft studies Arab Muslim converts who self-describe as "Christians." See Kraft, *Searching for Heaven in the Real World: A Sociological Discussion of Conversion in the Arab World*. Multiple other volumes have emerged exploring the factors involved in Muslims coming to faith and the qualities of different movements to Christ, both in popular and academic forms. See David Greenlee, ed. *From the Straight Path to the Narrow Way: Journeys of Faith*; David Greenlee, ed. *Longing for Community*; David Watson and Paul Watson, *Contagious Disciple Making: Leading Others on a Journey of Discovery*; Nik Ripken and Gregg Lewis, *The Insanity of God: A True Story of Faith Resurrected*; Jerry Trousdale, *Miraculous Movements: How Hundreds of Thousands of Muslims Are Falling in Love with Jesus*. Talman and Travis, eds. *Understanding Insider Movements: Disciples of Jesus Within Diverse Religious Communities*; Gene Daniels and Warrick Farah, eds. *Margins of Islam: Ministry of Diverse Muslim Contexts*.

45. See especially Walls, "The Gospel as Prisoner and Liberator of Culture."

46. Ibid., 7.

47. See my clarifications concerning the term and category "Muslim" earlier in the chapter. With ongoing caveats about "religious terms" still in place, I use the word here to reflect sociological, cultural, and ethnic categories of self-identification.

48. Parshall, "Lifting the Fatwa."

REFERENCES

Bailey, Kenneth. *Paul Through Mediterranean Eyes: Cultural Studies in 1 Corinthians*. Downers Grove, IL: IVP Academic, 2011.

Barclay, John M. *Jews in the Mediterranean Diaspora: From Alexander to Trajan (323 Bce–117 Ce)*. Edinburgh, Scotland: T&T Clark, 1999.

Barnett, Jens. "Living a Pun: Cultural Hybridity Among Arab Followers of Christ." In *Longing for Community: Church, Ummah, or Somewhere in Between*, edited by David H. Greenlee, 29-40. Pasadena, CA: William Carey Library, 2013.

Barnett, Jens. "Refusing to Choose: Multiple Belonging Among Arab Followers of Christ." In *Longing for Community: Church, Ummah, or Somewhere in Between*, 19-28. Pasadena, CA: William Carey Library, 2013.

Beale, G. K. *The Temple and the Church's Mission: A Biblical Theology of the Dwelling Place of God*. Downers Grove, IL: IVP Academic, 2004.

Berger, Peter L. *The Sacred Canopy: Elements of a Sociological Theory of Religion*. New York, NY: Doubleday, 1969.

Berger, Peter L., and Thomas Luckman. *The Social Construction of Reality: A Treatise in the Sociology of Knowledge*. New York, NY: Anchor Books, 1967.

Bishop, Bryan. *Boundless: What Global Expressions of Faith Teach Us About Following Jesus*. Grand Rapids, MI: Baker Books, 2015.

Blue, B. B. "Food Offered to Idols and Jewish Food Laws." In *Dictionary of Paul and His Letters*, edited by Gerald F. Hawthorne, Ralph P. Martin, and Daniel G. Reid, 306–10. Downers Grove, IL: InterVarsity Press, 1993.

Block, Corrie. *The Qur'an in Christian-Muslim Dialogue: Historical and Modern Interpretations (Culture and Civilization in the Middle East)*. New York: Routledge, 2013.

Brown, Rick. "Biblical Muslims." *International Journal of Frontier Missiology* 24, no. 2 (2007): 65–74.

Carson, D. A. "That By All Means I Might Win Some: Faithfulness and Flexibility in Gospel Proclamation." The Gospel Coalition National Conference (2009).

Carson, D. A. "That By All Means I Might Win Some: Faithfulness and Flexibility in Gospel Proclamation." (2017). https://www.thegospelcoalition.org/conference_media/means-might-win/.

Chandler, Paul-Gordon. *Pilgrims of Christ on the Muslim Road: Exploring a New Path Between Two Faiths*. Lanham, MD: Rowman & Littlefield Publishers, 2007.

Corwin, Gary. "A Humble Appeal to C5/insider Movement Muslim Ministry Advocates to Consider Ten Questions." *International Journal of Frontier Missiology* 24, no. 1 (2007): 5–21.

Crouch, Andy. *Culture Making: Recovering Our Creative Calling*. Downers Grove, IL: IVP Books, 2008.

Cumming, Joseph L. "Did Jesus Die on the Cross? The History of Reflection on the End of His Earthly Life in Sunni Tafsir Literature." Yale University (2001).

Cumming, Joseph L. "God, Word and Spirit: The Doctrine of the Trinity in the Qur'ān and Islamic Interpretation." PhD dissertation, Yale University, 2020.

de Lacey, D. R. "Gentiles." In *Dictionary of Paul and His Letters*, edited by Gerald F. Hawthorne, and Ralph P. Martin. Downers Grove, IL: InterVarsity Press, 1993.

Diaz, Carlos. "Insider Approach to Muslim Ministry: A Latino Perspective." *Evangelical Missions Quarterly* 46, no. 3 (2010): 312–19.

Donovan, Vincent J. *Christianity Rediscovered: An Epistle From the Masai*. London, UK: SCM Press, 1982.

Duerksen, Darren T. *Christ-Followers in Other Religions: The Global Witness of Insider Movements*. Oxford, UK: Regnum Books International, Kindle, 2022.

Duerksen, Darren T., and William A. Dyrness. *Seeking Church*. Carol Streams, IL: InterVarsity Press, 2019.

Fee, Gordon D. *The First Epistle to the Corinthians*. Grand Rapids, MI: William B. Eerdmans, 2014.

Flemming, Dean. *Contextualization in the New Testament: Patterns for Theology and Mission*. Downers Grove, IL: InterVarsity Press, 2005.

France, R. T. *Matthew: An Introduction and Commentary*. Downers Grove, IL: InterVarsity Press, 1985.

Garrison, David. *A Wind in the House of Islam: How God is Drawing Muslims Around the World to Faith in Jesus Christ*. Monument, CO: Wigtake Resources LLC, 2014.

Geertz, Clifford. "Religion as a Cultural System." In *Anthropological Approaches to the Study of Religion*, 1–46. New York, NY: Frederick A. Praeger Press, 1966.

Geertz, Clifford. *Islam Observed: Religious Development in Morocco and Indonesia*. Chicago, IL: University Of Chicago Press, 1971.

Gladwell, Malcolm. *The Tipping Point: How Little Things Can Make a Big Difference*. New York City, NY: Little, Brown and Company, 2006.

Grafas, Basil. "A View from the Bridge: Insider Movement Critics Speak Out." *St Francis Magazine* 6, no. 6 (2010): 934–38.

Green, Joel B. *Conversion in Luke-Acts: Divine Action, Human Cognition, and the People of God*. Grand Rapids, MI: Baker Academic, Kindle, 2015.

Hays, Richard B. *First Corinthians*. Louisville, KY: Westminster John Knox Press, 2011.

Hiebert, Paul G. "Critical Contextualization." *International Bulletin of Missionary Research* 11, no. 3 (1987): 104-112.

Hiebert, Paul G. "The Flaw of the Excluded Middle." *Missiology: An International Review* 10, no. 1 (1982): 35–47.

Higgins, Kevin. "Inside What? Church, Culture, Religion and Insider Movements in Biblical Perspective." *St Francis Magazine* 5, no. 4 (2009): 74–79.

Higgins, Kevin. "Speaking the Truth About Insider Movements: Addressing the Criticisms of Bill Nikides and 'Phil' Relative to the Article 'Inside What?'." *St Francis Magazine* 5, no. 6 (2009): 61–86.

Higgins, Kevin. "At Table in the Idol's Temple? Local Theology, Idolatry, and Identification in 1 Corinthians 8-10." *International Journal of Frontier Missiology* 31, no. 1 (2014): 27–36.

Houssney, Georges. "Jew to the Jew, Greek to the Greeks? Part 1." *Journal of Biblical Missiology* (2010). http://biblicalmissiology.org/2010/07/08/jew-to-jews-greek-to-greeks-part-i/.

Jones, Jeffrey M. "How Religious Are Americans?" *Gallup* (2021): Accessed June 1, 2023. https://news.gallup.com/poll/358364/religious-americans.aspx.

Jones, Rachel Pieh. *Pillars: How Muslim Friends Led Me Closer to Jesus.* Walden, NY: Plough Publishing House, 2021.

Kadir, Usman, and Daniel Roberts. *Seeing the World Through New Eyes: A Journey From Extremism to Love.* Fremantle, Australia: Vivid Publishing, Kindle, 2013.

Lewis, Rebecca. "Comment." On Jeff Morton, "Insider Movements and the Historical Approach." *Biblical Missiology* (2011). http://biblicalmissiology.org/2011/02/08/insider-movements-and-the-historical-approach/.

Lewis, Rebecca. "Promoting Movements to Christ Within Natural Communities." *International Journal of Frontier Missiology* 24, no. 2 (2007): 75–76.

Lingel, Josh, Jeff Morton, and Bill Nikkedes, eds. *Chrislam: How Missionaries Are Promoting an Islamized Gospel.* i2 ministries, 2012.

Mallouhi, Mazhar. "Comments on the Insider Movement." *St Francis Magazine* 5, no. 5 (2009): 3–14.

Manickam, J. A. "Race, Racism, and Ethnicity." In *Global Dictionary of Theology: A Resource for the Worldwide Church*, edited by William A. Dyrness, and Veli-Matti Kärkkäinen 718-24. Downers Grove, IL: IVP Academic, 2008.

Marranci, Gabrielle. *The Anthropology of Islam*. New York, NY: Berg Publishers, Kindle, 2008.

McGavran, Donald Anderson. *The Bridges of God: A Study in the Strategy of Missions*. Eugene, OR: Wipf and Stock Publishers, 2005.

Moo, Douglas J. *Galatians (Baker Exegetical Commentary on the New Testament)*. Grand Rapids, MI: Baker Academic, 2013.

Moreau, Scott. "Syncretism." In *Evangelical Dictionary of World Missions*, edited by A. Scott Moreau, 924. Grand Rapids, MI: Baker, 2000.

Mouw, Richard J. *When the Kings Come Marching in: Isaiah and the New Jerusalem*. Grand Rapids, MI: William B. Eerdmans Publishing Company, Kindle, 2002.

Muller, Roland. *The Messenger, the Message, the Community: Three Critical Issues for the Cross-Cultural Church-Planter*. CanBooks, 2006.

Nehrbass, Kenneth Robert. *Advanced Missiology: How to Study Missions in Credible and Useful Ways*. Eugene, OR: Cascade Books, 2021.

Nongbri, Brent. *Before Religion*. New Haven, CT: Yale University Press, 2013.

Piper, John. *Let the Nations be Glad!: The Supremacy of God in Missions*. Baker Academic, 2010.

Piper, John. "Minimizing the Bible?: Seeker-Driven Pastors and Radical Contextualization in Missions." *Mission Frontiers* (2006): 16–17.

Potok, Chaim. *Wanderings: Chaim Potok's History of the Jews*. New York, NY: Alfred A. Knopf, 1978.

Prenger, Henk. "Muslim Insider Christ Followers: A Grounded Theory Research." PhD dissertation, Biola University, 2014.

Priest, Robert. "Missionary Elenctics: Conscience and Culture." *Missiology: An International Review* 22, no. 3 (1994): 291–316.

Saeed, Abdullah. *Reading the Qur'an in the Twenty-First Century: A Contextualist Approach*. London, UK: Routledge, 2013.

Smith, Gregory A. "About Three-in-ten U.S. Adults Are Now Religiously Unaffiliated." *Pew Research Center* (2021). https://www.pewresearch.org/religion/2021/12/14/about-three-in-ten-u-s-adults-are-now-religiously-unaffiliated/.

Smith, Jay. "An Assessment of the Insider's Principle Paradigms." *St Francis Magazine* 5, no. 4 (2009): 20–51.

Steffen, Tom A. *Reconnecting God's Story to Ministry: Cross-Cultural Storytelling At Home and Abroad*. La Habra, CA: Center for Organizational & Ministry Development, 1996.

Steffen, Tom A. *Passing the Baton: Church-Planting That Empowers*. La Habra, CA: Center for Organizational & Ministry Development, 1997.

Steffen, Tom A. *The Facilitator Era: Beyond Pioneer Church Multiplication*. Eugene, OR: Wipf & Stock, 2011.

Steffen, Tom A. "Foundational Roles of Symbol and Narrative in the (Re)construction of Reality and Relationships." *Missiology: An International Review* 26, no. 4 (1998): 477–94.

Talman, Harley, and John Jay Travis, eds. *Understanding Insider Movements: Disciples of Jesus Within Diverse Religious Communities*. Pasadena, CA: William Carey Library, 2015.

Tennent, Timothy C. "Followers of Jesus (Isa) in Islamic Mosques: A Closer Examination of C-5 'High Spectrum' Contextualization." *International Journal of Frontier Missions* 23, no. 3 (2006): 101–15.

Tennent, Timothy C. *Theology in the Context of World Christianity: How the Global Church is Influencing the Way We Think About and Discuss Theology*. Grand Rapids, MI: Zondervan, 2007.

Thiselton, Anthony C. *1 Corinthians: A Shorter Exegetical and Pastoral Commentary*. Grand Rapids, MI: William B. Eerdmans Publishing Company, Kindle, 2006.

Travis, Anna. "Spiritual Power, World Religions, and the Demonic." In *Understanding Insider Movements*, edited by Harley Talman, and John Jay Travis, 521–36. Pasadena, CA: William Carey Library, 2015.

Travis, John. "The C1 to C6 Spectrum." *Evangelical Missions Quarterly* 34, no. 4 (1998): 407-408.

Travis, John. "Must all Muslims Leave Islam to Follow Jesus?" *Evangelical Missions Quarterly* 34, no. 4 (1998): 411-415.

Travis, John Jay. "The C1-C6 Spectrum After Fifteen Years: Misunderstandings, Limitations, and Recommendations." In *Understanding Insider Movements: Disciples of Jesus Within Diverse Religious Communities*, edited by Harley Talman, and John Jay Travis, 489–96. Pasadena, CA: William Carey Library, 2015.

Trousdale, Jerry. *Miraculous Movements: How Hundreds of Thousands of Muslims Are Falling in Love With Jesus*. Nashville, TN: Thomas Nelson, 2012.

Volf, Miroslav. *Exclusion and Embrace: A Theological Exploration of Identity, Otherness, and Reconciliation*. Nashville, TN: Abingdon Press, 1996.

Volf, Miroslav. *Allah: A Christian Response*. New York, NY: HarperCollins, Kindle, 2011.

Walls, Andrew F. "The Gospel as Prisoner and Liberator of Culture." In *Understanding Insider Movements*, 305–16. Pasadena, CA: William Carey Library, 2015.

Walls, Andrew F. *The Missionary Movement in Christian History: Studies in the Transmission of Faith*. Maryknoll, NY: Orbis books, 1996.

Walton, John H. *The Lost World of Genesis One: Ancient Cosmology and the Origins Debate*. Downers Grove, IL: InterVarsity Press, 2010.

Waterman, L. D. "Do the Roots Affect the Fruits?" *International Journal of Frontier Missiology* 24, no. 2 (2007): 57–63.

Watson, David, and Paul Watson. *Contagious Disciple Making: Leading Others on a Journey of Discovery*. Nashville, TN: Thomas Nelson, 2014.

"What Are Near, Far and Same Culture Mission Workers?" Operation Mobilization USA. Accessed 25 July 2023. https://www.omusa.org/what-are-near-far-and-same-culture-mission-workers.

Williams, Joseph S. "Two Decades of the Letter 'C'." In *The Life and Impact of Phil Parshall: Connecting With Muslims*, edited by Kenneth Nehrbass, and Mark Williams, 71–90. Littleton, CO: William Carey Publishing, 2021.

Williams, J. S. "Whose Story to Join? The Problem of Social Plausibility, Social Mission Stations, and Their Relationship to Church Planting Movements." *Great Commission Research Journal* 7, no. 2 (2016): 213–29.

Williams, Joseph S. "A Theology of Diversity With Special Reference to Translation Issues in Central Asia." *Missiology: An International Review* 45, no. 2 (2017): 156–68.

Woodberry, J. Dudley. "Contextualization Among Muslims Reusing Common Pillars." *International Journal of Frontier Missions* 13, no. 4 (1996): 171–86.

Wright, N. T. *Justification: God's Plan and Paul's Vision*. Downers Grove, IL: IVP Academic, 2009.

Wright, N. T. *How God Became King: The Forgotten Story of the Gospels*. New York, NY: HarperOne, 2011.

ABOUT THE AUTHOR

Dr. Joseph S. Williams has lived and worked for the past 20 years in Muslim Central Asia. He holds degrees in Religion, History, Literature, and Biblical Studies. He also holds a Doctorate in Intercultural Studies. He has published articles in *St. Francis Magazine*, *Missiology*, and the *Great Commission Research Journal*. He welcomes feedback at 4josephswilliams@gmail.com. Joseph S. Williams is a pen name to protect him and those around him.

www.ingramcontent.com/pod-product-compliance
Lightning Source LLC
Chambersburg PA
CBHW071423080526
44587CB00014B/1725